D1565925

CRITICAL INSIGHTS

The Red Badge of Courage

by Stephen Crane

CRITICAL INSIGHTS

The Red Badge of Courage

by Stephen Crane

Editor
Eric Carl Link
University of Memphis

Salem Press
Pasadena, California   Hackensack, New Jersey

Cover photo: Library of Congress

Published by Salem Press

© 2011 by EBSCO Publishing
Editor's text © 2011 by Eric Carl Link
"The *Paris Review* Perspective" © 2011 by Barry Harbaugh for *The Paris Review*

All rights in this book are reserved. No part of this work may be used or reproduced in any manner whatsoever or transmitted in any form or by any
means, electronic or mechanical, including photocopy, recording, or any information storage and retrieval system, without written permission from the
copyright owner except in the case of brief quotations embodied in critical articles and reviews or in the copying of images deemed to be freely licensed or
in the public domain. For information about the print edition address the publisher, Salem Press, http://salempress.com. For copyright information, contact EBSCO Publishing, 10 Estes Street, Ipswich, MA 01938.

∞ The paper used in these volumes conforms to the American National
Standard for Permanence of Paper for Printed Library Materials, Z39.48-1992
(R1997).

Library of Congress Cataloging-in-Publication Data
The Red badge of courage, by Stephen Crane / editor, Eric Carl Link.
    p. cm. — (Critical insights)
Includes bibliographical references and index.
ISBN 978-1-58765-707-8 (v. 1 : alk. paper)
    1. Crane, Stephen, 1871-1900. Red badge of courage. 2. United States—
History—Civil War, 1861-1865—Literature and the war. I. Link, Eric Carl.
PS1449.C85 R3977
813'.4—dc22
                                                                2010029186

PRINTED IN CANADA

Contents

The Book and Author

Critical Contexts

Critical Readings

Resources

About This Volume_____

Eric Carl Link

Stephen Crane's *The Red Badge of Courage* is one of the best-known and most widely read classics of American literature. This tale of a youth confronting combat for the first time on a Civil War battle-field was written by a youth. Crane was in his early twenties when he penned his masterpiece and had never—to that point in his young life—seen war in person. This was not evident to many of the early readers of *The Red Badge of Courage*, who, not knowing Crane, often imagined it was penned by a blood-soaked veteran, so powerful and immediate were its descriptions of combat.

Since its publication, *The Red Badge of Courage* has been the subject of a great deal of criticism. Readers have found it to be a rich and provocative text. It is not only well written—indeed, Crane's style in *Red Badge* is revolutionary is some ways—but it also tells a tale that speaks to contemporary readers with the same urgency as it did in the mid-1890s. A review of all that has been written about Crane's novel during the past century reveals that a great deal of the critical commentary, generation after generation, has gravitated toward a handful of key questions. Critics have studied *The Red Badge of Courage* as a novel of the Civil War, and they have attempted to trace Crane's use of historical source material. They have also looked at the novel as a meditation on the nature of manhood, growth, maturity, and courage. They have picked apart, with exacting detail, the symbolism and religious imagery in the novel. They have examined the novel as an aesthetic artifact, noting its relationship to impressionism, literary naturalism, and realism. They have looked at the novel in terms of deterministic ideologies and other themes that arose out of the scientific and philosophical milieu of the late nineteenth century. And, finally, what so many critics end up asking is the question all readers of *The Red Badge of Courage* ask upon finishing the final sentences of the novel: Has the youth become a man?

Collected in this volume are a wide variety of selections, some written specifically for this volume and published here for the first time and others that are reprinted, having originally appeared in a number of academic journals and books during the past half century. Collectively, they address—in their own individual ways—the core issues previously noted. The pieces range from general overviews of Crane's life and times and sweeping introductions to the critical commentary that has been written about the novel to minute analyses of Crane's symbolism and lengthy and penetrating commentary on the themes and ideas that emerge from Crane's story of a young man filled with heroic ideals who, when confronted with the raw fear of actual combat, must come face-to-face with his mortality.

THE BOOK
AND
AUTHOR

On *The Red Badge of Courage*

Eric Carl Link

In chapter 3 of Stephen Crane's *The Red Badge of Courage*, a brigade of soldiers—including the regiment of the novel's protagonist, Henry Fleming, an enlisted private in the Union army—encounters along the pathway the corpse of a soldier lying in eternal, open-eyed repose, staring skyward. The passing ranks of soldiers part in a wave around the dead man, as if the soldier possesses in death an unshakable power to move and shape others—a power, to which the corpse itself bears witness, the soldier did not have in life. This power does not, however, protect the corpse from indignity. Death has revealed—with the unforgiving force of a blunt instrument—things that the soldier would have kept hidden in life: as Fleming looks at the dead soldier, he is able to see that the soles of the man's shoes are worn through, exposing a poverty that the man may have kept private while alive. The living can shape how others see them; death reveals secrets.

Crane gives his readers few details about the corpse's appearance, but through them we can see his skillful use of the limited omniscient point of view. In the eyes of Henry Fleming, to whose perspective the narrative is limited, the wind-tossed waving of the corpse's beard suggests the stroking of a hand. One might extrapolate from Fleming's observation that this invisible hand is that of a contemplative man—a student of nature, perhaps, who, when confronted with a peculiar problem or a longed-for revelation, stops to ponder its depths in quiet reflection. But Crane does not reveal to his reader what the dead soldier's staring eyes might see in the heavens. Indeed, it is quite possible that death offers him no revelation other than the mere fact of dissolution. In effect, Crane's spare description makes the corpse, now an inert natural object, into a canvas upon which the observer, whether Fleming or the reader, paints significance.

To Fleming, the corpse hints at great revelations: if one could know what the dead soldier sees through his staring eyes, the passage suggests, one would have access to a type of knowledge forbidden to the living. The lure of this knowledge is a magnet pulling at Crane's youth, who "vaguely desired to walk around and around the body and stare; the impulse of the living to try to read in dead eyes the answer to the Question" (19). Crane does not tell the reader what the Question is, but the context and the emphasis suggest that it is an encapsulated version of the metaphysical mystery at the heart of all philosophy, all religion, all human striving after meaning: What lies beyond? No question is more compelling. It has fueled the human pursuit of knowledge for millennia and—since its answer would almost certainly have radical implications for an individual's sense of self-identity—humans search nature for such signs and symbols as will enable them to answer it, to understand themselves and the universe.

What *The Red Badge of Courage*, with its spare descriptions, makes its reader ask, however, is whether these signs and symbols might not exist in nature but, rather, only in the mind of the observer, making any interpretation of them nothing more than a projection of their ob-server's hopes and fears. But if this is the case, it does not necessarily mean that there is no answer to the Question: even though nature may not give a direct answer, one may still arise from the interaction be-tween the mind of the observer and the natural world. Still, the answer revealed through this interaction may not be pleasant or comforting. Just as easily as Fleming finds hints of some metaphysical answer in the corpse's gaze, one might also conclude that the corpse is just a corpse, that no hand strokes its beard, that the staring eyes contemplate nothing in the heavens, and that the Question itself is just the idealistic dream of a species that will not accept that its existence has no cosmic significance whatsoever.

Crane would toy with this last, bleak notion throughout his brief, whirlwind career, perhaps most famously in a poem from his 1899 col-lection *War Is Kind*:

A man said to the universe:
"Sir, I exist!"
"However," replied the universe,
"The fact has not created in me
A sense of obligation."

The Red Badge of Courage pulls the abstract cosmic irony of this poem down to earth. On the battlefield the individual is forced to confront the implications of human mortality in a direct and immediate manner. A single bullet is all that separates the living soldier from the corpse in quiet repose. Battles, as Fleming observes in chapter 8 of *The Red Badge of Courage*, are machines designed for the production of corpses. Still, in a sense, war itself is not the subject of the novel; rather, war is the background against which the real drama of the narrative is set: the drama of the human psyche as it is forced to confront self-doubt, fear, and dread.

Stephen Crane was twenty-three years old when he wrote *The Red Badge of Courage*. He was a veteran of no war; he had seen no combat, yet he composed what remains one of the finest war novels ever written. What he lacked in age and experience he made up for in skill, style, and research. He knew veterans of the American Civil War and in libraries had poured over voluminous accounts of the key figures and battles of that bloody national conflict. In particular, Crane had picked up details about the Battle of Chancellorsville—the battle on which *The Red Badge of Courage* is based—from reading portions of the long-running series *Battles and Leaders of the Civil War*, which ran in installments from 1884 to 1887 in *The Century Magazine* and was then compiled into a four-volume set of books. Readers of *Red Badge*, particularly upon its initial publication in book form in 1895, generally found the depiction of a young man's combat experiences so convincing that they easily assumed that its author must be older—almost certainly a veteran of the conflict. When, in the light of the fame that followed swiftly on the heels of publication, Crane's youth and inexperience became known, his having penned such a novel almost seemed like a minor sort of literary scandal.

Aside from the unmistakable importance of Crane's depth of talent and quality of imagination, a less obvious explanation for the convincing nature of his depiction of Civil War conflict may be found in the fact that *The Red Badge of Courage* is more about the psychology of dread than it is about the details of combat machinery. Yes, it is a Civil War novel, but to read the novel principally—if not exclusively—as a war novel is to overlook its depth and complexity. Indeed, Crane's novel is about many things: the fog of war, the nature of fear, the human capacity for self-doubt. It is also a novel about the relationship between humans and a seemingly indifferent universe. It is about the nature and significance of human heroism. It is about the complexities of human endeavor in the midst of crisis.

There has been no lack of criticism written about *The Red Badge of Courage*. From the earliest reviews in the mid-1890s to the studies of the present moment, Crane's masterpiece has generated a vast body of critical commentary. One issue that has received considerable attention is the genre of the novel. At various points and by various critics, *The Red Badge of Courage* has been treated as a work of literary naturalism, as a work of psychological realism, as an impressionistic work, as a modernist text, and as a symbolic novel. Much of the scholarly critique of the novel has been devoted to parsing the distinctions among these labels, and this debate has produced some excellent results, but it should be noted that these terms are not necessarily mutually exclusive. Much of the richness of *The Red Badge of Courage* derives from the fact that it can be seen as participating in each of these genres. Crane's novel is stylistically impressionistic. It uses with uncanny effect the limited omniscient point of view so favored by the psychological realists of the late nineteenth century. Thematically, it grapples with issues that were among the chief preoccupations of the literary naturalists, such as the relationship between post-Darwinian humans and their environment and the nature and scope of human agency within a network of deterministic and coercive pressures. It employs an evocative array of symbols that hearken back to the methods of the antebellum romantics. And it brings to bear a distinctively modernist sensibility that makes it look forward to the literary achievements of the 1920s and beyond.

There are other touchstone issues on which *Red Badge* critics have focused their attentions—such as examinations of the complex textual history of Crane's novel and investigations into the historical details of the Civil War battle upon which Crane based the historical framework of his narrative—but the issue that nearly all critics of Crane's novel eventually grapple with is the question of Henry Fleming's growth in the novel. Stated most simply, this is a novel about a young man, untried in combat, who flees from battle and must come to terms with his cowardice. The "red badge of courage" that Fleming receives from the blunt end of a fellow soldier's rifle is the passkey he needs to rejoin his regiment without having to admit his cowardice to his peers, and in subsequent combat Fleming performs with measurably more courage (even if the nature and quality of that courage are matters for debate). Taking stock of his actions at the end of the narrative, Fleming arrives at the conclusion that he is now a man.

If only it were that simple. All of the novel's key dichotomies crystallize around this moment at the end of the narrative. Courage and cowardice, freedom and determinism, man and boy, redemption and damnation, action and reflection—the narrative tensions created through the conflict between these oppositions make Fleming's status, his declared *manhood*, at the end of the work a matter of considerable complexity. Commentary on the novel's ending has run the gamut from very influential but hotly disputed readings of Fleming's transformation into manhood as an allegory of Christian redemption to extremely ironic, even cynical, readings of the ending that view Fleming as self-deluded, a victim of misperceptions and narcissistic impulses. Thus, critics of the novel often fall into one of two camps: those who view the ending as ironic and those who do not.

In a sense, however, this critical controversy is unsolvable, for the novel itself is *about* the difficulties inherent in any interpretive act. In order to make sense of the world, humans seek out and interpret signs and symbols. But in the interaction between the individual and his or her environment the mind is both mediator and commentator. This is the epistemological crux of Fleming's story. As one travels with Fleming through the narrative, one finds him engaged in a recursive process of interpretation: gathering streams of data through his interactions with his environment and endlessly recasting his opinions—most often opinions of himself—based on new interpretations of this stream of information. The reader finds Fleming in a continual shift between action and reflection, between engagement with the environment and the intellectual work of interpreting the meaning of his engagement as he views his sensory data as an array of potentially meaningful signs and symbols. In the end, after all, like Fleming, it is through the elements of perception that we draw conclusions about the world and what lies behind or beyond it; it is through examining the suggestive quality of signs and portents that, like the dead soldier staring in repose toward the heavens, we arrive at answers to the Question.

Works Cited

Crane, Stephen. *The Red Badge of Courage*. 1895. 4th ed. Ed. Donald Pizer and Eric Carl Link. New York: W. W. Norton, 2008.
_____. *War Is Kind*. 1899. *Stephen Crane: Prose and Poetry*. Ed. J. C. Levenson. New York: Library of America, 1984.

Biography of Stephen Crane_____

R. Baird Shuman

Stephen Crane, the youngest son of a youngest son, was the last of fourteen children born to the Reverend Jonathan Townley Crane and his wife, Mary Peck. Crane's father was a presiding elder of the Newark, New Jersey, district of the Methodist Church (1868-1872) when Stephen was born and served in a similar capacity in the Elizabeth, New Jersey, district of the church from 1872 until 1876. Because Methodist clergymen were subject to frequent transfer, the young Stephen was moved from Newark to Paterson, New Jersey, before he was old enough to attend school and to Port Jervis, New York, shortly before he began school. His *The Third Violet* (1897) and *Whilomville Stories* (1900) are set in villages modeled after Port Jervis.

Crane's father died in 1880, when the boy was eight years old, and, in 1883, Stephen and his mother moved to Asbury Park, New Jersey, a seaside resort some sixty miles from New York City, to be near the Methodist camp community of Ocean Grove, a town adjacent to Asbury Park, which Jonathan Crane had been instrumental in establishing. Stephen's brother Townley already ran a press bureau in Asbury Park, and soon their sister Agnes moved there to teach in the public schools.

As Stephen strayed from the religious teachings of the Methodist Church, his mother became concerned about his spiritual welfare, and, in 1885, she sent him to Pennington Seminary, some ten miles from both Trenton and Princeton, in the hope that he would receive a solid academic background and would simultaneously grow closer to the Church. Crane's father had been principal of Pennington Seminary for the decade from 1848 to 1858, and his mother had spent the first ten years of her marriage at Pennington.

Stephen, a handsome, dark-haired youth with a prominent nose, sensuous lips, and deep, dark eyes, rankled under Pennington's strong religious emphasis. In 1888, he enrolled in the Hudson River Institute in Claverack, New York, a coeducational institution with a military emphasis for its male students. It was perhaps during this period that Crane became extremely interested in war.

During the summers, Crane assisted his brother in his news bureau, learning something about journalism as he went about his work. He entered Lafayette College in 1890 to study engineering, but failed in his work there and left after the Christmas holiday to attend Syracuse University, where he played baseball, managed the baseball team, and worked on the school newspaper. He was not a strong student, and he left school in 1891 to seek his fortune in New York City. His mother died on December 7 of that year.

Stephen, who had met and established a friendship with Hamlin Garland in the summer of 1891, tried to make his living as a newspaperman, but he was not initially successful in this work. In 1892, however, the serial publication of seven of his "Sullivan County Sketches" gave him the encouragement he needed to pursue a literary career diligently.

Buoyed up by seeing his work in print, Crane, in 1893, paid for a private printing of *Maggie: A Girl of the Streets* (1893), a book gleaned from his experience of living in New York City's Bowery during the preceding two years. This early work, highly shocking in its time because it views with sympathy a girl who becomes pregnant out of wedlock and shows the hypocrisy of her lower-class family's morality, was first published under the pseudonym Johnston Smith.

Maggie was unabashedly naturalistic, somewhat in the tradition of Émile Zola. Despite William Dean Howells's attempts to get the book distributed, it sold hardly any copies in its original edition. In 1896, however, Crane revised it, cutting out much of its offensive profanity, omitting some of its graphic description, and regularizing the grammar and punctuation. His reputation had by this time been established with the publication, the preceding October, of *The Red Badge of Courage*, a book that grew out of Crane's fascination with war, battles, and men in combat. *The Red Badge of Courage* was initially published in an abbreviated form in 1894 as a serial appearing in the Bacheller Syndicate's newspapers. *George's Mother* (1896) appeared two years later, and in its use of realistic detail it goes far beyond that of William Dean Howells, who had become Crane's friend. *Maggie*, although it still was deemed shocking to delicate sensibilities, was more favorably received when it was republished in 1896 than it had been three years earlier.

With the publication of both *The Black Riders, and Other Lines* and *The Red Badge of Courage* in 1895, Crane became an overnight celebrity. In March of that year, he also went to Mexico for the first time, and the trip made a substantial impression upon him. With the appearance of *George's Mother, Maggie, The Little Regiment, and Other Episodes of the American Civil War* (1896), and *The Third Violet*, it was quite apparent that Crane, still only twenty-five years old, was on the way to becoming one of the leading literary figures in the United States. If readers complained because he wrote about subjects that depressed them, they could not reasonably contend that the conditions about which he wrote did not exist or that he wrote badly about them.

Although Crane was fascinated by war and by 1896 had written much about the subject, he had never known the battlefield, and he was keenly aware of this lack in his experience. Therefore, when the Bacheller Syndicate offered to send him as a correspondent to join the insurgents who were fighting against Spanish rule in Cuba, Crane enthusiastically accepted the assignment. He went first to Jacksonville, Florida, to wait for a ship, the *Commodore*, to be outfitted for the short trip to Cuba. Arriving in Jacksonville in November, he met Cora Stewart, who owned a brothel and nightclub, the Hotel de Dream.

It took until December 31 for the *Commodore* to be ready to sail, and by that time Crane and Stewart, who already had a husband, had fallen in love. Nevertheless, Crane sailed for Cuba as planned. The ship, however, got only several miles down the St. John's River before it ran aground. Crane and some of his shipmates were forced to put to sea in a small, flimsy lifeboat before the *Commodore* capsized with some loss of life.

It was fifty-four hours before Crane and his companions were able to ride the heavy surf to shore at Daytona. One of his companions was drowned as they came to shore. From his frightening experience in the lifeboat, Crane wrote what is probably his best known and most artistically confident short story, "The Open Boat." The shipwreck scuttled, for the time, Crane's plans to go to Cuba. Instead, he and Stewart sailed for Greece in late March, both of them to report on Greece's war with Turkey.

In mid-1897, Crane and Stewart, who was six years older than he, went to England, where he wrote some of his most memorable short fiction, including the novella *The Monster* and the short stories "Death and the Child" and his much-anthologized "The Bride Comes to Yellow Sky." He introduced Cora Stewart as his wife, although the two had never been married because she was not free to do so. It was at this time that Crane met Joseph Conrad and became his close friend.

After Crane's collection *The Open Boat, and Other Tales of Adventure* (1898) was published, the author returned to the United States to join the armed forces in the Spanish-American War, which the United States had just entered. He was, however, rejected for military service and instead went to Cuba as a war correspondent for Joseph Pulitzer. He was fearless in combat situations, but his health began to fail. He did some work in Puerto Rico and in Cuba for the Hearst newspapers, but in 1899, the year in which *War Is Kind* (1899), *Active Service* (1899), and *The Monster, and Other Stories* (1899) were published, he returned to England, this time to live in the stately Brede Place in Sussex. While celebrating Christmas, Crane had a massive hemorrhage brought on by tuberculosis.

In the spring of 1900, the year in which *Whilomville Stories* and *Wounds in the Rain* were published, Crane's health declined, and in May, he and Cora, accompanied by a retinue consisting of their butler, maids, nurses, and a doctor, went to Badenweiler in Germany's Black Forest, hoping that the climate would benefit the ailing writer's health.

There Crane died on June 5. Three of his works, *The Great Battles of the World* (1901), *Last Words* (1902), and *The O'Ruddy* (1903), were published shortly after his death.

From *Dictionary of World Biography: The 19th Century.* Pasadena, CA: Salem Press, 1999. Copyright © 1999 by Salem Press, Inc.

Bibliography

Benfey, Christopher E. G. *The Double Life of Stephen Crane.* New York: Alfred A. Knopf, 1992. A narrative of Crane's life and literary work that argues that the writer attempted to live the life his works portrayed. Includes bibliography and index.

Berryman, John. *Stephen Crane.* New York: William Sloane Associates, 1950. This combined biography and interpretation has been superseded as a biography, but it continues to be an absorbing Freudian reading of Crane's life and work. Berryman, himself a major American poet, eloquently explains the patterns of family conflict that appear in Crane's fiction. Furthermore, Berryman's wide-ranging interests allow him to tackle such large topics as Crane's influence on the birth of the short story, a form which, though existing earlier, came to prominence only in the 1890's. Includes notes and index.

_____. *Stephen Crane: A Critical Biography.* New York: Cooper Square, 2001. A reissue of the first major biography of the author. Still valuable for its detail and insight.

Bruccoli, Matthew J. *Stephen Crane, 1871-1971.* Columbia: Department of English, University of South Carolina, 1971. Extremely valuable bibliography, although not easily accessible.

Cady, Edwin H. *Stephen Crane.* Rev. ed. Boston: Twayne, 1980. An excellent introductory, chronological account of Crane's career, with chapters on his biography, his early writing, *The Red Badge of Courage*, notes, a chronology, an updated bibliographical essay, and an index.

Colvert, James B. *Stephen Crane.* New York: Harcourt Brace Jovanovich, 1984. This biography, aimed specifically at the nonspecialist, is highly readable and is enhanced by numerous illustrations. Its bibliography is limited but well selected. The author's research is impeccable.

_____. "Stephen Crane and Postmodern Theory." *American Literary Realism* 28 (Fall, 1995): 4-22. A survey of postmodern approaches to Crane's fiction. Summarizes the basic premises of postmodern interpretation, examining how these premises have been applied to such Crane stories as "The Open Boat," "The Upturned Face," and "Maggie"; balances such interpretive strategies against critics who affirm more traditional, humanistic approaches.

Davis, Linda H. *Badge of Courage: The Life of Stephen Crane.* Boston: Houghton Mifflin, 1998. This biography of Crane depicts him as a perpetual adolescent who was very much an enigma.

Gibson, Donald B. *The Fiction of Stephen Crane.* Carbondale: Southern Illinois University Press, 1968. This study, although badly dated, is valuable in suggesting the sources of much of Crane's fiction and in establishing some of Crane's literary relationships.

Gullason, Thomas A., ed. *Stephen Crane's Career: Perspectives and Evaluations.* New York: New York University Press, 1972. The contributors to this book consider Crane in the light of his times and his background. They trace sources of his stories, review Crane research, consider Crane's short fiction quite thoroughly, and present some of Cora Stewart's original writing.

Halliburton, David. *The Color of the Sky: A Study of Stephen Crane.* New York: Cambridge University Press, 1989. Though somewhat thematically disorganized, the author's philosophical grounding and ability to look at Crane's works from unusual angles make for many provocative readings. In his discussion of "The Blue Hotel," for example, he finds much more aggression directed against the Swede than may at first appear, coming not only from seemingly benign characters but also from the layout of the town. Notes, index.

Johnson, Claudia D. *Understanding "The Red Badge of Courage": A Student Casebook to Issues, Sources, and Historical Documents.* Westport, Conn.: Greenwood Press, 1998. An excellent accompaniment to the novel. Essential for students.

Katz, Joseph, ed. *Stephen Crane in Transition: Centenary Essays.* De Kalb: Northern Illinois University Press, 1972. The nine essays in this centenary edition that commemorates Crane's birth consider the novels, the stories, Crane's journalistic career, his literary style, and his radical use of language. The introduction is astute, and the afterword gives a fine overview of resources for study.

Knapp, Bettina L. *Stephen Crane.* New York: Frederick Ungar, 1987. A succinct introduction to Crane's life and career, with a separate chapter on his biography, several chapters on his fiction, and an extensive discussion of two poetry collections, *The Black Riders, and Other Lines,* and *War Is Kind.* Includes a detailed chronology, a bibliography of primary and secondary sources, and an index.

Metress, Christopher. "From Indifference to Anxiety: Knowledge and the Reader in 'The Open Boat.'" *Studies in Short Fiction* 28 (Winter 1991): 47-53. Shows how the structure of "The Open Boat" (made up of four key moments) creates an epistemological dilemma for readers, moving them from a position of indifference to a state of epistemological anxiety. By suggesting that the survivors have become interpreters, Crane implies that we must get rid of indifference to the difficulty of gaining knowledge and embrace the inevitable anxiety of that failure.

Monteiro, George. *Stephen Crane's Blue Badge of Courage.* Baton Rouge: Louisiana State University Press, 2000. A demonstration of the ironic role of temperance propaganda, in which Crane was immersed as a child, in the imagery and language of his darkest work.

Nagel, James. *Stephen Crane and Literary Impressionism*. University Park: Pennsylvania State University Press, 1980. Nagel carefully delineates what he considers Crane's application of impressionist concepts of painting to fiction, which involved Crane's "awareness that the apprehension of reality is limited to empirical data interpreted by a single human intelligence." This led the writer to a stress on the flawed visions of men and women and a depiction of the dangers of this natural one-sidedness in works such as *Maggie: A Girl of the Streets*, as well as depictions of characters who transcended this weakness through an acceptance of human inadequacies in such works as "The Open Boat." Notes, index.

Robertson, Michael. *Stephen Crane: Journalism and the Making of Modern American Literature*. New York: Columbia University Press, 1997. Argues that Crane's success inspired later journalists to think of their work as preparatory for writing fiction; claims the blurring of fact and fiction in newspapers during Crane's life suited his own narrative experiments.

Solomon, Eric. *Stephen Crane: From Parody to Realism*. Cambridge, Mass.: Harvard University Press, 1966. A penetrating study that shows Crane's remarkably swift development as a writer who found his metier in realism despite his sallies into naturalism and impressionism.

Sorrentino, Paul, ed. *Stephen Crane Remembered*. Tuscaloosa: University of Alabama Press, 2006. A more recent complementary volume to Stallman's still valuable biography of Crane. Sorrentino brings together nearly one hundred documents from acquaintances of the novelist and poet for a somewhat more revealing look at Crane than has heretofore been available.

Stallman, Robert W. *Stephen Crane: A Critical Bibliography*. Ames: Iowa State University Press, 1972. This book is now somewhat dated; it is still useful to scholars, however, and is more easily available generally than Matthew J. Bruccoli's splendid bibliography, which was completed the year before Stallman's.

Weatherford, Richard M., ed. *Stephen Crane: The Critical Heritage*. Boston: Routledge & Kegan Paul, 1973. Divided into sections which provide contemporary British and American reviews of Crane's work as it was published. Similarly, the introduction charts Crane's career in terms of each published text, noting the critical reception of his work and the details of his publishing career. Includes a brief annotated bibliography and an index.

Wertheim, Stanley. *A Stephen Crane Encyclopedia*. Westport, Conn.: Greenwood Press, 1997. A very thorough volume of Crane information. Includes bibliographical references and an index.

Wertheim, Stanley, and Paul Sorrentino. *The Crane Log: A Documentary Life of Stephen Crane, 1871-1900*. New York: G. K. Hall, 1994. Wertheim and Sorrentino, editors of *The Correspondence of Stephen Crane* (1988), have attempted to counter many of the falsehoods that have bedeviled analyses of Crane's life and work by providing a documentary record of the author's life. Opening with biographical notes on persons mentioned in the text and lavishly sourced, this volume is divided into seven chapters, beginning with the notation in Crane's father's diary of the birth of his fourteenth child, Stephen, and ending with a newspaper report of Crane's funeral, written by Wallace Stevens.

Wolford, Chester L., Jr. *The Anger of Stephen Crane*. Lincoln: University of Nebraska Press, 1983. Describes Crane as a semiliterate genius and presents his work as a repudiation of the epic tradition and of conventional religion. Although the book is not always convincing, it is engaging and original in its approach.

_____. *Stephen Crane: A Study of the Short Fiction*. Boston: Twayne, 1989. Brief but useful look at Crane's short fiction provides sensitive readings as well as commentary on the major points that have been raised in critical discussions of the Crane pieces. In describing "The Bride Comes to Yellow Sky," for example, Wolford explains his view of how the story fits into the archetypical patterns of the passing of the West narratives while also exploring why other critics have seen Crane's story as a simple parody. About half of the book is given over to selected Crane letters and extractions from other critics' writings on Crane's short pieces. Includes a chronology, bibliography, and index.

The *Paris Review* Perspective

Barry Harbaugh for *The Paris Review*

Stephen Crane lived twenty-eight years on this earth, from late 1871 to early 1900, and we know only a glimmer of his short life. John Berryman's 1950 "psychological biography" sought to reintroduce Crane to the public, but by that point it was too late: too much from the record of Crane's life had been lost or destroyed—or maybe there simply was not enough to begin with. "His friends while alive and his critics since have found Stephen Crane mysterious, inscrutable," Berryman wrote. We have a better sense of Henry Fleming, the protagonist of Crane's masterpiece *The Red Badge of Courage*, than we have of Crane himself.

What we know: Crane was born in Newark, New Jersey, to a Methodist minister. He had eight brothers and sisters. He read Tolstoy, Emerson, Twain, and Poe. As a boy, he got into a fistfight over Tennyson (whose work he'd called "swill"). At Lafayette College, he pulled a revolver on his brothers at Delta Upsilon after they played a prank on him. He was sickly and penniless before he published *The Red Badge of Courage* at age twenty-three and sickly and poor thereafter (blowing the profits to fund his war correspondence from Cuba and travels to the American West). He couch-surfed, took loans in the tiniest of amounts, and, unmindful of the holes in his shoes, accepted invitations from New York literary types to eat steak and potatoes and talk about Truth. He worked summers reporting for his brother at the *New York Tribune* and developed his deft ear—"Ye'd oughta see th' swad a' chil'ren I've got, an' all like that"—while writing daily sketches of life in the Bowery or dispatches from Asbury Park. His chagrined editors often had to remove some of the more fanciful passages. "Of all human lots for a person of sensibility," he later said, "that of an obscure free lance in . . . journalism is, I think, the most discouraging."

In his fiction Crane advanced a style of deadpan naturalism that he adapted from writers such as Émile Zola and Ambrose Bierce (whose wanderlust—Bierce died fighting with Pancho Villa—Crane would later emulate). He had a dim view of man's place in the world: human beings were mere "lice . . . clinging to a whirling, fire-smote, ice-locked, disease-stricken, space-lost bulb." Crane's was a cynicism that would have seemed callous were it not often rescued, in his prose, by the earnestness of his ambition to "picture the daily life in the most exact terms possible." His first book, *Maggie: A Girl of the Streets*, which he self-published for nine hundred dollars and self-marketed (he allegedly paid four fashionably dressed men to read it while riding up and down the New York rail lines), made for an early study in suffering. Maggie is born to a drunken family in the Bowery, is sexed up prematurely, disowned by her mother, and abandoned to a life of prostitution. She finally kills herself by jumping into a river. No newspaper would serialize it, no magazine would run an excerpt, and no bona fide publisher would touch it. The critic Hamlin Garland placed a positive review of *Maggie* in *The Arena* some months after Crane published the manuscript ("It is the voice of the slums. . . . Mr. Crane is only twenty-one years of age, and yet he has met and grappled with the actualities of the street in almost unequalled grace and strength") but, the book was, initially at least, a failure. Garland's review may have bolstered the young writer's confidence, but the encouragement could not then, as it does not now, pay the rent. Crane stored three hundred copies of his *Maggie* at a friend's and left New York and its pecuniary burdens for his brother's home in New Jersey. He played football with his nieces and began in earnest what would become *The Red Badge of Courage*.

It has become an object of fascination how Crane intuited so much about war without ever fighting in one. Though one senile veteran would later testify to having fought beside Crane at Antietam, the truth was Crane had not even been born at the time of that battle. He dreamed of one day becoming a soldier—he'd had a childhood fascination with toy soldiers and wanted to go to West Point for college—but he was too frail to enlist. Nevertheless the book is esteemed for its battle scenes. The young soldier Fleming, during the course of a two-day battle, comes to terms with death, bravery, and the torment of whether or not in the face of violence he might simply up and run. Though Crane set out to write a "potboiler," *The Red Badge of Courage* is, like his most famous poem, "Do not weep maiden, for war is kind," imbued with both unrelenting sarcasm and moral seriousness. The "red badge" is a lie: our hero Fleming, a sympathetic hypocrite, gets walloped in the head by a fellow Union soldier's rifle butt but later claims to have been shot. He spends most of the novel an immature boy, a coward. But, in the last pages, he is redeemed. He becomes "capable of profound sacrifices, a tremendous death . . . he [thinks] of the bullets only as things that could prevent him from reaching the place of his endeavor."

There might have been a kind of courage, too, in Crane's pushing forward with his writing in the face of so much discouragement. Crane's first biographer, Thomas Beer, described the bedraggled Crane handing over his stained, handwritten manuscript to the newspaper that would serialize it (at half the length) as "a boy who went confidently off to make war on a world and a city. He had been beaten to shelter and had lurched up a lane in darkness. . . . He had been praised for his daring while his [first] novel, like a retreating army, lay in unsold heaps." If naturalism has to do with man's struggle for meaningful existence in an indifferent world, then Crane lived his art. Back in New York, he shared a bed with two other men in order to help make his rent payments while he waited for fame to set in.

Gore Vidal told *The Paris Review* in 1974 that Stephen Crane "did everything that Hemingway did and rather better. Certainly *The Red Badge of Courage* is superior to *A Farewell to Arms*." The book indeed made Crane famous, but it could not save him. He fled New York after the trial of a pair of chorus girls charged with prostitution exposed his sex life and stirred rumors. He set off into the world, trying to live a life worth writing about. He was shipwrecked with four men off the coast of Florida and wrote his best short story, "The Open Boat," based on the experience. He covered the Spanish-American War and made friends with Joseph Conrad. But perhaps he never entirely lived up to *The Red Badge*, not that he had time enough to do so, or maybe much cared to. He said he was "disappointed with success."

"It was," Crane wrote, before he died of tuberculosis in the Black Forest, married to a prostitute, "an effort born of pain."

Bibliography

Benfey, Christopher. "The Courage of Stephen Crane." *New York Review of Books* 36.4 (1989).

Berryman, John. *Stephen Crane: A Critical Biography*. New York: Cooper Square, 2001.

Crane, Stephen. *"The Red Badge of Courage" and Other Stories*. New York: Penguin Books, 2005.

CRITICAL CONTEXTS

The Red Badge of Courage
in the Context of the 1890s_____

So vivid and affecting were Stephen Crane's depictions of battle in his 1895 novel *The Red Badge of Courage* that many readers assumed the book must have been written by a soldier. One veteran even claimed, "I was with Crane at Antietam." It was a remarkable myth to spring up around a young man of twenty-four, who had been born six years after the Civil War ended. Crane had seen no battlefield nor had he ever been a civilian during a time of war. The Civil War belonged not to his own generation but to that of his parents. Yet Crane's novel would become the definitive representation of this war—and, indeed, one of best novels to depict any war. Crane so powerfully evokes the hardships of camp life and the horrors of battle that it is easy to forget that he did not experience these realities firsthand. The novel is often read and taught as a quasi-historical document, a faithful record of the war that divided the nation in the 1860s. In survey courses, it is often held up as the definitive example of Civil War literature. Yet *The Red Badge of Courage* is also a novel of Crane's own time and is informed by some of the social and cultural developments of New York City in the 1890s: immigration, industrialization, the rise of the tenement and the factory, clashes over labor conditions, an increasingly militant national mood and foreign policy, and the emergence of the unsentimental literary movement known as naturalism. Understanding something of both Crane's personal history and the larger historical forces that shaped the nation in the 1890s can broaden one's understanding of the scope and importance of Crane's great novel.

Growing up in the wake of the Civil War, Crane had several formative experiences that would contribute to his realistic portrayal of war. Born in Newark, New Jersey, in 1871, Crane was named for an ancestor who had fought in the Revolutionary War. Crane's father, a Methodist minister, died when Stephen was eight years old, and subse-

The Red Badge of Courage in the Context of the 1890s **23**

quently his mother wrote for religious journals to support the family. For a time the boy lived with one of his adult brothers; later he joined his mother in Asbury Park, New Jersey. Crane, who was already writing stories and essays of his own, often helped his mother by doing research for her articles. Despite—or because of—growing up in a strictly religious family, Crane was a rebellious and irreverent youth. An indifferent student, he preferred playing baseball and writing his own stories to doing his schoolwork. As an effort to provide Crane with a more stable and disciplined environment, his mother sent him to Claverack College, a military academy.

While Crane was not particularly successful at his military school, and would eventually leave without receiving a degree, he loved the martial environment of the place. He would later call his time at Claverack "the happiest period of my life." Though he often skipped classes to play baseball, Crane seemed to take the school's rank system seriously. He was drawn to the uniforms and titles that figure so prominently in a military school's ethos and for some time considered pursuing a career in the military itself. Crane's fascination with the military was also evident in his lifelong interest in war stories. He grew up surrounded not only by veterans of the Civil War but also by an ever-multiplying body of work representing that war. Crane's relationship to military culture and to the legacy of war is a fascinating one. He came of age during one of the most peaceful stretches of American history, for the United States waged no wars between the end of the Civil War in 1865 and the start of the Spanish-American War in 1898. Crane might well have sympathized with Henry Fleming, the protagonist of *The Red Badge of Courage*, who believes "there was a portion of the world's history which he had regarded as the time of wars, but it, he thought, had been long gone over the horizon and had disappeared forever" (3). But whereas Fleming's understanding of war is drawn from Homer, Crane's is drawn from stories of the war that his father's generation had waged. Crane spent "the happiest period of [his] life" in an environment of sanitized, formalized militarism. The veterans of the generation before his had endured the privations of camp life and battle, but Crane's military experience consisted of adding stripes and medals to his dress uniform. The groundwork for his unsentimental portrayal of the Civil War may therefore have been laid in military school—or, more precisely, in Crane's eventual realization that most war stories treated a soldier's life as if it were an extension of the clean, orderly rituals of a military school.

After studying intermittently at two colleges, Crane left school at the age of twenty without taking a degree. Drawing on a journalist brother's connections, he obtained a job as a reporter for the *New York Tribune* and soon branched out to write for other newspapers and journals as well. He found himself drawn to the Bowery, a Lower Manhattan neighborhood that had been transformed over the preceding twenty years from a middle-class enclave to an alternately vibrant and desperate lower-class one. Crane soon moved to an apartment on Avenue A on the Lower East Side. Living there in the 1890s, Crane was in the midst of one of the most dramatic demographic shifts in world history.

By the time Crane moved to the Lower East Side, the area south of Fourteenth Street and east of Third Avenue had become one of the most densely populated neighborhoods in the world. Swelled by wave after wave of European immigrants, the area had become a crucible of urbanization and industrialization. By 1890, more than 40 percent of the population of New York City was made up of first-generation immigrants (Cashman 146). These new immigrants gravitated toward the burgeoning ethnic neighborhoods of Lower Manhattan: *Kleindeutschland*, Little Italy, Chinatown, the Bend, the Five Points, and countless other enclaves. Single-family homes were sold and torn down to make way for tenements, large apartment buildings designed to house dozens of families. Historian Sean Dennis Cashman describes New York's demographic shift this way: "In 1890, 1 million people, two-thirds of the population, were packed like sardines in 32,000 dumbbell tenements in New York" (146). Named for the air shafts on either side of them—which gave them, from above, a dumbbell shape—these tenements were dark, dirty, and overcrowded. This was more or less what their landlords had in mind: the tenements were designed for maximum occupancy and hence for a maximum return on their owners' investment.

Jacob Riis documented conditions on the Lower East Side in his photojournalistic book *How the Other Half Lives* (1890). In words and pictures, Riis brought the plight of the immigrant communities into the public eye. A photographer, Riis brought his cameraman's gaze to his prose. In so doing, he walked millions of middle-class readers through the dark passageways of a New York tenement:

> Be a little careful, please! The hall is dark and you might stumble over the children pitching pennies back there. Not that it would hurt them; kicks and cuffs are their daily diet. They have little else. Here where the hall turns and dives into utter darkness is a step, and another, another. A flight of stairs. You can feel your way, if you cannot see it. Close? Yes! What would you have? All the fresh air that ever enters these stairs comes from the hall-door that is forever slamming, and from the windows of dark bedrooms that in turn receive from the stairs their sole supply of the elements God meant to be free. (43)

Riis was a reformer, and he set his sights on the tenement as the single most important factor contributing to crime, disease, and poverty in the American city. In fact, Riis saw his "other half" as being isolated from mainstream society by the tenement itself: "The gap that separates the man in the patched coat from his wealthy neighbor is, after all, perhaps but a tenement" (87).

Crane, too, would see tenement life up close, for his reporting career focused on the same neighborhoods that Riis documented. In addition, Crane had the benefit of writing after Riis and being able to learn from his example. In 1892, Crane even attended one of Riis's lectures and reported on it for the *New York Tribune* (Bowers 514). Several passages in Crane's first novel would echo descriptions from Riis; both men, for example, wrote of a young boy being sent into a bar to bring back alcohol for a bedridden father. On the Lower East Side, Riis and Crane alike saw scenes that were entirely alien to their middle-class readership. Crane's newspaper stories gave him a platform from which to report on these ethnic urban neighborhoods and an apprenticeship in how to craft prose that would capture a concrete scene as surely as would a camera's eye.

The squalor of the tenements was matched by the hardships of the factories and sweatshops in which most immigrants worked. In fact, the tenement and the factory were inseparable conditions: the one was a means of housing the workforce that labored in the other. The prosperity of the Gilded Age, both in New York City and across the United States, was founded on an exponential increase in the industrial and manufacturing base. Cashman describes the boom this way:

> Between 1865 and 1900 more and more workers were drawn into factories, foundries, and mills on the same low terms as common laborers. The total number of people employed in manufacturing increased from 1.3 million to 4.5 million. The number of factories or sweatshops rose from 140,000 to 512,000. In factories, foundries, and mills wages were low, hours of work long, and conditions unhealthy. . . . Progress and poverty were, apparently, inseparable. (100)

Crane knew the realities of life in the tenements and the factories firsthand, for his news beat was the Lower East Side. He had also experienced some measure of this poverty himself: he was living among the people about whom he wrote and, like his subjects, was often cold, hungry, and exhausted. Crane had options the truly poor did not and would occasionally retreat to one of his brothers' houses in various well-to-do New Jersey towns. Nevertheless, Crane was for some years the equivalent of an embedded reporter, experiencing some measure of the hardscrabble existence about which he wrote.

Crane set out on his career as a reporter in the midst of a sea change in the field of journalism itself. Newspapers were an expanding business, taking on new advertising and increasing their circulation dramatically. The 1890s was the era of yellow journalism, in which the daily newspapers were in stiff competition to scoop each other by being the first to uncover—or, in some cases, invent—a given story. By the middle of the decade, William Randolph Hearst and Joseph Pulitzer were vying to dominate New York City's newspaper market. With this increased circulation and competition came a demand for more reporters and for a wider range of stories. Young men who had graduated from the best colleges were joining the ranks of the city newsrooms, while editors were increasingly seeking a broader scope in terms of both the style and the substance of the features they ran. The newspapers introduced a new mode of expression into American discourse. Michael Robertson argues that the "abrupt style" that Crane cultivated was in fact "a journalistic convention of the era" (79). Adrian Hunter makes a similar point, saying of Crane's articles for the *New York Tribune*:

> He learned to write about a wide range of material, even that which was considered salacious or provocative, with an impassive irony. See, for example, how he brings issues of poverty, homelessness, vandalism, cruelty, and violence to the fore without any evaluative narrational commentary. (22)

In the impassive reportage of Crane and his contemporaries one can see the origins of the style that Ernest Hemingway would make his own a generation later. The newspapers of the 1890s gave birth to what would eventually be termed the "hard-boiled" tradition, in which the narrator serves as an unflinching and laconic witness to the injustices around him.

Crane would bring this same impassive irony to his fictional portrayals of the cruel poverty of the Lower East Side. In his first novel, *Maggie: A Girl of the Streets*, Crane tells the story of an impoverished girl who struggles and fails to survive on the Bowery. Crane's Maggie is inherently decent and virtuous, but, faced with appalling conditions at home and the duplicity of a man she trusts, she becomes a prostitute. In the 1890s, there were no child labor laws, no minimum wage requirements, no labor unions, and no federal aid programs—in short, there was no legal or social safety net for the working poor. Rejected by both her family and the man she thought she would marry, Maggie has few options available to her. Crane's apprenticeship in the newspapers served him well, for the book succeeds precisely because of the impassive, unsentimental tone of its narration. Crane presents Maggie's case but leaves it to the reader to voice the measure of outrage or sanctimony that her case inspires.

Maggie would eventually be recognized as a great novel and as one of the first instances of the new school of literature known as naturalism. The naturalists—writers such as Frank Norris, Theodore Dreiser, and Crane—could have come into existence only in the wake of Darwinism and of the rapid industrialization of the modern landscape. These writers were fascinated by the effects that environment wrought on the individual. Crane scholar Donald Pizer defines the naturalist project this way:

> The naturalist often describes his characters as though they are conditioned and controlled by environment, heredity, instinct, or chance. But he also suggests a compensating humanistic value in his characters or their fates which affirms the significance of the individual and of his life. The tension here is that between the naturalist's desire to represent in fiction the new, discomfiting truths which he has found in the ideas and life of his late nineteenth-century world, and also his desire to find some meaning in experience which reasserts the validity of the human enterprise. (11)

Surrounded not by nature but by the human-made environment of the modern industrial city, writers such as Crane tried to trace out the ways in which this environment worked on individual men and women.

With *Maggie*, Crane had written something radically new, and it was perhaps for this reason that he could not find an editor willing to publish the novel. Crane used his inheritance from his mother's death to self-publish the work, and even then he could do little more than give away copies of his book. The problem did not lie in Crane's subject matter. In fact, the late 1880s and early 1890s saw a boom in so-called slum fiction. Most of these titles—such as *The Evil That Men Do* and *Tenement Tales of New York*—are now forgotten. Crane's novel failed to sell because it did not condescend or moralize in the way the best sellers did; as one critic put it, "The scandal of Crane's work was not its setting but, rather, his refusal to judge slum life according to middle class standards" (Gandal 39). Maggie fell into prostitution not because of some inherent moral failing on her part but because of the indifferent social and economic structures that make up her environment. Crane's unwillingness to cast slum life in the conventions of the melodrama—that milieu of heroes and villains, virtuous women and fallen ones, noble sacrifices and poetic justice—made his novel both an artistic success and a commercial failure.

It was after the debacle of self-publishing *Maggie* that Crane began to spend a great deal of time in an artist friend's studio. Reading some special issues of *The Century Magazine* that featured stories about the Civil War, Crane was struck by a sudden inspiration. Something was missing from all of these accounts; Crane would later recall his reaction to the stories: "I wonder that some of those fellows don't tell how they *felt* in those scraps. They spout enough of what they *did*, but they're as emotionless as rocks" (qtd. in Wertheim and Sorrentino 89). The *Century* series was called "Battles and Leaders of the Civil War." Crane's novel would take a dramatically different perspective on the war, focusing not on leaders and battles but on the struggles of an individual soldier with his environment and his emotions.

Three powerful elements came together for Crane as he began to work on *The Red Badge of Courage*. First, there was his lifelong interest in the military and in war stories. He was steeped in the contemporary literature of the Civil War and knew exactly where the genre's weaknesses lay. The second element, of course, was that Crane had developed through his reporting and his first novel a clean, unsentimental, hard-lined style that would allow him to avoid the purple prose and inflated sentimentality of this overblown genre. Finally, while Crane had not been to war, he had experienced the grinding poverty of the slums of the Lower East Side. *The Red Badge of Courage* was born out of the confluence of Crane's various experiences and interests. One might see Crane as evoking the hardships of war through a mode of triangulation: between his abstract knowledge of the Civil War (as well as the literary genre it had inspired) and his firsthand experiences of hardship in New York, he produced a novel that centered not on the noble exploits of the officers but on the day-to-day suffering of the soldier.

Crane wrote the novel quickly, working by night, since he was still reporting for the *New York Tribune* by day. Reading *The Red Badge of Courage* in the light of Crane's biography, one might see Fleming as a stand-in for Crane himself: both are young men struggling not only with hunger, cold, and exhaustion but also with living up to the expectations they had set for themselves. Fleming hopes to shine in battle and to be true to the Homeric visions of martial bravery that led him to enlist in the first place. Instead, he runs when he first comes under fire and must somehow recover from the crisis that this failure precipitates in him. Crane, too, may have been torn between his hopes to make a name for himself as a novelist and his fear that this new book would fail as *Maggie* had. Crane wrote the novel remarkably quickly—in a matter of weeks—and this speed itself may speak to the degree to which the author identified with his subject.

As with his first novel, Crane was again writing a book that would utterly transform a popular, established genre. In the 1890s, any number of Civil War novels and short stories were already on the market. Most of these were sentimental and melodramatic, featuring subplots in which a Union soldier falls in love with a southern belle or brothers fighting on either side of the war are tearfully reunited. Scenes of battle were important to these popular novels, but at least equally important were the romantic and familial subplots that sought to present the war as ultimately affirming the Union. Just as Crane had rejected the moralizing of the slum novel, so did he reject a similar strain in the literature of the Civil War. His novel would be as relentlessly unsentimental and objective as *Maggie* had been. Perhaps not surprisingly, Crane again had trouble publishing his book. Eventually he made an end run around the publishing industry itself by serializing *The Red Badge* in a daily newspaper syndicate. In this sense, Crane's work came full circle, and it is perhaps fitting that a book shaped largely by Crane's work as a newspaper reporter first came to readers' attention in the context of the newspaper itself.

The serial form of *The Red Badge of Courage* received some good reviews, and the work was published as a novel a year and a half later. Reactions to the novel ran the gamut: some reviewers assumed Crane was a veteran who had seen battle himself, while others questioned his patriotism for writing an account of the war that was so unrelentingly grim. What most critics agreed on, however, was that Crane was doing something new and different. An anonymous reviewer wrote of Crane's realistic approach to war:

> The description is so vivid as to be almost suffocating. The reader is right down in the midst of it where patriotism is dissolved into its elements. . . . This is war from a new point of view, and it seems more real than when seen with an eye only for large movements and general effects. (in Weatherford 86)

Crane's objectivity re-created the actual conditions of war rather than the vague sentiments and platitudes that are so readily found in the earlier dime novels.

As with *Maggie*, Crane is concerned in *The Red Badge* with how brutal living conditions break down and reshape the individual's identity and will. If in Crane's earlier novel it was tenement and factory life that made up this oppressive environment, in *The Red Badge* it is camp life and the battlefield. Yet Crane's experience in the former environment informs his depiction of the latter. He applies the hardships of urban life, which he has witnessed firsthand, to those of the soldier's life that he can only imagine. In fact, one of the most striking patterns of imagery running through the novel is explicitly industrial: war, the army, and the individual man are all compared to parts of a machine. Fleming imagines that the enemy soldiers "must be machines of steel" (39). The Union army, of which he is a part, is a "mighty blue machine" (66). Later he sees his own men, who stand their ground rather than run, as "machine-like fools!" (41). Battle is "like the grinding of an immense and terrible machine," and Fleming "must go see it produce corpses" (48). Likewise, "The torn bodies expressed the awful machinery in which the men had been entangled" (50). Fleming comments on "the furnace roar of the battle" (61) and after combat finds himself "grimy and dripping like a laborer in a foundry" (35). During a fight, Fleming, like the men around him, loses his individuality and becomes part of a single mechanism: "Directly he was working at his engine like an automatic affair. . . . He became not a man but a member" (32). Again and again, Crane re-creates the dehumanizing effects of war through the vocabulary and imagery of the modern, industrialized city and factory.

In another one of Crane's striking images, Fleming thinks of himself not as a soldier but as a laborer. He compares firing his gun to the work of a carpenter:

> He was at a task. He was like a carpenter who has made many boxes, making still another box, only there was furious haste in his movements. He, in his thoughts, was careering off in other places, even as the carpenter who as he works whistles and thinks of his friend or his enemy, his home or a saloon. (33)

This, too, might be read as a postwar image of labor, for the carpenter in a small town or a rural setting is a jack-of-all-trades. He might build a box one day, frame out a house the next, and put up some cabinets the next. It is industrialized labor that compels a worker to make the same thing again and again; to build box after box, the carpenter of Crane's analogy must be functioning not in a small-town setting but in that of an industrialized market. He is less a craftsman than he is an automaton. His thoughts of the saloon—the institution that Riis in particular railed against—further locate his labors in a modern, urban setting.

Against this trope of war as a mechanized and industrial environment Crane juxtaposes a pattern of images in which Henry Fleming becomes aware of the indifference of the natural world to his own plight. In one of the novel's most famous passages, Fleming emerges from battle to find that nature itself is unaffected by the trauma he has just witnessed:

> As he gazed around him the youth felt a flash of astonishment at the blue, pure sky and the sun gleaming on the trees and fields. It was surprising that Nature had gone tranquilly on with her golden process in the midst of so much devilment. (37)

These juxtaposed images of industrialized warfare and indifferent nature go to the heart of Crane's philosophical outlook. Man, though once a part of the natural world, has chosen to live in an unnatural environment of his own making. Whether one looks at Maggie's tenement and factory or at Fleming's camp and battlefield, modern men and women have forsaken nature for the industrialized streetscape and the mechanized battlefield. The romantics, writing at the start of the nineteenth century, argued that men and women must return to nature in order to assert their own *human* nature. Crane seems to argue that such a return is impossible: men and women have been reshaped in the image of their human-made environments and hence are alienated from a natural world that is entirely indifferent to their fate. Naturalism therefore involves seeing men and women as being shaped by two forces: their own human nature as manifested in the unnatural setting of an industrial society.

Ironically, Crane's depiction of the Civil War is grounded in images and in a narrative voice that are inherently anachronistic. This is true not only of his mechanized imagery but also of his dialogue. The slang that his soldiers use in speaking to each other, for example, is really a patois of the 1890s rather than one of the 1860s. Alfred Habegger notes the paradox of Crane's language:

> Anyone who immerses himself or herself in letters or journals from the early 1860s will at once realize (though the point is evident anyway) that Crane was no more concerned to reproduce the exact talk of Civil War combatants than he was to establish battle coordinates. Yet the reviews of the novel tell us that its first readers regarded it as fascinatingly historical. The narrative took them back to the Civil War in a way no other account succeeded in doing. (231-32)

Perhaps the "fascinatingly historical" quality of The Red Badge of Courage is located in the immediacy and the verisimilitude of Crane's dialogue and description. Despite being grounded in the discourse of the 1890s, his narration and his soldiers' talk are realistic and unsentimental in a way that earlier depictions of the war were not. Crane's contemporaries were struck by how *real* his depiction was and associated that sense of verisimilitude with historical accuracy. In The Red Badge of Courage, Crane used his modern sensibility and modern techniques to animate a historical period, making his soldiers convincingly alive. Louis Menand, in his preface to his study The Metaphysical Club, sees the Civil War as a watershed event not only for the country's political, social, and economic structures but also for its ideological and intellectual ones:

The Civil War swept away the slave civilization of the south, but it also swept away almost the whole intellectual culture of the North along with it. It took nearly half a century for the Unites States to develop a culture to replace it, to find a set of ideas, and a way of thinking, that would help people cope with the conditions of modern life. (x)

Crane's book helps to develop this new intellectual culture, for the ironic, objective, and dispassionate narration of *The Red Badge of Courage* would become a hallmark of modernism. Crane may be writing about a war that ended thirty years before, but he does so in an idiom that looks forward rather than back.

There is another great irony in the relationship that Crane establishes between the industrialized city and the war that divided the nation. In *The Red Badge of Courage*, he uses what he knew about life on the Lower East Side to create a convincing portrait of men at war. Yet the forces of industrialization in the second half of the nineteenth century were themselves often violent ones, and Crane may in fact know of war precisely because he lived through the upheavals of the 1880s and 1890s. Robert Shulman catalogs the many faces of industrial violence during this period, underscoring that, while the nation was not at war between 1865 and 1898, it was torn by internicene conflicts:

Crane . . . has created an enduring myth that draws on, universalizes, and puts in perspective the immediate violence of militia and Federal troops, of Pinkerton strike breakers and corporate warfare, of lynchings and the armed counter-attacks of black men, of the subjugation of the Indians, entire industries shut down, cities under martial law, workers and police killed, dynamite exploding, and men either baffled and unemployed or deeply uncertain about their position in a rapidly changing urban, industrial war. (214)

The 1880s and 1890s might be seen as a time of intermittent violence that was tantamount to warfare: these skirmishes were fought not on battlefields but on the streets and outside the contested mines and factories.

In fact, the mood of the nation as a whole was becoming increasingly militant throughout the 1890s. In the same year that Crane published his novel, the U.S. Congress passed a resolution approving of Cuba's use of force to resist Spanish domination. Within three years, the country would declare war on Spain, and the quarter century of official peace would come to an end. Amy Kaplan sees *The Red Badge of Courage* as commenting on and participating in this mood:

> The heightened militarism in America and Europe at the end of the nineteenth century shapes his novel as does the historical memory of the Civil War. The novel looks back at the Civil War to map a new arena into which modern forms of warfare can be imaginatively projected. (78)

Teddy Roosevelt, who soon after fighting with his Rough Riders in Cuba would be elected president of the country, knew that the sentiments of the nation were shifting in favor of war. And, in fact, Roosevelt himself hoped for a war; it fit his ideal of the strenuous life, in which men exerted themselves in sport, politics, and battle. In a remarkably candid letter of 1897, he confided to a friend: "In strict confidence . . . I should welcome almost any war, for I think this country needs one" (qtd. in Zinn 290). Why would any country "need" a war? Howard Zinn links Roosevelt's desire for war to the struggles of labor over the last quarter century, asking, "Would not a foreign adventure deflect some of the restless energy that went into strikes and protest movements toward an external enemy?" (290). What the country needed, according to men like Roosevelt, was to find some foreign target on which to vent its anger over domestic policies, living standards, and working conditions.

The Red Badge of Courage is therefore a remarkably prescient book, for it looks not only back on the history of the Civil War but also ahead to an increasingly militaristic U.S. foreign policy. In a fascinating example of life imitating art, Crane would accompany U.S. soldiers to Cuba and the Philippines as a war correspondent. It was a role that Crane helped to define and one that would figure prominently in twentieth-century literature. In fact, it is hard to imagine an Ernest Hemingway or a Norman Mailer without Crane's example. Crane's own career therefore mirrors a larger national process that began in the 1890s and continues through to the present day: the gradual entanglement of interests among the media, industries, and the military.

Works Cited

Bowers, Fredson. *Tales, Sketches, and Reports*. Vol. 8 of *The Works of Stephen Crane*. Charlottesville: U of Virginia P, 1973.

Cashman, Sean Dennis. *America in the Gilded Age: From the Death of Lincoln to the Rise of Theodore Roosevelt*. New York: New York UP, 1984.

Crane, Stephen. *The Red Badge of Courage*. 1895. New York: Bantam Dell, 2004.

Gandal, Keith. *The Virtues of the Vicious: Jacob Riis, Stephen Crane, and the Spectacle of the Slum*. New York: Oxford UP, 1997.

Habegger, Alfred. "Fighting Words: The Talk of Men at War in *The Red Badge of Courage*." *Critical Essays on Stephen Crane's "The Red Badge of Courage."* Ed. Donald Pizer. Boston: G. K. Hall, 1990.

Hunter, Adrian. Introduction. *Maggie: A Girl of the Streets*. 1893. By Stephen Crane. Ontario: Broadview, 2006.

Kaplan, Amy. "The Spectacle of War in Crane's Revision of History." *New Essays on "The Red Badge of Courage."* Ed. Lee Clark Mitchell. New York: Cambridge UP, 1986.

Menand, Louis. *The Metaphysical Club*. New York: Farrar, Straus and Giroux, 2001.

Pizer, Donald. *Realism and Naturalism in Nineteenth-Century American Fiction*. Rev. ed. Carbondale: Southern Illinois UP, 1984.

Riis, Jacob. *How the Other Half Lives*. 1890. New York: Penguin, 1997.

Robertson, Michael. *Stephen Crane: Journalism and the Making of Modern American Literature*. New York: Columbia UP, 1997.

Shulman, Robert. "*The Red Badge of Courage* and Social Violence: Crane's Myth of His America." *Critical Essays on Stephen Crane's "The Red Badge of Courage."* Ed. Donald Pizer. Boston: G. K. Hall, 1990.

Weatherford, Richard M., ed. *Stephen Crane: The Critical Heritage*. London: Routledge & Kegan Paul, 1973.

Wertheim, Stanley, and Paul Sorrentino. *The Crane Log: A Documentary Life of Stephen Crane*. New York: G. K. Hall, 1994.

Zinn, Howard. *A People's History of the United States*. New York: HarperCollins, 1980.

The Red Badge of Courage:
Criticism and Commentary

Patrick K. Dooley

The Red Badge of Courage was enormously popular when it was first published, and it rapidly gained an iconic, then canonical, status. Its impact on other late-nineteenth- and early-twentieth-century American and British authors is remarkable, and today its compactness makes it an ideal length for high school and college classes. The novel's stylistic firepower and energy make it not only student friendly but also a compelling read.

Red Badge has never gone out of print. From the beginning and without pause, generations of Crane scholars have found in it ample complexity and controversy to fuel a cottage industry of commentary.

Editions

Before we turn to the commentary on this American classic, a word of clarification and a warning about the various versions of *Red Badge*. Because of uncertainty about how Crane wished his novel to be published, scholars make use of four versions: the shorter, serialized version that appeared in newspapers in 1894; the book-length version published by Appleton in 1895; the 1982 edition edited by Henry Binder, which restored sections and an entire chapter that appear in Crane's manuscripts but not the Appleton version; and the University of Virginia Press Critical Edition, edited by Fredson Bowers, which attempts to mediate between the Appleton and Binder editions by excluding materials Bowers believes Crane wished to discard from the final version of his novel and restoring materials Bowers believes Crane's editor pressured him to discard. Even readers who decide to steer clear of this controversy need to know its basic outlines, as the versions vary enough to affect interpretations of the novel deeply. In a word, readers and teachers of *Red Badge* need to be alert to which version of the novel they are studying because significant textual, artistic, and interpretive matters are at stake.

Red Badge's first appearance was in a truncated form as a newspaper serial running between December 3 and December 9, 1894. Charles Johanningsmeier gives a comprehensive account of these appearances as well as Crane's dealings with the Bacheller-Johnson newspaper syndicate, which purchased the story for $90 (the equivalent of approximately $2,500 in 2009). While it may cause a bit of eyestrain, it is instructive to read the entire story as it appeared in the *New York Press* on December 9, 1894, a facsimile of which was reproduced by Joseph Katz in 1967. Seeing this version with its installment divisions, chapter headings, and illustrations gives modern-day readers a sense of the story's flavor and the powerful impact that Crane's story had on its first readers. Willa Cather, for instance, was just one of many readers captivated by this serialized version. Less than three weeks after Crane's death, she wrote a tribute, "When I Knew Stephen Crane," which, among other things, describes her meeting Crane in Lincoln, Nebraska, a scant two months after she had read the installments of *Red Badge* in the *State Journal*, where she worked during her senior year at the University of Nebraska. An eye-friendly, conventional print transcription of this abbreviated version of the novel is available in Thomas A. Gullason's *Complete Novels of Stephen Crane* (1967).

In early 1895, Crane signed with D. Appleton & Company to publish a book-length version of *Red Badge*, and in October 1895 the novel appeared. Though the Appleton version was long considered authoritative, in the late twentieth century scholars began reviewing Crane's manuscripts and noting discrepancies between them and the Appleton text; naturally, several enterprising Crane scholars could not resist poking at the hornet's nest that these manuscript variants presented.

The complete *Red Badge* manuscript is held in the special collections of the University of Virginia, but a four-fifths sized, photographic facsimile of it was also produced by Fredson Bowers in 1972. Seeing

Red Badge "in the flesh" gives readers not only a sense of immediacy but also a chance to see how Crane worked on the text. His newspaper background made him conscious of the jobs of typesetters and compositors, so he took exquisite care to make his handwriting neat and legible, even carefully circling the period at the end of each sentence. The manuscript also provides a chance to see how remarkably clean and lightly revised Crane's copy texts are. Even so, the manuscript and its facsimile reveal Crane's corrections: the false-start or dead-end sections he abandoned, plus a complete chapter he discarded.

With a flare for the dramatic and controversy, in 1982 Henry Binder produced a version of *Red Badge* that reinstated the excised sections as well as the abandoned chapter. The edition met with great interest from both scholars and general readers, with a front page article in the *New York Times* by Herbert Mitgang announcing that *"Red Badge* Is Due out as Crane Wrote It." While it can be argued that this is the version "as Crane wrote it," Binder went on to claim that his new text presents both a different and an improved novel. Different to be sure, but the question of whether the version is improved or faithful to Crane's intentions has occasioned heated, noisy, and protracted debate among scholars. Readers wishing to study this controversy will want to consider, in defense of the Binder edition, essays by Binder (1978, 1978a, 1979, 1982), Kevin J. Hayes, Steven Mailloux (1978, 1982), and Hershel Parker (1984, 1986, 1995); and, in criticism of the Binder edition, essays by James B. Colvert (1990), Regina Domeraski, Michael Guemple, and Donald Pizer (1979, 1985). Scholars in the Binder camp tend to justify his edition by portraying Crane as a poor, pliable, and hungry writer who succumbed to the wishes of his overbearing Appleton editor, Ripley Hitchcock. While in the Appleton version the reader is unsure about how much irony to factor into the narrator's descriptions of Henry in chapter 24—"he saw that he was good . . . he felt a quiet manhood . . . he was a man"—Binder's expanded version substantially alters the novel's ending by rendering it unambiguously ironic. In Binder's version, Henry without doubt remains a deluded, preening, and posturing adolescent. The *contra* Binder camp maintains that, like many great classic authors, Crane wished *Red Badge* to contain a calculated and teasing ambivalence, which the Appleton version preserves.

One other version of *Red Badge*, the University of Virginia edition, is worth noting. It briefly complicated matters after it was published in 1972, but a growing and now all but complete scholarly consensus has emerged concerning it. As to be expected, Fredson Bowers, supervisor of the University of Virginia editions of Crane's works, took care to correct the Appleton edition's transcription errors and textual inconsistencies, but, unlike Binder, he decided against including the excised passages and the abandoned chapter. However, Bowers muddied the waters when he attempted to discern which revisions to the manuscript Crane made on his own (such as his deletion of the names of his three main characters except when they are engaged in direct discourse and his revisions of several passages of dialect, all changes that were prompted by suggestions from Hamlin Garland) and which revisions Crane only made at Hitchcock's insistence. As a result, the Virginia critical edition of *Red Badge* presents readers with a fourth version of Crane's novel. Criticism of the edition can be found in Hershel Parker's 1976 review of it, and Bowers himself published a defense in 1989. Unfortunately, despite the time, expense, care, and painstaking effort that went into it, the Virginia critical edition has been discredited, and most scholars have returned to the Appleton text or turn to an amalgamation of the Appleton text and Crane's manuscript.

The now standard resource for Crane texts, J. C. Levenson's 1984 Library of America volume, *Stephen Crane: Prose and Poetry*, for example, reprints nearly all the texts from the Virginia edition of Crane's works but takes its *Red Badge* text from the Appleton edition. Most subsequent reprintings of *Red Badge* have followed Levenson's lead, though a few, such as Pizer's very helpful Norton editions (1994, 2008) and those edited by Sculley Bradley et al., Richard Lettis et al., and Phyllis Frus and Stanley Corkin, include as appendices the excised passages and the dropped chapter so those interested in revisiting this textual controversy can judge for themselves. General readers, students, and teachers looking for a guide to the various texts may wish to consult Joseph Katz's survey of classroom editions (1972) and Robert M. Myers's analysis of popular editions (1997).

In a word, while the Binder edition created a great stir and spawned tremendous controversy, the Appleton version deserves to be regarded as *the* standard edition. As Domeraski convincingly argues in her introduction to the Bantam edition: Crane prepared and proofread the Appleton version, he made no further attempt to revise the Appleton text after it was published, and it is the Appleton version that made Crane an overnight celebrity and introduced him to millions of readers.

Contemporary Responses

The contemporary reaction to *Red Badge* was immediate and nearly universally enthusiastic. Crane's book was quickly a best seller on both sides of the Atlantic, and a mere six months after it appeared it was seventh in sales in England and second in the United States (Hackett 96). Weatherford's invaluable volume *Stephen Crane: The Critical Heritage* (1973) has done Crane scholars and students the tremendous favor of reprinting the three dozen initial American reviews of *Red Badge*. (Since all of these contemporary reviews have been reprinted in Weatherford's volume, my citations of them will refer to the page numbers in his collection.) The earliest American notice was a short item by E. J. Edwards in the Philadelphia *Press* that called attention to the newspaper's publication of the syndicated version and enthusiastically announced that Crane had been offered "a very flattering offer from one of the largest publishing houses in the city for a contract of that story in book form and he has accepted it" (82).

Edwards's commentary on Crane's novel opened two refrains that marked its early reception: the remarkable power of Crane's style and the equally remarkable accuracy of his depictions of combat. A *New*

York Times review titled "A Green Private Under Fire," for example, commented on Crane's "terse and vigorous sentences" (90), and Nancy Huston Banks, writing for *Bookman* in November 1895, noted that "the short, sharp sentences hurled without sequence give one the feeling of being pelted from different angles by hail—hail that is hot" (97). A January *New York Times* review by Harold Frederic praised the novel as a "photographic revelation, which startles and fascinates" (119). On the point of Crane's accuracy, many reviewers wondered how the writer, born years after the war, could have, as a reviewer for the Philadelphia *Press* put it, "evolved from his imagination purely what strikes the reader as a most impressive and accurate record of actual personal experience" ("Rev. of *Red Badge*" 84). Other reviewers, unsure of Crane's age and his war experience, straddled the fence. So Sydney Brooks in the January 1896 *Saturday Review* averred, "Certainly, if his book were altogether a work of imagination, unbiased on personal experience, his realism would be nothing short of a miracle" (101). Among the initial reactions to *Red Badge*, the lengthy notice by George Wyndham in the January 1896 *New Review* should not be missed. More than a century later, its perceptive, clear, and nuanced examination, with an interesting comparison of Crane with Émile Zola, remains among the best analyses of *Red Badge*.

Still, despite most reviewers' enthusiasm for the novel, not all of Crane's initial reviews were positive. General Alexander C. McClurg's April 1896 letter to the *Dial* denounced the book and the American and British critics who praised it. Believing that *Red Badge* had been first published in England, he charged that its appearance in the United States was a surreptitious campaign to ridicule the competence and patriotism of ordinary American soldiers. He also claimed that there were no positive notices of Crane's book. In the next issue of the *Dial*, D. Appleton & Co.'s response, most likely penned by Ripley Hitchcock, corrected McClurg's mistake about the publishing history of *Red Badge* and, as evidence of the "almost universal chorus of eulogy" it received, listed nearly two dozen papers' favorable reviews (144). A final contemporary review is noteworthy. Colonel John Burleigh was not only enthusiastic about the vibrant verisimilitude of Crane's prose, the veteran officer also explained the source of Crane's accuracy by testifying, in an article in *The Roycroft Quarterly*, "I was with Crane at Antietam" (158). Of course, Antietam was fought in 1862, nine years before Crane was born. Sharon Carruthers offers informative commentary on Colonel Burleigh, and Lyndon Upson Pratt and Thomas F. O'Donnell have discussed Crane's knowledge of Antietam, which he likely gained through his history teacher at Claverack College, General John Van Patten, whose regiment was forced into flight during that famous battle. Readers wishing to explore the reviews of Crane's contemporaries further can find close examinations of the American reviews in articles by Eric Solomon (1965) and James B. Colvert (1999) and of the British reviews in two articles by Benjamin F. Fisher (1999, 2000).

The Crane Revivals

The first rebirth of interest in Crane was triggered by the 1925 Knopf edition of *Red Badge* and Thomas Beer's 1923 biography *Stephen Crane: A Study in American Letters*. Beer's portrait of Crane was poignant and his insights into his works penetrating, but it was not long before suspicions about Beer's sources surfaced. Stanley Wertheim and Paul Sorrentino (1990; see also Sorrentino, 2003) and John Clendenning have now established that Beer manufactured several letters, invented Crane quips, and fabricated numerous events in his life. For a good history of this first revival, see Wertheim (1971).

Beginning in the early 1950s, about midway in the fifty years between the Knopf and Virginia editions, the work of Robert Stallman ushered in a second renaissance of Crane scholarship. Much of Crane's apprentice fiction and many of his newspaper stories were unattributed, and so, in the wake of the great interest that followed the Beer biography (and another by John Berryman in 1950), scholars vied to discover Crane's unknown works. The undisputed leader in this search was Robert Stallman, whose *Stephen Crane: An Omnibus* (1952) reprinted the best of Crane, both items long known and those recently discovered. This volume also printed the portions of the *Red Badge* manuscript that Binder added to his edition, so, in reality, Stallman is the scholar who opened the debates about which version of Crane's novel has superior literary merit and which version reflects Crane's true intentions.

General Overviews

Before we turn to commentary on specific issues and themes in *Red Badge*, several overview treatments are notable. Donald B. Gibson's monograph *"The Red Badge of Courage": Redefining the Hero* (1988) deserves special attention. His short and tightly argued treatise stresses the tension between *Red Badge* as a typical initiation story and Crane's use of irony to critique Fleming's maturity. Gibson argues that Crane portrays a somewhat schizophrenic heroic/antiheroic protagonist who both grows and regresses. "Throughout the text," he writes, "Henry appears more or less sympathetic, more or less deserving of blame or censure. This modulation of the reader's response is carefully and intentionally managed, largely through irony—and, as well, through editing of irony when the negative or positive response elicited toward Henry seems too great or too little" (58-59). John E. Curran, Jr., also offers a nice analysis of Crane's ironic use of the gaps between Henry's ignorance and his comrades' (and, thereby, the reader's) wealth of knowledge. Valuable overview treatments can also be found in the chapters devoted to *Red Badge* in the established and well-regarded book-length treatments of Crane by Edwin Cady, David Halliburton, Marston LaFrance (1971), James Nagel, and Eric Solomon (1966).

Though not as lengthy as these book chapters, also not to be missed are Joseph Hergesheimer's introduction to the *Red Badge* that appeared in the opening volume of the *The Work of Stephen Crane*, edited by Wilson Follett and published by Knopf in 1925, and, despite what has been said about the discredited Bowers edition, J. C. Levenson's introduction to the *Red Badge* volume of the 1975 Virginia critical edition of *The Works of Stephen Crane*. Here Levenson carefully and clearly sorts out the literary, historical, and political influences to which Crane was responding. Andrew Delbanco's sophisticated examination of Crane's use of war to explore what it means to be a person and an American should also be consulted. Further, as one would expect from one of our most celebrated Civil War historians, Shelby Foote's introduction to the 2000 Modern Library edition of the novel offers an elegant and poignant general essay, which concludes that "any true work having to do with war is bound, by definition, to turn out antiwar in its effect, and so, of course, does this one" (xl). Finally, three of the best recent short essays on Crane and *Red Badge* can be found in reference books. Mark Richardson argues in *American Writers Classics* that the breakthrough style of *Red Badge*—including its ironic, sardonic prose—enables Crane to narrate "at once from inside and outside his hero's sensibilities" (242). James Woodress in the *Reference Guide to American Literature* examines Crane's deft and novel handling of metaphors that startle both the casual and the careful reader. Claudia Durst Johnson's *Student Casebook* is several notches above the usual CliffsNotes reference pamphlet; accordingly, high school students facing a term paper on *Red Badge* will find much help in her analyses.

Historical Sources

As an outgrowth of Crane's extraordinarily accurate depictions of combat, scholars have long been occupied with identifying the historical sources on which he drew while writing the novel. Though Crane did not identify the battlefield actions that initiate young Fleming into war, critics generally agree that his historical source was the Battle of Chancellorsville. Harold R. Hungerford and Alexander R. Tamke have convincingly established that the novel's charge-and-retreat pattern over three battles fits Chancellorsville, and Roy Morris (2007) provides a survey of the numerous historical sources he believes Crane studied. Charles LaRocca (1991) has identified Fleming's unit as the 124th New York State volunteers; Cecil D. Eby (1960), however, traces the book's title to the patch worn by General Philip Kearny's New Jersey "red badge" division. More on this link to Kearny can be found in Thomas Kearny's 1937 work *General Philip Kearny: Battle Soldier of Five Wars* (267-68). For the full workup on the novel's historical analogues, see Morris and LaRocca's annotated historical edition of *Red Badge* and the very ambitious volume by Perry Lentz, *Private Fleming at Chancelorsville: "The Red Badge of Courage" and the Civil War*. Equipped with reliable information about all aspects of the Civil War—including details about uniforms, tactics, strategy, maps, photographs, muskets, sharpshooters, artillery and cavalry, battlefield hospitals and medical care—Lentz's volume concludes that "the more readers know about the American Civil War, the more they can appreciate Crane's depiction of 'An Episode' within it" (2).

Still, whether and how such comprehensive background knowledge enhances our appreciation of Crane's fictional narrative is not obvious. The benefits of searching out every historical reference and each factual analogue are limited. Donald Pizer (2007) has written a fine essay on this question in which he explores the points at which historical facts fit *Red Badge* and the points at which the search for an exact historical source is a distraction. Pizer concludes that Crane "was not interested in rendering the battle and its participants in a manner consistent with full historical accuracy . . . rather he shaped a narrative closer to the pattern in his [Crane's] head" (11). And so, though Lentz's study is replete with interesting information about the life and times of soldiers during the Civil War, Pizer wonders how important it is to establish, for example, to which regiment the *fictional* Henry Fleming belonged?

Religious Symbolism

All of Robert W. Stallman's insightful and seminal commentary on Crane's works has to be reckoned with, but none more so than his introduction to the 1951 Modern Library edition of *Red Badge*. In this essay Stallman proposes that Christian symbols are the key to Crane's novel. Focusing on Jim Conklin as a Christ figure (see Robert Detweiler for more on this), Stallman argues that the novel's central theme is redemption and asserts, in support of his reading, that the iconic sentence at the end of chapter 9—"the red sun was pasted in the sky as a wafer"—refers to the communion wafer of the Holy Eucharist.

Alfred North Whitehead famously remarked that the history of Western philosophy is best understood as a series of footnotes to the thought of Plato. With regard to religious readings of *Red Badge*, Stallman stands in as Plato. His religious reading attracted some enthusiastic supporters, such as John E. Hart, whose fine essay analyzes the ways in which Fleming is reborn through a cluster of redemptive moments and symbolic encounters, and Edward Stone (1964), who argues that life as a "pilgrim's progress" is a prominent motif of Crane's novel.

William R. Linneman, on the other hand, while sidestepping Stallman's claims regarding religious symbolism, hails his choice of the wafer as an especially pregnant image in Crane's narrative. Linneman explains that Crane's works were a touchstone for the satires and parodies of the period's humor magazines. The April 23, 1896, issue of *Life*, for example, offered this parody, "The sun hung like a custard pie in a burnt blanket," and Frank Norris's 1897 collection *Perverted Tales* offered, among parodies of Rudyard Kipling, Bret Harte, Ambrose Bierce, and Anthony Hope, the "Green Stones of Unrest," an uncanny mimicry of Crane. A number of other notable parodies have been located: Richard M. Weatherford (1973a) comments on O. Henry's "A Blue Blotch of Cowardice," and Stallman (1952) lists several contemporary takeoffs. Edward Stone (1957), in his examination titled "The Many Suns of *The Red Badge of Courage*," partly agrees with Stallman, conceding that Crane's novel appeals to both religious and secular meanings.

Though Stallman's gospel attracted a few devotees, the more numerous skeptics have suggested alternative readings to the wafer image and, more generally, argued that naturalism and Darwinism offers better accounts of Crane's novel. Among the critics taking a naturalistic view are Eric W. Carlson and Scott C. Osborn, who think Crane's wafer more plausibly refers to the red wax used to seal letters or notarize documents, and Jean G. Marlowe, who argues for the red paper wads that were part of the black powder explosive charges of Civil War artillery. Edmund Wilson also objects to Stallman's view of the wafer on the grounds that Crane was a Methodist, not a Catholic, and Thomas L. Kent suggests that since Crane was skeptical about apprehending reality and understanding human experiences, "no single meaning given to the wafer simile is finally correct" (627).

Certainly many elements of *Red Badge*, notably the chapel scene, with its "religious half light," in chapter 7, seem to be explicitly religious. On that memorable scene see the analyses of Ben Satterfield and James W. Tuttleton. Contrarily, what are we to make of Crane's paradoxical narration in chapter 17: "These incidents made the youth ponder. It was revealed to him that he had been a barbarian, a beast. He had fought like a pagan who defends his religion"? Stanley B. Greenfield is cautious as he warns commentators of a false scent, and he argues that Crane's "religious phrasing unfortunately predisposes the reader toward an interpretation of spiritual redemption" (563). Several critics are leery of any religious interpretations, to the extent of contending that Stallman's intensely religious readings are far-fetched and not particularly helpful. Eby (1963) suggests that nothing more is involved in the red sun and wafer sentence and, for that matter, in the title of the book than Crane's fondness for the color and the word "red"; Reid Maynard also calls attention to Crane's fondness for red.

Frederic Gwynn scoffs at the easy identification of Jim Conklin with Jesus Christ. Mordecai and Erin Marcus contend that Crane's persistent use of animal imagery makes him a naturalistic instead of a religious novelist; Richard Chase pushes further, contending that, as a good Darwinian, Crane could be expected to use all sorts of color symbolism; also on this point see James Trammell Cox and Darryl Hattenhauer. More generally on Crane's use of colors, in 1960 Claudia C. Wogan examined 24 color words used in *Red Badge*; ten years later, Robert Stowell offered a slightly expanded tabulation; and in 1999, armed with a computer, William E. Newmiller found 343 matches of 39 base color words that he then examined for themes, patterns, and percentages. (Readers keen on computer analyses should see Dorothy Margaret Guinn's analysis of Crane's composition and revision of *Red Badge*.)

With reference to both color and Darwinism, Bert Bender's "Hanging Stephen Crane in the Impressionist Museum" explores Crane's gift of using colors to evoke moods. Also, the second chapter of Bender's well-regarded recent book *Evolution and "the Sex Problem": American Narratives During the Eclipse of Darwinism*, which is titled "'The Chaos in His Brain': Evolutionary Psychology in *The Red Badge of Courage*," provides a definitive examination of Crane's psychological (that is, naturalistic, evolutionary, and materialistic) portraits of fear and rage in battle. Eric Carl Link, too, provides a penetrating analysis of Crane's particular brand of naturalism. Olaf W. Fryckstedt argues for a naturalistic pessimism akin to nihilism instead of the redemption that Stallman and others see in *Red Badge*. Philip Rahv broadens the attack on Stallman, holding that the fixation on religious symbolism has become a debilitating bias that fails to yield important interpretive insights. If for no other reason than to gain a sense of the heat and smoke sparked by Stallman's claims about religion and the communion wafer, see his contentious rebuttals (1955, 1957), wherein he first directly responds to his critics and then restates and reaffirms the merits of his religious readings.

Fleming's Growth or Regression

The degree of self-awareness and maturity that Fleming acquires in his two days of combat is a perennial scholarly and classroom discussion topic. As previously noted, the Binder edition had a significant impact on the controversy, presenting readers with an unambiguously cocky, even pompous and self-deluded, adolescent. However, because it provides textual evidence in support of an interesting range of opinions about Fleming, for this section I will regard the Appleton version as canonical.

The prevalent reading is that Fleming does mature, though scholars disagree about the extent and catalysts of his growth. The most straightforward account is Warren French's, which proposes that it is only common sense that three days of combat would hasten anyone—young or old—toward maturity. Hence, for French, Crane has given us a pragmatic Henry who is open to and learns from experience. Robert C. Albrecht also finds that Fleming becomes substantially more mature, even if he is still left short of manhood. Robert M. Rechnitz and Robert Shulman argue that the impact and depersonalization of combat bring Fleming to the threshold of a new self. Daniel G. Hoffman agrees that Henry achieves a measure of maturity, but he argues that Henry's advances toward personal integrity can be traced to his faulty and genuine responses to ethical imperatives. John E. Hart traces Henry's rebirth after his battlefield desertion to a group identification, especially the embrace he receives in chapter 13 when he returns to his regiment. Solomon (1959) argues that, through his contact with five separate soldiers, Fleming appropriates the value of group loyalty, which enables him gradually to take responsibility for his actions. Edward Stone (1962) builds on Solomon's argument, locating a sixth soldier, Private Smithers, as a steady and reliable soldier whom Fleming adopts as a role model. John Fraser's analysis of the ethical norms that continue in force and those held in abeyance in war provides a context for his account of how Fleming recovers moral equilibrium. Pizer's (2001) careful examination of four incidents that Henry experiences during his flight away from the front lines—his retreat to the chapel in nature, his encounter with Jim Conklin, his desertion of the tattered man, and his being wounded—gives added weight to a nonironic interpretation of the novel's end. Pizer explains that Henry is sufficiently matured by his experiences with basic human emotions—anguish, terror, and anger at death, plus the real pain and suffering of his wound—to merit initiation into manhood. Regarding the extent of Fleming's growth and the factors responsible for it, my own *Pluralistic Philosophy of Stephen Crane* reminds us that Henry is very young and that we have witnessed only two days in his life; nonetheless, by the novel's end he has made significant steps. As William Wasserstrom puts it, "Henry has come a long way from home" (227), and now on the cusp of maturity,

> his growth to adulthood is not due to battlefield heroics and public deeds. Rather, his quiet manhood is the fruit of three separate moral realizations: his confrontation with a serious ethical choice, his acknowledgment that he had failed to respond morally [when he abandoned the tattered man], and his most difficult and humbling experience, the decision to forgive and to accept himself. (89)

Kapil Kapoor also holds that Fleming's most severe failure is with regard to the tattered man, so his growth toward adulthood has to start there.

A smaller number of scholars see neither growth nor regression. Marvin Klotz finds that Crane's protagonist does not significantly change; moreover, he excuses Fleming's abandonment of the tattered man as neither worse nor better than the actions of the other young soldiers in his regiment. Klotz's claim, then, is that the fidelity of Crane's depictions of typical soldiers and their reactions to combat resonated with veteran soldiers such as the previously noted Colonel Burleigh. Philip D. Beidler argues that Fleming measures up to the standards for the common Civil War soldier, and Myers (1999) agrees that, on balance, he is a "good soldier." For more on this topic, also see John H.

Irsfeld and Thomas M. Lorch, both of whom find Henry little changed from when he started as a green recruit.

A significant but insistent minority of scholars argue that the narrator's summative comment in chapter 24, "he was a man," is *the* locus of Crane's fully ironic—and thereby negative—verdict on Fleming. Kirk M. Reynolds supports this conclusion with a close scrutiny of the full range of Crane's ironic statements, calling particular attention to Fleming's tenuous hold on reality and his faulty self-awareness. John J. McDermott and Frederic Newberry concentrate on Fleming's hidden wound and his reasoning in chapter 15 that since "he had performed his mistakes in the dark . . . he had license to be pompous and veteran like." Stressing Henry's rationalizations, these two scholars also point out similarities between Fleming and Arthur Dimmesdale of *The Scarlet Letter*, both of whom suffer from secret sins they refuse to divulge. Clinton Burhans asks against whose standard we ought to judge: Henry's, the narrator's, or the reader's common sense? It is not clear which standard Burhans is using, however, when he concludes that Fleming remains a deluded dreamer. For other damning indictments of Fleming's immaturity and dishonesty, see N. E. Dunn and Neil Schmitz: the former argues that, while Henry appears to grow, in reality he regresses, and the latter concludes, "Fleming stumbles out of his ordeal a supple neurotic, busily revising his delusions" (450). And, of course, Binder (1978), using his own edition as support, sees Crane's final chapter as a full-blown exercise in irony and naturally insists, "Henry does not change."

A recent resurgence of the view that Fleming is less mature and even more self-deluded at the end needs to be acknowledged. Michael Schaefer (2006a) offers an interesting reexamination of the perennial debate about Crane's ending, opting to take it as ironic. He bolsters his case with an examination of "A Mystery of Heroism," which he notes was the first Civil War story Crane wrote after *Red Badge*. Another forceful proponent of this position is Randal W. Allred, who argues that, when confronted by the chaos, confusion, and complexity of combat, Fleming orients himself by "invent[ing] a text where none exists" (103). Accordingly, "*Red Badge* is not so much a portrayal of Henry Fleming in battle as it is a portrayal of Henry Fleming's portrayal of himself in battle" (105). As expected, Allred appeals to the Binder version to marshal evidence for his case, but then, contrary to the usual readings of Crane's short story "The Veteran," which is a sort of sequel to *Red Badge*, he argues that in this story Fleming, now an old man, manufactures one last self-deceptive text of vindication.

However, generally scholars do not read "The Veteran" as Crane's coded condemnation of Henry. Instead, most find it striking that three months after *Red Badge* appeared in book form Crane himself was apparently undecided about Henry's character. In this story, Fleming, now an old man and grandfather, is asked by the cracker-barrel philosophers at the country store, "Mr. Fleming, you never was frightened much in them battles, was you?" To his grandson Jimmie's chagrin, Fleming answers, "'Well, I guess I was, . . . you bet I was scared. . . . Of course, afterward I got kind of used to it. A man does'" ("The Veteran" 666-67). (Note that in his Norton Critical Edition of *Red Badge* [1994, 2008], Pizer places "The Veteran" in the section of criticism devoted to "early estimates of *Red Badge*.")

Given the perennial and persistent controversy about the pace, direction, and outcome of Henry's struggles, perhaps the most challenging and balanced account of Henry's character at the close of the novel is to be found in Harold C. Horsford's essay "He Was a Man." Horsford argues not only that "no single statement expressing his [Fleming's] state of mind is ever really final" (124) but also that neither the Appleton nor the Binder edition settles the matter, for "either version of the novel authenticates a reader's skepticism regarding Fleming's concluding self-satisfaction" (110). Christopher Benfy, too, decides that, by the end of *Red Badge*, Crane has left us with two incompatible Henrys, and he speculates that this is due to the fact that it is not clear which of the two Cranes wrote the novel, "the intrepid and heroic reporter, or the master of pretense and pose" (5).

Race, Gender, and Class

Verner D. Mitchell thoughtfully examines race in *Red Badge*, correctly observing that "signs of 'gender' and 'race' in Crane's fiction have gone largely uninterrogated" (60). Andrew Lawson examines *Red Badge* in terms of class, paying special attention to the tensions between the recruits and their officers. Myers (1999) sees a similar tension, but his diagnosis focuses on the democratically conditioned recruits who chafe at their order-giving superiors. Scott Derrick looks for "homosexual interests or anxieties" in Crane's biography that might find their way into *Red Badge*.

Literary Resources

In Crane's Whilomville story "The Angel Child," the narrator comments, "Men spoke to other men saying, 'How do you pronounce the name of that barber up there on Bridge Street hill?' And, then, before anyone could prevent it, the best minds in the town were splintering their lances against William Neeltje's signboard" (1177). Similarly, all would-be Crane biographers have so far continued splintering their lances on the stubbornly illusive life of Crane, thus bringing added complications to the task of identifying the literary influences on his writings. As will soon be obvious, essays attempting to do so tend to be conjectural, circumstantial, contradictory, and tentative.

Warren D. Anderson seeks out Homeric references in *Red Badge*, and Robert Dusenbery lays out parallels between the *Iliad* and *Red Badge*. Dunn argues that "Crane had in mind, and wished the reader to keep in mind, the Homeric epic as background pointing up the satiric absurdity of the situation in *Red Badge*" (272) and, as a result, Henry, like Ulysses before him, remains deluded. Gibson (1966) extends his source hunting to several classical myths beyond Homer. Not searching so far back, Vickery proposes Dante's *Inferno* as a model; Abraham Feldman and Benfy (1997) find Shakespearean influences, specifically from *Henry IV, Part 2*.

Also tenuous is the claim, for example by E. C. Brody, that Tolstoy was a *Red Badge* influence. Colvert (1956) proposes Zola as a mentor, contending that while it is not likely that Crane read *La Débâcle*, he probably read the long review of it in the July 10, 1892, *New York Tribune*. In that light, Colvert shows several passages of clear resemblance. Mangum (1976), however, believes that Crane had probably read *La Débâcle* in translation. Edward Stone (1963) also cites Zola, but another of his novels: *L'Assommoir*. LaFrance (1970) dismisses any Zola influence.

Gordon S. Haight and Thomas F. O'Donnell suggest that Crane was emulating John William De Forest's popular 1867 Civil War novel *Miss Ravenel's Conversion from Secession to Loyalty*. Solomon (1958, 1965) and Alexander Tamke see traces of Joseph Kirkland's *The Captain of Company K*; Solomon also finds influences from a number of *Century Magazine* articles. Inge (1993, 1994) finds striking parallels between *Red Badge* and Sam R. Watkins's 1882 memoir *"Co. Aytch," Maury Grays, First Tennessee Regiment; Or, A Side Show of the Big Show*. H. T. Webster is certain that "unless chance violates probability" (285) Crane learned much from Wilbur F. Hinman's 1889 depiction of a regular soldier in his *Corporal Si Klegg and His "Pard."* Wertheim (1973) explores parallels with several Civil War soldiers' autobiographies. And none other than Ernest Hemingway is confident that the photographs of Mathew Brady reappear as images in *Red Badge*. On Brady and other Civil War photographers, also see Lewis Renza.

Beyond the religious readings previously noted, several source hunters posit direct biblical influences: Mangum (1975) traces the "hot plow shares" phrase in *Red Badge*'s final chapter to Isaiah 2:4, and Robert McIlvaine sees interesting parallels between Fleming and Jacob in Genesis 32:11. See Donald Thomas for comments on several other biblical allusions. A pioneering 1957 essay by Thomas A. Gullason also suggests that the sermons, essays, and books of Crane's father, Reverend Jonathan Crane, deserve a close look as literary influences.

Varieties of Courage

Crane's lifelong preoccupations were the varieties of courage and heroism (and cowardice) humans exhibit under stress and during crises. The opening chapters of *Red Badge* are replete with Fleming's worried calculations about whether he will stand or run in battle. Of course, he does both, giving commentators on *Red Badge* material for perceptive analyses of Fleming's motivations, which range from craven selfishness to the highest sorts of altruism, as well for an elaborate taxonomy of responses to danger and fear: moral versus muscular heroism, bravery versus cowardice, reflexive versus calculated responses. Also, in the view of several recent commentators, Crane's graphic depiction of modern warfare radically calls into question traditional notions of battlefield heroism.

Harold Beaver, William B. Dillingham, Pizer, and I find little reason to believe Fleming exhibits cool self-possession or courage. Beaver finds Fleming's passionate, rash actions pseudoheroic; Dillingham argues that his acts of "heroism" are driven by subhuman urges; Pizer (1966) retranslates Crane's poetic description of "a temporary but sublime absence of selfishness" into "a temporary delirium derived from animal fury . . . and fear" (25); and I find (as I discuss in "'Matters of Conscience' and 'Blunders of Virtue'") that, both when Fleming holds the line and when he leads with the regiment flag, his deeds are instances of amoral, unconscious muscular heroism quite unlike, for example, the cool and deliberate moral courage of Dr. Trescott in Crane's last novel, *The Monster.* Daniel Weiss's psychoanalytic examination of Crane's account of the psychology of fear is one of the best places to begin a study of *Red Badge.* Whereas John Conder stresses that Henry's baseline behaviors are group governed—when his mates advance, so does he, and when they run, he does too—because all of them are "in a moving box" that is wonderfully described in chapter 3, Weiss extends this line of reasoning, arguing that in the adrenaline-charged chaos of war, personal responsibility is obliterated. John Fraser, Leland Krauth, and Andrew Rutherford, however, counter that this is not so.

Fraser holds that Crane preserves for Henry an admittedly small but nevertheless significant zone of human freedom that is sufficient to ethical action; Krauth is more suspicious yet still argues that the ambiguities contained in the conclusion of Crane's story can accommodate both military heroism and acts of human compassion. Rutherford is more emphatic: his thesis is that the demanding reality of war is precisely what makes truly heroic conduct possible, since such supererogative actions are, by definition, above and beyond the call of duty.

A quantum leap in destructive technologies and the total war policy embodied in General William T. Sherman's slash-and-burn March to the Sea have led military historians to suggest that perhaps the traditional rules of war, including a meaningful distinction between civilians and combatants, were rendered moot in the Civil War. Five excellent commentaries explore this. Carol B. Hafer sees the ending of *Red Badge* not ironic but absurd. Wayne Charles Miller argues that heroism is "absurd" in modern war and that, consequently, Crane's novel is mistitled—it is not about a badge of courage or, for that matter, *any* sort of courage. Mary Neff Shaw sees Crane's novel as a mostly satiric critique of romanticized heroism, the sort that had been possible in earlier, less savage wars. Along this line, Moorhead Wright proposes that modern war has deconstructed heroism and courage. Donald Pease's convoluted, dense, and somewhat jargon-infested essay broadens this claim, holding that as a result of his acute depersonalization of war Crane's soldiers become mere machines devoid of any possibility of moral agency. Recall, for example, Crane's comments in chapter 8 that "the battle was like the grinding of an immense and terrible machine to him," and how in his first battle, as soon as Henry "fired a first wild shot, directly he was working his weapon like an automatic affair." Daniel Shanahan, on the other hand, after conceding Crane's fondness for machine images, nonetheless holds that Fleming has sufficient resources and opportunities to grow into manhood. For more on Crane and machines, see Terry Mulcaire.

In a word, critics have found that Crane's *Red Badge* provides ample illustration for a wide spectrum of opinion about Fleming's action, from those that commend him for exhibiting the highest sort of bravery to those that condemn him for the most despicable and groveling cowardice. And between those extremes, Rudolph F. Dietz notes that although many readers have assumed that the narrator's comment in chapter 6—"He ran like a rabbit"—refers to Fleming, it is actually directed toward another soldier. After several soldiers around him have begun to run, Fleming then reacts "like a proverbial chicken [who] . . . had lost the direction of safety." Dietz's fine-grained clarification is crucial: careful attention to Crane's text reveals a less cowardly young, green private. Finally, Crane's treatment of the varieties of courage is expansive enough to include the heroism of a noncombatant. Kermit Vanderbilt and Daniel Weiss astutely point out that in his finest hour Fleming, without his weapon, leads the charge bearing the regiment's flag.

Film, TV, Classic Comics, and Young Reader Resources

The redoubtable John Huston struggled mightily to bring *Red Badge* to film in 1951. Even with Audie Murphy, a Medal of Honor recipient and the most highly decorated veteran of World War II, playing Henry, Huston could not bridge the novel/film divide. (On Murphy, see William Mauldin.) For a full account of Huston's film see Lillian Ross's book—or, better yet, the five serialized installments that appeared in *The New Yorker* between May 24 and June 21, 1952. Reading Ross's essays alongside the other articles, advertisements, and cartoons of the magazine gives a fascinating glimpse into the America of the 1950s during the Eisenhower years. See also Fred Silva on Huston's film, which, although neither a critical nor a box-office success, nicely captured how "nature remains a totally indifferent constant . . . unmoved by men's subtle activities, be they the confusion of Henry Fleming's early fears or his subsequently courageous behavior" (123).

Further afield, James A. Stevenson makes interesting comparisons between Crane's novel and Stanley Kubrick's 1987 film *Full Metal Jacket*. A popular, more successful adaptation, a made-for-TV version directed by Lee Philips and starring Richard Thomas, appeared in 1974. Finally, in 1999 the Discovery Channel's Great Books series presented a one-hour program on *Red Badge* produced by Nancy LeBrun, written by James McPherson, and narrated by Donald Sutherland. With respected Crane biographer James B. Colvert appearing as one of the talking heads, the film provides a helpful context that combines Civil War history and details about Crane's life and his other works as it does justice to the breakthrough achievement of his novella.

In 1952, Gilbertson Publishers released its Classic Comics Illustrated version of *Red Badge*. It originally sold for twenty-four cents (in 2010 it was selling for about fifteen dollars at online sites). Its drawings and liberal quotations of the dialogue between Henry and his fellows do a surprisingly good job of capturing Crane's story. See Schaefer's essay (2006b) for a detailed examination of the Classic Comics Illustrated version.

Several books for juveniles deserve notice. Sorrentino's *Student Companion to Stephen Crane* (2006) has a reliable sketch of Crane's life and literary heritage, and its twenty-page chapter on *Red Badge* is useful for both young students and their teachers. (Colvert's 1984 biography is aimed at a general audience and so is also accessible for younger students.) Caroline Kepnes's *Classic Story Tellers: Stephen Crane*, one volume in Mitchell Lane Publishers' academic children's books series, has a mostly reliable biography of Crane, but the main reason to recommend the book is its pictures. It includes five good ones of Crane from the Syracuse University Special Collection, all of which Crane scholars are likely familiar with, but in Kepnes's book they have been stunningly "colorized" and skillfully cropped. The strong suit of Linda Bickerstaff's short book *"The Red Badge of Courage" and the Civil War*, which is written for middle-school readers, is also its photographs; her biographical sketch of Crane, however, is flawed. Gibson's (1996) introduction to his 1996 reprinting of *Red Badge* is also aimed at beginning readers.

Bibliographies

In 1972, Stallman released a nearly seven-hundred-page, and purportedly definitive, volume titled *Stephen Crane: A Critical Bibliography*. Unfortunately, Stallman resisted few opportunities to celebrate his own discoveries of unattributed Crane pieces, and he regularly privileged his literary interpretations over those of other scholars (and often denigrated their commentary). As a result, this potentially valuable book assumed a polemical tone and stirred further controversy. My own 1992 *Annotated Bibliography* is now the standard resource, and updates to it can be found in the 1999 special issue of *War, Literature & the Arts* edited by James H. Meredith and in essays in *Stephen Crane Studies* (1999, 2001, 2003, 2005, and 2009).

Works Cited

Albrecht, Robert C. "Content and Style in *The Red Badge of Courage*." *College English* 27 (1966): 487-92.

Allred, Randal W. "'The Gilded Images of Memory,' *The Red Badge of Courage*, and 'The Veteran.'" *Stephen Crane in War and Peace*. Ed. James H. Meredith. Spec. issue of *War, Literature & the Arts* (1999): 100-15.

Anderson, Warren D. "Homer and Stephen Crane." *Nineteenth-Century Fiction* 19 (1964): 77-86.

Banks, Nancy Huston. "The Novels of Two Journalists." *Bookman* 2 (1895): 217-20. Rpt. in *Stephen Crane: The Critical Heritage*. Ed. Richard M. Weatherford. London: Routledge & Kegan Paul, 1973. 96-99.

Beaver, Harold. "Stephen Crane: The Hero as Victim." *Yearbook of English Studies* 12 (1982): 186-93.

Beer, Thomas. *Stephen Crane: A Study in American Letters*. New York: Alfred A. Knopf, 1923.

Beidler, Philip D. "Stephen Crane's *The Red Badge of Courage*: Henry Fleming's Courage in Its Contexts." *CLIO* 20 (1991): 235-51.

Bender, Bert. "'The Chaos of His Brain': Evolutionary Psychology in *The Red*

Badge of Courage." *Evolution and "the Sex Problem": American Narratives during the Eclipse of Darwinism.* Ed. Burt Bender. Kent, OH: Kent State UP, 2004. 52-71.

_____. "Hanging Stephen Crane in the Impressionist Museum." *Journal of Aesthetics and Art Criticism* 35 (1976): 47-55.

Benfy, Christopher. "Badges of Courage and Cowardice: A Source for Crane's Title." *Stephen Crane Studies* 6.2 (Fall 1997): 2-5.

_____. "Two Cranes, Two Henrys." *Stephen Crane in War and Peace.* Ed. James H. Meredith. Spec. issue of *War, Literature & the Arts* (1999): 1-10.

Berryman, John. *Stephen Crane.* New York: William Sloane, 1950.

Bickerstaff, Linda. *"The Red Badge of Courage" and the Civil War.* New York: Rosen, 2003.

Binder, Henry. "Donald Pizer, Ripley Hitchcock, and *The Red Badge of Courage.*" *Studies in the Novel* 11 (1979): 216-23.

_____. *"The Red Badge of Courage* Nobody Knows." *Studies in the Novel* 10 (1978a): 9-47.

_____. *"The Red Badge of Courage* Nobody Knows." *The Red Badge of Courage,* by Stephen Crane. Ed. Henry Binder. New York: W. W. Norton, 1982. 111-58.

_____. "Unwinding the Riddle of Four Pages Missing from *The Red Badge of Courage* Manuscript." *Papers of the Bibliographical Society of American* 72 (1978b): 100-06.

Bowers, Fredson. "Regularization and Normalization in Modern Critical Texts." *Studies in Bibliography* 42 (1989): 79-102.

Brody, E. C. "Tolstoy and Crane's *The Red Badge of Courage.*" *Studia Slavica Hungaricae* 23 (1978): 39-54.

Brooks, Sydney. Rev. of *The Red Badge of Courage,* by Stephen Crane. *Saturday Review* 11 Jan. 1896: lxxxi, 44-45. Rpt. in *Stephen Crane: The Critical Heritage.* Ed. Richard M. Weatherford. London: Routledge & Kegan Paul, 1973. 99-103.

Burhans, Clinton. "Judging Henry Judging: Point of View in *The Red Badge of Courage.*" *Ball State University Forum* 15.2 (1974): 38-48.

Cady, Edwin. *Stephen Crane.* Boston: Twayne, 1980.

Carlson, Eric W. "Crane's *The Red Badge of Courage.*" *Explicator* 16 (1958): item 34.

Carruthers, Sharon. "'Old Soldiers Never Die': A Note on Col. John L. Burleigh." *Studies in the Novel* 10 (1978): 158-60.

Cather, Willa. "When I Knew Stephen Crane." *Library* 1 (23 June 1900): 17-18. Rpt. in *Prairie Schooner* 23 (1949): 231-36.

Chase, Richard. Introduction. *The Red Badge of Courage.* 1895. By Stephen Crane. Cambridge, MA: Riverside, 1960.

Clendenning, John. "Stephen Crane and His Biographers: Beer, Berryman, Schoberlin, and Stallman." *American Literary Realism* 28 (1995): 23-57.

_____. "Thomas Beer's *Stephen Crane*: The Eye of His Imagination." *Prose Studies* 14 (1991): 68-80.

Colvert, James B. "Crane, Hitchcock, and the Binder Edition of *The Red Badge of Courage*." *Critical Essays on Stephen Crane's "The Red Badge of Courage."* Ed. Donald Pizer. Boston: G. K. Hall, 1990. 238-63.

_____. *"The Red Badge of Courage* and a Review of Zola's *La Débâcle*." *Modern Language Notes* 71 (1956): 98-100.

_____. *Stephen Crane*. New York: Harcourt Brace Jovanovich, 1984.

_____. "Unreal War in *The Red Badge of Courage*." *Stephen Crane in War and Peace*. Ed. James H. Meredith. Spec. issue of *War, Literature & the Arts* (1999): 35-47.

Conder, John J. *"The Red Badge of Courage*." *Modern American Fiction: Form and Function*. Ed. Thomas Daniel Young. Baton Rouge: Louisiana State UP, 1989. 28-38.

Cox, James Trammell. "The Imagery of *The Red Badge of Courage*." *Modern Fiction Studies* 5 (1959): 209-19.

Crane, Stephen. "The Angel Child." *Harper's New Monthly Magazine* Aug. 1899: 358-65. Rpt. in *Stephen Crane: Prose and Poetry*. Ed. J. C. Levenson. New York: Library of America, 1984. 1174-83.

_____. "The Veteran." *McClure's Magazine* Aug. 1896: 222-23. Rpt. in *Stephen Crane: Prose and Poetry*. Ed. J. C. Levenson. New York: Library of America, 1984. 666-70.

Curran, John E., Jr. "'Nobody Seems to Know Where We Go': Uncertainty, History, and Irony in *The Red Badge of Courage*." *American Literary Realism* 26 (1993): 1-12.

D. Appleton & Co. [Ripley Hitchcock]. "Reply to McClurg." *Dial* 1 May 1896: xx, 263. Rpt. in *Stephen Crane: The Critical Heritage*. Ed. Richard M. Weatherford. London: Routledge & Kegan Paul, 1973. 144-45.

Delbanco, Andrew. "The New Stephen Crane: The Context for *The Red Badge of Courage*." *New Essays on "The Red Badge of Courage."* Ed. Lee Clark Mitchell. New York: Cambridge UP, 1986. 49-76.

Derrick, Scott. "Behind the Lines: Homoerotic Anxiety and the Heroic in Stephen Crane's *The Red Badge of Courage*." *Monumental Anxieties: Homoerotic Desire and Feminine Influence in 19th Century U.S. Literature*. New Brunswick, NJ: Rutgers UP, 1997. 170-90.

Detweiler, Robert. "Christ and the Christ Figure in American Fiction." *Christian Scholar* 47 (1964): 111-24.

Dietz, Rudolph F. "Crane's *The Red Badge of Courage*." *Explicator* 42 (1984): 36-38.

Dillingham, William B. "Insensibility in *The Red Badge of Courage*." *College English* 25 (1963): 194-98.

Domeraski, Regina. "A Note on the Text." *The Red Badge of Courage*. By Stephen Crane. New York: Bantam, 1983. 133-35.

Dooley, Patrick K. *An Annotated Bibliography of Secondary Scholarship on Stephen Crane*. New York: G. K. Hall, 1992.

_____. "'Matters of Conscience' and 'Blunders of Virtue': Crane on the Varieties of Heroism, or Why Moral Philosophers Need Literature." *A Commu-*

nity of Inquiry: Conversations Between Classical American Philosophy and American Literature. Kent, OH: Kent State UP, 2008. 42-54.

_____. *The Pluralistic Philosophy of Stephen Crane*. Urbana: U of Illinois P, 1993.

_____. "Stephen Crane: An Annotated Bibliography of Secondary Scholarship: An Update." *Stephen Crane in War and Peace*. Ed. James H. Meredith. Spec. issue of *War, Literature & the Arts* (1999): 250-98.

_____. "Stephen Crane: An Annotated Bibliography of Secondary Scholarship: Book Chapters Through 1997." *Stephen Crane Studies* 8.2 (1999): 13-27.

_____. "Stephen Crane: An Annotated Bibliography of Secondary Scholarship: Book Chapters Through 1999." *Stephen Crane Studies* 10.2 (2001): 12-34.

_____. "Stephen Crane: An Annotated Bibliography of Secondary Scholarship: Book Chapters Through 2001." *Stephen Crane Studies* 12.1 (2003): 2-19.

_____. "Stephen Crane: An Annotated Bibliography of Secondary Scholarship: Book Chapters Through 2004." *Stephen Crane Studies* 14.2 (2005): 10-23.

_____. "Stephen Crane: An Annotated Bibliography of Secondary Scholarship: Book Chapters Through 2007." *Stephen Crane Studies* 18.1 (2009).

Dunn, N. E. "The Common Man's *Illiad*." *Comparative Literature Studies* 21 (1984): 270-81.

Dusenbery, Robert. "The Homeric Mood in *The Red Badge of Courage*." *Pacific Coast Philology* 3 (1968): 31-37.

Eby, Cecil D. "The Source of Crane's Metaphor, *Red Badge of Courage*." *American Literature* 32 (1960): 204-7.

_____. "Stephen Crane's 'Fierce Red Wafer.'" *English Language Notes* 1 (1963): 128-30.

Edwards, E. J. Edit. on *The Red Badge of Courage*. *Philadelphia Press* 8 Dec. 1894: 7. Rpt. in *Stephen Crane: The Critical Heritage*. Ed. Richard M. Weatherford. London: Routledge & Kegan Paul, 1973. 82-83.

Feldman, Abraham. "Crane's Title from Shakespeare?" *American Notes and Queries* 8 (1950): 185-86.

Fisher, Benjamin F. "*The Red Badge of Courage* Under British Spotlights." *Stephen Crane in War and Peace*. Ed. James H. Meredith. Spec. issue of *War, Literature & the Arts* (1999): 72-81.

_____. "*The Red Badge of Courage* Under British Spotlights Again." *War, Literature & the Arts* 12.2 (2000): 203-12.

Foote, Shelby. Introduction. *The Red Badge of Courage & "The Veteran."* New York: Modern Library, 2000. vi-lii.

Fraser, John. "Crime and Forgiveness: *The Red Badge* in Time of War." *Criticism* 9 (1967): 243-56.

Fredrick, Harold. Rev. of *The Red Badge of Courage,* by Stephen Crane. *New York Times* 26 Jan. 1896: 22. Rpt. in *Stephen Crane: The Critical Heritage*. Ed. Richard M. Weatherford. London: Routledge & Kegan Paul, 1973. 115-20.

French, Warren. "Stephen Crane: Moment of Myth." *Prairie Schooner* 55 (1981): 155-67.

Fryckstedt, Olaf W. "Henry Fleming's Tuppenny Fury: Cosmic Pessimism in Stephen Crane's *The Red Badge of Courage*." *Studia Neophilologia* 33 (1961): 265-81.

Gibson, Donald B. "Crane's *The Red Badge of Courage*." *Explicator* 24 (1966): item 49.

_____. Introduction. *The Red Badge of Courage*. 1895. By Stephen Crane. New York: Washington Square P, 1996. vii-xxiii.

_____. *The Red Badge of Courage: Redefining the Hero*. Boston: Twayne, 1988.

"A Green Private Under Fire." *New York Times* 19 Oct. 1895: 3. Rpt. in *Stephen Crane: The Critical Heritage*. Ed. Richard M. Weatherford. London: Routledge & Kegan Paul, 1973. 87-90.

Greenfield, Stanley B. "The Unmistakable Stephen Crane." *PMLA* 73 (1958): 562-72.

Guemple, Michael. "A Case for the Appleton *Red Badge of Courage*." *Resources for American Literary Study* 21 (1995): 43-57.

Guinn, Dorothy Margaret. "The Making of a Masterpiece: Stephen Crane's *The Red Badge of Courage*." *Computers and the Humanities* 14 (1980): 231-39.

Gullason, Thomas A. "New Sources from Stephen Crane's War Motif." *Modern Language Notes* 72 (1957): 572-75.

Gwynn, Frederic. "Editorial Note." *College English* 16 (1955): 427.

Hackett, Alice Payne. "1896." *60 Years of Best Sellers*. New York: Bowker, 1956. 96.

Hafer, Carol B. "The Red Badge of Absurdity: Irony in *The Red Badge of Courage*." *CLA Journal* 14 (1971): 440-43.

Haight, Gordon S. Introduction. *Miss Ravenel's Conversion from Secession to Loyalty*. 1867. By John W. De Forest. New York: Rinehart, 1955. v-xix.

Halliburton, David. *The Color of the Sky: A Study of Stephen Crane*. New York: Cambridge UP, 1989.

Hart, John E. "*The Red Badge of Courage* as Myth and Symbol." *University of Kansas City Review* 19 (1953): 240-56.

Hattenhauer, Darryl. "Crane's *The Red Badge of Courage*." *Explicator* 50 (1992): 160-61.

Hayes, Kevin J. "How Stephen Crane Shaped Henry Fleming." *Studies in the Novel* 22 (1990): 296-307.

Hemingway, Ernest. Introduction. *Men at War*. New York: Bramhill, 1942. xvii.

Hergesheimer, Joseph. Introduction. *"The Red Badge of Courage" and "The Veteran."* Vol. 1 of *The Work of Stephen Crane*. Ed. Wilson Follett. New York: Alfred A. Knopf, 1925. ix-xvii.

Hoffman, Daniel G. Introduction. *"The Red Badge of Courage" and Other Stories by Stephen Crane*. New York: Harper, 1959. vii-xxix.

Horsford, Howard C. "He Was a Man." *New Essays on "The Red Badge of Courage."* Ed. Lee Clark Mitchell. New York: Cambridge UP, 1986. 109-27.

Hungerford, Harold R. "'That Was at Chancellorsville': The Factual Framework of *The Red Badge of Courage*." *American Literature* 34 (1963): 520-31.

Inge, M. Thomas. "Sam Watkins and the Fictionality of Fact." *Rewriting the South: History and Fiction.* Ed. Lothar Hönninghauser and Valeria Luda. Tübingen: Franke, 1993. 176-84.

_____. "Sam Watkins: Another Source for Crane's *Red Badge of Courage.*" *Stephen Crane Studies* 3.1 (1994): 11-16.

Irsfeld, John H. "Art and History in *The Red Badge of Courage.*" *American Notes and Queries*, Supp. 1 (1978): 297-300.

Johanningsmeier, Charles. "The 1894 Syndicated Newspaper Appearances of *The Red Badge of Courage.*" *American Literary Realism* 40.3 (2008): 226-47.

Johnson, Claudia Durst. *Understanding "The Red Badge of Courage": A Student Casebook to Issues, Sources and Historical Documents.* Westport, CT: Greenwood Press, 1999.

Kapoor, Kapil. "Desertion in the Fields: A Note on the Interpretation of *The Red Badge of Courage.*" *Journal of the School of Languages* 7 (1980): 65-69.

Katz, Joseph. Introduction. *"The Red Badge of Courage" by Stephen Crane: A Facsimile Reproduction of the New York Press Appearance of December 9, 1894.* Gainesville, FL: Scholars' Facsimiles and Reprints, 1967. 9-42.

_____. "Practical Editions: Stephen Crane's *The Red Badge of Courage.*" *Proof* 2 (1972): 302-19.

_____. "The *Red Badge of Courage* Contract." *Stephen Crane Newsletter* 2.4 (1968): 5-10.

Kearny, Thomas. *General Philip Kearny: Battle Soldier of Five Wars.* New York: Putnam's, 1937.

Kent, Thomas L. "Epistemological Uncertainty in *The Red Badge of Courage.*" *Modern Fiction Studies* 27 (1982): 621-28.

Kepnes, Caroline. *Classic Storytellers: Stephen Crane.* Hockessin, DE: Mitchell Lane, 2005.

Klotz, Marvin. "Crane's *The Red Badge of Courage.*" *Notes & Queries* 6 (1959): 58-69.

Krauth, Leland. "Heroes and Heroics: Stephen Crane's Moral Imperative." *South Dakota Review* 11 (1973): 86-93.

LaFrance, Marston. "Crane, Zola, and the Hot Ploughshares." *English Language Notes* 7 (1970): 285-87.

_____. *A Reading of Stephen Crane.* Oxford: Clarendon, 1971.

LaRocca, Charles. "Stephen Crane's Inspiration." *American Heritage* 42.3 (1991): 108-09.

Lawson, Andrew. "The Red Badge of Class: Stephen Crane and the Industrial Army." *Literature and History* 14 (2005): 53-68.

Lentz, Perry. *Private Fleming at Chancellorsville: "The Red Badge of Courage" and the Civil War.* Columbia: U of Missouri P, 2006.

Levenson, J. C. Introduction. *The Red Badge of Courage.* 1895. Vol. 2 of *The Works of Stephen Crane.* Ed. Fredson Bowers. Charlottesville: UP of Virginia, 1975. xiii-xvii.

_____, ed. *Stephen Crane: Prose and Poetry.* New York: Library of America, 1984.

Link, Eric Carl. "Stephen Crane's Accurate Romanticism." *The Vast and Terrible Drama: American Literary Naturalism in the Late Nineteenth Century.* Tuscaloosa: U of Alabama P, 2004. 57-61.

_____. "Subjectivism and *The Red Badge of Courage.*" *The Vast and Terrible Drama: American Literary Naturalism in the Late Nineteenth Century.* Tuscaloosa: U of Alabama P, 2004. 129-40.

Linneman, William R. "Satires of American Realism, 1880-1900." *American Literature* 34 (1962): 80-93.

Lorch, Thomas M. "The Cyclical Structure of *The Red Badge of Courage.*" *CLA Journal* 10 (1967): 220-38.

McClurg, General Alexander C. Letter on *The Red Badge of Courage. Dial* 16 Apr. 1896: xx, 277-78. Rpt. in *Stephen Crane: The Critical Heritage.* Ed. Richard M. Weatherford. London: Routledge & Kegan Paul, 1973. 128-41.

McDermott, John J. "Symbolism and Psychological Realism in *The Red Badge of Courage.*" *Nineteenth-Century Fiction* 23 (1968): 324-31.

McIlvaine, Robert. "Henry Fleming Wrestles with an Angel." *Pennsylvania English* 12 (1985): 21-27.

Mailloux, Steven. "Literary History and Reception Study." *Interpretive Conversations: The Reader in the Study of American Fictions.* Ithaca, NY: Cornell UP, 1982. 159-91.

_____. "*The Red Badge of Courage* and Interpretive Conventions: Critical Response to a Maimed Text." *Studies in the Novel* 10 (1978): 48-63.

Mangum, A. Bryant. "Crane's *Red Badge* and Zola." *American Literary Realism* 9 (1976): 279-80.

_____. "The Latter Days of Henry Fleming." *A N&Q* 13 (1975): 136-38.

Marcus, Mordecai, and Erin Marcus. "Animal Imagery in *The Red Badge of Courage.*" *Modern Language Notes* 74 (1959): 108-11.

Marlowe, Jean G. "Crane's Wafer Image: Reference to an Artillery Primer?" *American Literature* 43 (1972): 645-47.

Mauldin, William. "A Buddy's Tribute to Audie Murphy." *Life* 70.22 (1971): 77.

Maynard, Reid. "Red as a Leitmotiv in *The Red Badge of Courage.*" *Arizona Quarterly* 30 (1974): 135-41.

Meredith, James H., ed. *Stephen Crane in War and Peace.* Spec. issue of *War, Literature & the Arts* (1999).

Miller, Wayne Charles. "A New Kind of War Demands a New Kind of Treatment: The Civil War and the Birth of American Realism." *An Armed America, Its Face in Fiction: A History of the American Military Novel.* New York: New York UP, 1970. 58-91.

Mitchell, Verner D. "Reading 'Race' and 'Gender' in Crane's *The Red Badge of Courage.*" *CLA Journal* 40 (1996): 60-71.

Mitgang, Herbert. "'Red Badge' Is Due out as Crane Wrote It." *New York Times* 2 Apr. 1982: Sections A1 and C30.

Morris, Roy. "On Whose Responsibility? Historical Underpinnings of *The Red Badge of Courage.*" *Memory and Myth: The Civil War in Fiction and Film.* David Sachsman, ed. Lafayette, IN: Purdue UP, 2007. 137-150.

Mulcaire, Terry. "Progressive Views of War in *The Red Badge of Courage* and *The Principles of Scientific Management*." *American Quarterly* 43 (1991): 46-72.

Myers, Robert M. "A Review of Popular Editions of *The Red Badge of Courage*." *Stephen Crane Studies* 6.1 (1997): 2-15.

_____. "'The Subtle Battle Brotherhood,' The Construction of Military Discipline in *The Red Badge of Courage*." *Stephen Crane in War and Peace*. Ed. James H. Meredith. Spec. issue of *War, Literature & the Arts* (1999): 128-41.

Nagel, James. *Stephen Crane and Literary Impressionism*. University Park: Penn State UP, 1980.

Newberry, Frederic. "*The Red Badge of Courage* and *The Scarlet Letter*." *Arizona Quarterly* 38 (1982): 101-15.

Newmiller, William E. "The Color of War: A Computer Analysis of Color in *The Red Badge of Courage*." *Stephen Crane in War and Peace*. Ed. James H. Meredith. Spec. issue of *War, Literature & the Arts* (1999): 141-46.

Norris, Frank. "The Green Stones of Unrest." Norris, *"Perverted Tales."* San Francisco *Wave* 18 Dec. 1897: 5-7. Rpt. in *The Red Badge of Courage*. 4th ed. Ed. Donald Pizer and Eric Carl Link. New York: W. W. Norton, 2008. 248-50.

O'Donnell, Thomas F. "DeForest, Van Patten, and Stephen Crane." *American Literature* 27 (1956): 578-80.

Osborn, Scott C. "Stephen Crane's Imagery: 'Pasted Like a Wafer.'" *American Literature* 23 (1951): 362.

Parker, Hershel. "The Auteur-Author Paradox: How Critics of the Cinema and the Novel Talk About Flawed or Even 'Mutilated' Texts." *Studies in the Novel* 27.3 (1995): 413-26.

_____. "Getting Used to the 'Original' Form of *The Red Badge of Courage*." *New Essays on "The Red Badge of Courage."* Ed. Lee Clark Mitchell. New York: Cambridge UP, 1986. 25-47.

_____. "*The Red Badge of Courage*: The Private History of a Campaign That—Succeeded?" *Flawed Texts and Verbal Icons: Literary Authority in American Fiction*. Evanston, IL: Northwestern UP, 1984. 147-79.

_____. "Review of Recent Editions of *The Red Badge of Courage*." *Nineteenth-Century Fiction* 30 (1976): 558-62.

Pease, Donald. "Fear, Rage, and Mistrials of Representation in *The Red Badge of Courage*." *American Realism: New Essays*. Ed. Eric J. Sundquist. Baltimore: Johns Hopkins UP, 1982. 155-75.

Pizer, Donald. "Henry Behind the Lines and the Concept of Manhood in *The Red Badge of Courage*." *Stephen Crane Studies* 10.1 (Spring 2001): 2-7.

_____. "Late Nineteenth-Century American Naturalism." *Realism and Naturalism in Nineteenth-Century American Literature*. Carbondale: Southern Illinois UP, 1966. 11-32.

_____. "'*The Red Badge of Courage* Nobody Knows': A Brief Rejoinder." *Studies in American Fiction* 11 (1979): 77-81.

_____. "*The Red Badge of Courage*: Text, Theme, and Form." *South Atlantic Quarterly* 84 (1985): 302-13.

_____. "What Unit Did Henry Belong to at Chancellorsville, and Does It Matter?" *Stephen Crane Studies* 16.1 (Spring 2007): 2-13.

Pratt, Lyndon Upson. "A Possible Source of *The Red Badge of Courage.*" *American Literature* 11 (1939): 1-10.

Rahv, Philip. "Fiction and the Criticism of Fiction." *Kenyon Review* 18 (1956): 276-99.

Rechnitz, Robert M. "Depersonalization and the Dream in *The Red Badge of Courage.*" *Studies in the Novel* 6 (1974): 76-87.

Renza, Louis. "Crane's *The Red Badge of Courage.*" *Explicator* 56.2 (1998): 82-83.

Rev. of *The Red Badge of Courage. Philadelphia Press* 13 Oct. 1895: 30. Rpt. in *Stephen Crane: The Critical Heritage.* Ed. Richard M. Weatherford. London: Routledge & Kegan Paul, 1973. 84-85.

Reynolds, Kirk M. "*The Red Badge of Courage:* Private Henry's Mind as Sole Point of View." *South Atlantic Quarterly* 52 (1987): 59-69.

Richardson, Mark. "Stephen Crane's *The Red Badge of Courage.*" Vol. 1 of *American Writers Classics.* Ed. Jay Parini. New York: Scribner's, 2003. 237-55.

Ross, Lillian. "Picture." *Reporting.* New York: Simon & Schuster, 1964. 223-442.

Rutherford, Andrew. "Realism and the Heroic: Some Reflections on War Novels." *Yearbook of English Studies* 12 (1982): 194-207.

Satterfield, Ben. "From Romance to Reality: The Accomplishment of Private Fleming." *CLA Journal* 24 (1980-81): 451-64.

Schaefer, Michael. "'Heroes Had No Shame in Their Lives': Heroics and Compassion in *The Red Badge of Courage* and 'A Mystery of Heroism.'" *War, Literature & the Arts* 18.1-2 (2006a): 104-113.

_____. "Sequential Art Fights the Civil War: The *Classics Illustrated* Version of *The Red Badge of Courage.*" *Stephen Crane Studies* 15.2 (Fall 2006b): 2-17.

Schmitz, Neil. "Stephen Crane and the Colloquial Self." *Midwest Quarterly* 13 (1972): 437-51.

Shanahan, Daniel. "The Army Motif in *The Red Badge of Courage* as a Response to Industrial Capitalism." *Papers in Language and Literature* 32 (1996): 399-409.

Shaw, Mary Neff. "Henry Fleming's Heroics in *The Red Badge of Courage*: A Satiric Search for a 'Kinder, Gentler' Heroism." *Studies in the Novel* 22 (1990): 418-28.

Shulman, Robert. "*The Red Badge* and Social Violence: Crane's Myth of America." *Canadian Review of American Studies* 12 (1981): 1-19.

Silva, Fred. "Uncivil Battles and Civil Wars." *The Classic American Novel and the Movies.* Ed. Gerald Peary and Roger Shatzkin. New York: Frederick Ungar, 1977. 114-23.

Solomon, Eric. "Another Analog for *The Red Badge of Courage.*" *Nineteenth-Century Fiction* 13 (1958): 64-67.

_____. "Stephen Crane, English Critics, and American Reviewers." *Notes and Queries* 12 (1965): 62-64.

_____. *Stephen Crane: From Parody to Realism.* Cambridge, MA: Harvard UP, 1966.

_____. "The Structure of *The Red Badge of Courage*." *Modern Fiction Studies* 5 (1959): 220-34.

_____. "Yet Another Source for *The Red Badge of Courage*." *English Language Notes* 2 (1965): 215-17.

Sorrentino, Paul. "The Legacy of Thomas Beer in the Study of Stephen Crane and American Literary History." *American Literary Realism* 35 (2003): 187-211.

_____. *Student Companion to Stephen Crane*. Westport, CT: Greenwood Press, 2006.

Stallman, Robert W. "Fiction and Its Critics: A Reply to Mr. Rahv." *Kenyon Review* 19 (1957): 290-99.

_____. Introduction. *The Red Badge of Courage*. 1895. By Stephen Crane. New York: Modern Library, 1951. v-xxxiii.

_____. "The Scholar's Net; Literary Sources." *College English* 17 (1955): 20-27.

_____. *Stephen Crane: A Critical Bibliography*. Ames: Iowa State UP, 1972.

Stevenson, James A. "Beyond Stephen Crane: *Full Metal Jacket*." *Literature/Film Quarterly* 16 (1988): 238-342.

Stone, Edward. *The Battle and the Books: Some Aspects of Henry James*. Athens: Ohio UP, 1964. 150.

_____. "Crane and Zola." *English Language Notes* 1 (1963): 46-47.

_____. "Introducing Private Smithers." *Georgia Review* 16 (1962): 442-44.

_____. "The Many Suns of *The Red Badge of Courage*." *American Literature* 29 (1957): 322-26.

Stone, Robert. Introduction. *The Red Badge of Courage*. 1895. By Stephen Crane. New York: Vintage/Library of America, 1990. xi-xvii.

Stowell, Robert. "Stephen Crane's Use of Colour in *The Red Badge of Courage*." *Literary Criterion* 9 (1970): 36-39.

Tamke, Alexander R. "The Principal Source of Stephen Crane's *Red Badge of Courage*." *Essays in Honor of Esmond Linworth Marilla*. Eds. Thomas Austin Kirby and William John Olive. Baton Rouge: Louisiana State UP, 1970. 299-311.

Thomas, Donald. "Biblical Parallelism in *The Red Badge of Courage*." *Stephen Crane: A Collection of Critical Essays*. Ed. Maurice Bassan. Englewood Cliffs, NJ: Prentice-Hall, 1967. 137-40.

Tuttleton, James W. "The Imagery of *The Red Badge of Courage*." *Modern Fiction Studies* 8 (1963): 410-15.

Vanderbilt, Kermit, and Daniel Weiss. "From Rifleman to Flagbearer: Henry Fleming's Separate Peace in *The Red Badge of Courage*." *Modern Fiction Studies* 11 (1966): 371-80.

Vickery, Olga W. "The Inferno of the Moderns." *The Shaken Realist: Essays in Modern Literature in Honor of Frederick J. Hoffman*. Ed. Melvin J. Friedman and John B. Vickery. Baton Rouge: Louisiana State UP, 1970. 147-64.

Wasserstrom, William. "Hydraulics and Heroics: William James and Stephen Crane." *Prospects* 4 (1979): 215-35.

Weatherford, Richard M. "Stephen Crane and O. Henry: A Correction." *American Literature* 44 (1973a): 666.

_____, ed. *Stephen Crane: The Critical Heritage*. London: Routledge & Kegan Paul, 1973b.

Webster, H. T. "Wilbur F. Hinman's *Corporal Si Klegg* and Stephen Crane's *The Red Badge of Courage*." *American Literature* 11 (1939): 285-93.

Weiss, Daniel. "*The Red Badge of Courage*." *Psychoanalytic Review* 52 (1965): 176-96, 460-84.

Wertheim, Stanley. "*The Red Badge of Courage*, and Personal Narratives of the Civil War." *American Literary Realism* 6 (1973): 61-65.

_____. *A Stephen Crane Encyclopedia*. Westport, CT: Greenwood Press, 1997.

_____. "Stephen Crane." *Hawthorne, Melville, Stephen Crane*. Ed. Theodore Gross and Stanley Wertheim. New York: Free Press, 1971. 201-301.

Wertheim, Stanley, and Paul Sorrentino. *The Crane Log: A Documentary Life of Stephen Crane, 1871-1900*. New York: G. K. Hall, 1994.

_____. "Thomas Beer: The Clay Feet of Stephen Crane Biography." *American Literary Realism* 22 (1990): 2-16.

_____, eds. *The Correspondence of Stephen Crane*. 2 vols. New York: Columbia UP, 1988.

Whitehead, Alfred North. *Process and Reality*. New York: Free Press, 1929.

Wilson, Edmund. Rev. of Robert W. Stallman's introduction to his 1951 Modern Library edition of *The Red Badge of Courage*. *The New Yorker* 2 May 1953: 124.

Wogan, Claudia C. "Crane's Use of Color in *The Red Badge of Courage*." *Modern Fiction Studies* 6 (1960): 168-72.

Woodress, James. "*The Red Badge of Courage*." *Reference Guide to American Literature*. Ed. D. L. Kirkpatrick. Chicago: St. James Press, 1978. 677-78.

Wright, Moorhead. "The Existential Adventurer and War: Three Case Studies in American Fiction." *American Thinking About Peace and War: New Essays on American Thought and Attitudes*. Ed. Ken Booth and Moorhead Wright. New York: Barnes & Noble, 1978. 101-110.

Wyndham, George. "A Remarkable Book." *New Review* 14 (Jan. 1896): 30-40. Rpt. in *Stephen Crane: The Critical Heritage*. Ed. Richard M. Weatherford. London: Routledge & Kegan Paul, 1973. 106-14.

Editions of *The Red Badge of Courage*

Binder, Henry, ed. *The Red Badge of Courage: An Episode of the American Civil War*. New York: W. W. Norton, 1982.

Bowers, Fredson, ed. *The Red Badge of Courage*. Vol. 2 of *The Works of Stephen Crane*. Charlottesville: UP of Virginia, 1975.

_____. *Stephen Crane, "The Red Badge of Courage": A Facsimile Edition of the Manuscript*. 2 vols. Washington, DC: NCR/Microcard Editions, 1972.

Bradley, Sculley, et al., eds. *"The Red Badge of Courage" by Stephen Crane: An*

Annotated Text, Backgrounds and Sources, Essays in Criticism. New York: W. W. Norton, 1962.

Follett, Wilson, ed. *The Red Badge of Courage.* Vol. 1 of *The Work of Stephen Crane.* New York: Alfred A. Knopf, 1925.

Frus, Phyllis, and Stanley Corkin, eds. *Stephen Crane: "The Red Badge of Courage," "Maggie: A Girl of the Streets," and Other Selected Writings.* Boston: Houghton Mifflin, 2000.

Gullason, Thomas A., ed. *The Complete Novels of Stephen Crane.* New York: Doubleday, 1967.

Katz, Joseph, ed. *"The Red Badge of Courage" by Stephen Crane: A Facsimile Reproduction of the New York "Press" Appearance of December 9, 1894.* Gainesville, FL: Scholars' Facsimiles and Reprints, 1967.

LaRocca, Charles, annotator. *Stephen Crane's Novel of the Civil War: "The Red Badge of Courage"—A Historically Annotated Edition.* Fleischmanns, NY: Purple Mountain Press, 1995.

Lettis, Richard, Robert F. McDonnell, and William E. Norris, eds. *Stephen Crane's "The Red Badge of Courage": Text and Criticism.* New York: Harcourt Brace, 1960.

Levenson, J. C., ed. *Stephen Crane: Prose and Poetry.* New York: Library of America, 1984.

Pizer, Donald, ed. *The Red Badge of Courage.* 3rd ed. New York: W. W. Norton, 1994.

Pizer, Donald, and Eric Carl Link, eds. *The Red Badge of Courage.* 4th ed. New York: W. W. Norton, 2008.

The Red Badge of Courage. Classic Comic Illustrated, no. 98. New York: Gilbertson, 1952.

Stallman, Robert, ed. *Stephen Crane: An Omnibus.* New York: Alfred A. Knopf, 1952.

The Red Badge of Courage and the Existential Nature of Combat_____

Matthew J. Bolton

Philosophy and literature have always been in dialogue with each other. In *The Republic*, for example, Plato famously bans poets from his ideal state, perhaps in recognition of the power that literature holds. Aristotle takes a different tack in his *Poetics*, drawing on the tragedies of Sophocles to illustrate his own philosophical positions. By the same token, many great poets, playwrights, and novelists are concerned with abiding philosophical questions. Hamlet's soliloquies, George Eliot's omniscient narration, the poetry of T. S. Eliot, and the dilemma faced by Vladimir and Estragon in Samuel Beckett's *Waiting for Godot* might all be read as expressions of a philosophical position about an individual's place in the universe. Moreover, some of the most important philosophers of the past century have written both philosophy and literature. The French existentialist Jean-Paul Sartre, for example, wrote not only philosophical tracts such as *Being and Nothingness* but also plays, novels, and memoir. Perhaps it is not surprising that an author would want to work in the fields of both philosophy and literature, for the two offer such different resources. Critic Martha Nussbaum has written of the relationship between philosophy and literature:

> There may be some views of the world and how one should live in it . . . that cannot be fully and adequately stated in the language of conventional philosophical prose . . . but only in a form that itself implies that life contains significant surprises. (3)

Philosophy and literature may approach similar questions, and may even postulate similar answers, but their modes of expressing these questions and answers are radically different. As such, it is a valuable exercise to read works of literature and works of philosophy in light of each other, for a story and a formalized system of thought can be mutually illuminating.

Taking a comparative approach to philosophy and literature allows one to draw connections across different time periods, genres, and traditions. A novel or play from a given period may present characters or situations that seem to illustrate a particular school of philosophical thought—even if that school of thought did not yet exist at the time the author was writing. This is only natural, for if creative writers and philosophers alike are asking the most fundamental questions about the nature of human existence, then they will, in different times and in different forms, reach some common conclusions. In reading Stephen Crane's 1896 novel *The Red Badge of Courage*, for example, one may be struck by the degree to which the behavior of the novel's protagonist demonstrates the principal tenets of Sartre's version of existentialism, a philosophy that was not fully articulated until several decades after Crane's death. Sartre's writings on existentialism are a powerful lens through which to view Crane's novel, for both writers seem to believe that identity and character are constructs that one can create for oneself only by reflecting on one's own actions. Crane's novel of the Civil War presents combat as a phenomenon so traumatic and disturbing that no man may determine in advance how he will behave when in its midst. Half a century later, Sartre himself and his nation as a whole lived through a traumatic experience: the military defeat of France and the Nazi occupation of Paris. In a series of seminal books written during and after World War II, Sartre developed his philosophy of existentialism, which revolves around the idea that even in everyday life one battles to maintain a consciousness of one's freedom over situation and existence. Comparing Crane's novel with Sartre's seminal works can help a reader to understand both, for both explore an individual's obligation to reflect on his or her actions and to create out of these reflections a coherent and valid sense of self. The crisis Crane's young protagonist faces is, at its core, an existential crisis, and Sartre's writings provide some sense of both the nature of this crisis and the key to resolving it.

The Red Badge of Courage tells the story of Henry Fleming, a young soldier who runs away from his first battle and then must reconcile his actions with the heroic ideals that led him to enlist in the first place. The youth had meant to return home in glory, but once he has fled and found himself safe and unharmed, he faces a spiritual crisis. Having failed to live up to the ideal to which he once subscribed, he no longer knows who he is. Fleming believes that his retreat has revealed his essential character: since he showed cowardice, he must be a coward. Shaken by this new conception of himself, he spends much of the rest of the novel determining how he may redeem himself by adopting a new, more heroic identity. By novel's end, the youth will again face combat, and this time he will prove himself to be full of reckless courage.

Henry Fleming's personal journey makes for a compelling story line: he fails at first, but then he reflects on his failure, makes a resolution, and ultimately succeeds. In many ways, this is a quintessentially American story. Like Jay Gatsby or a character in a Horatio Alger novel, Fleming is a self-made man who determines to reinvent himself. Such a reading, however, ignores the deeper complexities of this novel, for Crane presents war itself in the most brutal and unsentimental of terms. War is the "the red animal . . . the blood-swollen god" in the face of which retreat seems sane and valor an act of madness (23). As Fleming and his companions engage the enemy, the youth sees men around him fall from rifle fire and cannonballs. The youth's heroic notion of war is supplanted by a grim, absurd reality as war takes its toll on the bodies of the men around him:

> The men dropped here and there like bundles. The captain of the youth's company had been killed in an early part of the action. His body lay stretched out in the position of a tired man resting, but upon his face there was an astonished and sorrowful look, as if he thought some friend had done him an ill turn. The babbling man was grazed by a shot that made the blood stream widely down his face. He clapped both hands to his head.

"Oh!" he said, and ran. Another grunted suddenly as if he had been struck by a club in the stomach. He sat down and gazed ruefully. In his eyes there was mute, indefinite reproach. Farther up the line a man, standing behind a tree, had had his knee joint splintered by a ball. Immediately he had dropped his rifle and gripped the tree with both arms. And there he remained, clinging desperately and crying for assistance that he might withdraw his hold upon the tree. (35)

This is a deliberately frank and unsentimental portrayal of war; there is no room for glory in this kind of anonymous combat. Only when the enemy briefly withdraws does the youth feel some measure of relief, the "joy of a man who at last finds leisure in which to look about him" (35). The scene around him, however, immediately undercuts his briefly felt elation:

Under foot there were a few ghastly forms motionless. They lay twisted in fantastic contortions. Arms were bent and heads were turned in incredible ways. It seemed that the dead men must have fallen from some great height to get into such positions. They looked to be dumped out upon the ground from the sky. (36)

Again and again, Crane's novel makes the point that war can seem glorious only in the abstract. The further one gets from the experience of combat, the more one can minimize, romanticize, or valorize it. In reality, war is a hellish experience, and those who survive it are simply luckier than the men who fall around them.

Crane has been widely praised for the verisimilitude with which he portrays war; from the drudgery of camp life to the horrors of the battlefield, his gaze is unflinchingly realistic. Some of Crane's contemporaries assumed that the author, who was born some five years after the Civil War ended, must himself have been a veteran (Kazin xii). Crane's book would also have a tremendous impact on the novelists of the next generation. Ernest Hemingway believed *The Red Badge of Courage* was the first "real literature of our Civil War" (xvii), while William Faulkner called it "the only good war story I know" (69). In his treatment of war and in his impact on the next generation of American authors, Crane is a powerfully modern novelist, but the novel's modernism lies not just in its unsentimental depiction of external reality. Rather, *The Red Badge of Courage* is essentially a psychological novel, and its great accomplishment lies in its articulation of the relationship between war and the youth's psyche.

Consider the scene in which Fleming finally turns and runs. It is not merely the horror of war that compels him to flee but rather that horror as registered in the faces of the men and boys around him. Their expressions serve to mirror his own fear, and when his comrades run he joins them as if by instinct:

> A man near him who up to this time had been working feverishly at his rifle suddenly stopped and ran with howls. A lad whose face had borne an expression of exalted courage, the majesty of he who dares give his life, was, at an instant, smitten abject. He blanched like one who has come to the edge of a cliff at midnight and is suddenly made aware. There was a revelation. He, too, threw down his gun and fled. There was no shame in his face. He ran like a rabbit.
>
> Others began to scamper away through the smoke. The youth turned his head, shaken from his trance by this movement as if the regiment was leaving him behind. He saw the few fleeting forms.
>
> He yelled then with fright and swung about. (39-40)

Crane's scene is psychologically profound, portraying the extent to which a soldier's preconceived notions about courage under fire disappear when the battle starts in earnest. It is interesting to note that Crane chooses to dramatize this transformation through two stand-ins for his protagonist rather than through the protagonist himself. The protagonist watches "a man nearby" turn and run howling and then, in an exquisitely drawn scene, watches the expression change on the face of "a lad" who must be positioned even closer to the protagonist. This lad serves not only to mirror Fleming's fears but also to teach him the "normal" response to the horrific experience of combat. The lad's "revelation" is one that the protagonist himself will soon share in, for he, too, "yelled then with fright and swung about."

The experience of the protagonist and the soldiers around him illustrates a central tenet of Sartre's existentialism. Sartre wrote that "existence precedes essence," a formulation that radically reinterprets the traditional understanding of human character ("Existentialism" 24). According to Sartre, one *is* before one is *something*, and, in fact, one can say what or who one is only by reflecting on what one has already done or been. In other words, there is a "prereflective stage" in which one acts and then a "reflective stage" in which one thinks back on those actions and draws conclusions. It is in this "reflective stage" that the ego is formed and that one attains a conception of selfhood. The ego—an individual's notion of his or her essential character—is constructed only after the fact. One can see this process at work in the lad whom Fleming observes. At first, his "face had borne an expression of exalted courage, the majesty of he who dares give his life," but with the battle raging around him these preconceived notions evaporate. "Smitten abject," the boy no longer thinks in abstract terms of courage and majesty. In fact, he is not thinking at all; he is simply acting: "He, too, threw down his gun and fled. There was no shame in his face. He ran like a rabbit." There is "no shame" here because there is no ego—he has no more sense of self in relation to others than does "a rabbit."

Sartre gives more commonplace examples of how one may, through one's actions, transcend the ego: "When I run after a streetcar, when I look at the time, when I am absorbed in looking at a portrait, no I is present" (*Transcendence* 100). It is only after catching the streetcar, to build on Sartre's example, that an individual might think, *Perhaps I looked foolish running down the street*, or *I am proud of myself for having caught up with this car*. Emotions and value judgments come rushing in only after the action has been taken, and to a very real extent the individual is free to choose how he or she will interpret his or her own actions. If "existence precedes essence"—if a person acts in a prere-flective stage and then forms his or her ego in a reflective one—then emotions such as pride or shame are all ex post facto (i.e., after-the-fact) constructions. Furthermore, abstract qualities such as bravery and cowardice are even further removed from the realm of action. In the moment, an individual simply *is* and simply *acts*. Indeed, this is what Fleming does. During this most pivotal of scenes, Crane gives us no di-rect access into the youth's thought processes. Fleming has become an observer, watching the behavior of the solders around him. Then, all at once, "He yelled then with fright and swung about." Fleming does not reflect—he simply acts. In making his retreat, he is like Sartre's exam-ple of a man running for a streetcar: in this moment of decisive action, "no I is present."

To understand how radical Sartre's notion is, one might contrast it with Heraclitus's maxim that "character is destiny." There is a com-monsense, logical appeal to this formulation: it argues that each person possesses an essence that will manifest itself in the sort of life he or she leads. A courageous man, for example, will shine in battle. Because bravery is somehow essential to his nature, he will act bravely when the situation calls for it. Conversely, the man who behaves bravely in battle has revealed his essential self. Henry Fleming certainly sub-scribes to a Heraclitean notion of character and destiny. In fact, the an-cient Greeks—and particularly Homer—are the basis of his romanti-cized notion of warfare:

> He had long despaired of witnessing a Greeklike struggle. Such would be no more, he had said. Men were better, or more timid. . . . He had burned several times to enlist. Tales of great movements shook the land. They might not be distinctly Homeric, but there seemed to be much glory in them. He had read of marches, sieges, conflicts, and he had longed to see it all. His busy mind had drawn for him large pictures extravagant in color, lurid with breathless deeds. (3)

Fleming's vision of battle is drawn from the *Iliad*, in which heroes square off for single combat on the field and each man's victories and defeats are duly recorded by an omniscient narrator. In Homer's world-view, as in Heraclitus's, each man has an essential character that determines his destiny. The first word of the *Iliad*, for example, is *mênin*, or "rage." "Rage—Goddess, sing the rage of Peleus's son Achilles," Homer calls out to the muses, identifying at the start of the epic the characteristic that will determine the hero's fate (77). Fleming might sympathize with Roquentin, the protagonist of Sartre's novel *Nausea*, who envies the surety with which a life unfolds in a book or a story; he says, "I wanted the moments of my life to follow each other and order themselves like those of a life remembered" (59). Yet he also realizes the impossibility of living this way, saying, "I might as well try to catch time by the tail" (59). Homer may start his epic with the word *mênin*, for he already knows the end of Achilles' story before he begins to tell it. For a person, however, such retrospective living is impossible; as Roquentin notes: "Life moves in one direction and stories move in the opposite" (59).

Fleming tries to see himself through the Homeric lens of the essential quality. As a new recruit, he has devoted much energy to self-analysis, trying "to mathematically prove to himself that he would not run from a battle" (8). In the Homeric epics that he idealizes, a man's essential character can be neatly proven and defined: Achilles is full of wrath (*mênin*), Odysseus is wily (*polytropos*), and so on with any Homeric figure. The even light of Homer's omniscient narrator reveals not merely the patronage and history of each new character but also their essential qualities. In the real world, Fleming discovers, there is no such clarity. Instead, he reaches a profoundly unsettling conclusion:

> He was forced to admit that as far as war was concerned he knew nothing of himself. . . . He was an unknown quantity. . . . He must accumulate information of himself, and meanwhile he resolved to remain close upon his guard lest those qualities of which he knew nothing should everlastingly disgrace him. (8)

It is in scenes such as this one that the fundamentally modern quality of *The Red Badge of Courage* becomes clear. Fleming still retains a Homeric or Heraclitean notion of war, character, and heroism and believes himself to have "qualities of which he knew nothing" that will determine his destiny. Yet, in the act of searching for and failing to locate these qualities, he draws ever closer to the existential vision of himself as one whose actions will precede—rather than be determined by—his essence. It is telling that Fleming uses a word that will be so central to Sartre's philosophy: "nothing." If being is the state of actual objects and people in the world, then nothingness is that realm of possibility that people usher into existence by asking questions and by imagining alternative scenarios. Sartre might argue that nothingness has inserted itself between what Fleming is now and what he fears he may be in the future. In his seminal work *Being and Nothingness*, Sartre argues that this inability to know how one will behave in the future is a source of anguish, for "the decisive conduct will emanate from a self that I am not yet" (32). Fleming hopes that he will behave bravely, but ultimately he has no control over how he will act, for the version of himself who imagines battle in the abstract is not synonymous with the future self who will experience the reality of battle.

Sartre illustrates the notion of anguish by using an example very similar to Fleming's situation:

> The artillery preparation which precedes the attack can provoke fear in the soldier who undergoes the bombardment, but his anguish begins when he tries to foresee the conduct with which he will face the bombardment, when he asks himself if he is going to be able to "hold out." Similarly the recruit who reports for active duty at the beginning of the war can in some instances be afraid of death, but more often he is "afraid of being afraid"; that is, he is filled with anguish before himself. (*Being* 29)

One feels fear in the face of actual danger but anguish in the face of the nothingness that stands between one's present hopes and resolutions and one's future actions. In the terms Sartre uses elsewhere, Fleming is "condemned to be free," and his fear is that he will freely choose to run rather than to fight (39). In another example, Sartre writes of a gambler who has resolved not to play cards again and who then finds himself within view of a card game. In the presence of the actual game of cards, he feels alienated from his heartfelt promise not to gamble: "What he apprehends then in anguish is precisely the total inefficacy of the past resolution. . . . I am not subject to it, it fails in the mission which I have given it" (*Being* 33). Sartre's concept of anguish helps explain Fleming's crisis before the battle; unlike Achilles or another Homeric hero, Fleming is "an unknown quantity." This notion of anguish also helps to explain why Fleming's resolution to be brave fails him on the battlefield. Like Sartre's gambler, Fleming finds that in the heat of battle his earlier resolution has no hold over him.

It is only after the immediate danger has passed that Fleming realizes the magnitude of his decision. Upon learning that his regiment did, in fact, hold off the enemy attack, Fleming is filled with shame. He has run while his comrades have stood their ground, and hence he must be a coward. The youth's response is visceral: he "cringed as if discovered in a crime" (43). Fleming has moved from Sartre's prereflective stage to the ego-formation stage. Reflecting on his actions, he is now reaching conclusions about what essential traits those actions revealed:

> He shambled along with bowed head, his brain in a tumult of agony and despair. When he looked loweringly up, quivering at each sound, his eyes had the expression of those of a great criminal who thinks his guilt and his punishment great, and knows that he can find no words. (44)

Like "a great criminal," Fleming feels that he has done something wrong. As he thinks back on his actions, he is filled with shame. It little matters that he and the men around him felt no such emotion during the battle itself—the youth next to Fleming is described in this way: "There was no shame in his face. He ran like a rabbit." Crane's depiction of battle and its aftermath illustrates an idea that is central to Sartre's philosophy: shame is an ex post facto construction. People are ashamed only after they have acted, and that shame centers on their relation to others. Fleming, finding himself among a troop of wounded men, suddenly sees the gap between how these soldiers acted and how he himself acted. For the first time since retreating, he thinks of how he must appear to the gaze of the men around him:

> But he was amid wounds. The mob of men was bleeding. Because of the tattered soldier's question he now felt that his shame could be viewed. He was continually casting sidelong glances to see if the men were contemplating the letters of guilt he felt burned into his brow. (52)

In battle, Fleming's thoughts were entirely centered on external danger. Now, with that danger passed, he instead thinks of himself as an object for other people's scrutiny.

Sartre uses shame to illustrate the distinction between a person in a state of action and that same person in a state of reflection. In *Being and Nothingness*, Sartre famously gives the example of a Peeping Tom who is intent on looking through a keyhole. He is so absorbed in his project of looking into the other room that he has no real consciousness of himself. It is only when he realizes that he is being watched that this relationship reverses itself; the Peeping Tom suddenly thinks of his own appearance rather than of the view through the keyhole. Whereas before he was a subject and the room on the far side of the keyhole was an object, the Peeping Tom now sees himself as an object caught in the gaze of another. With the sudden return of self-consciousness comes a sudden awareness of shame. Sartre writes that shame is "shame of *self*; it is the *recognition* of the fact that I *am* indeed the object which the other is looking at and judging. . . . I *am* this being. I do not for an instant think of denying it; my shame is a confession" (261). The most social of emotions, shame cannot exist without the gaze of the other.

Like Sartre's Peeping Tom, Fleming becomes self-consciousness, and hence ashamed of himself, only when he finds himself the object of the other's gaze. Were he to have remained alone, he might have continued to think only of his own safety and well-being, but when he joins the group of wounded soldiers, he is forced outside of his own thoughts and emotions. Fleming must define himself in relation to these men; the soldiers serve as a collective other whose presence turns him from subject to object.

Fleming's crisis is therefore an existential one, for he is struggling to reconcile his past behavior (his existence) with the abstract principle of courage (which he has always hoped would be his essence). Ironically, it is a chance encounter with a fleeing soldier that helps lead Fleming out of this crisis. When Fleming tries to hold the soldier to get information about the battle, the terrified man strikes him in the head with his rifle. Fleming has received the wound—the "red badge of courage" of the novel's title—that he had so envied in the party of brave and injured soldiers. Returning to his own regiment with a wound, and hence a plausible explanation for his absence, Fleming is welcomed by his comrades. In fact, they treat him as a hero. When the soldiers find themselves in the midst of a new battle, Fleming acts in accordance with this new image of himself. Carrying the regiment's flag, he distinguishes himself through his courage on the field. A colonel even asks Fleming's lieutenant for the name of the soldier who carried the flag, saying, "He's a good 'un" (116). Fleming has earned a kind of recognition that is not so different from what he once dreamed of in his Homeric reveries. In the novel's last scene, Fleming has made a tenuous peace with himself. He is defined neither by the "brass and bombast of his earlier gospels," which he now "despised," nor by his cowardice, for he has "put the sin at a distance" (130). Instead, "he was a man," and his thoughts are already turning from war to "an existence of soft and eternal peace" (131).

Sartre's writings on existentialism offer many insights into Fleming's behavior in the first half of the novel, but what might Sartre say about the youth's final transformation? One might offer three interpretations of Fleming's behavior in light of Sartre's writings. First, Fleming's redefinition of himself as a brave soldier could be read as an act of what Sartre calls *mauvaise foi*, or bad faith. Sartre writes that bad faith "has in appearance the structure of falsehood. Only what changes everything is the fact that in bad faith it is from myself that I am hiding the truth" (49). One who acts in bad faith assumes a defining role or posits a determining essence that limits his or her natural freedom. Sartre cites as an example a waiter who is too studied, solicitous, and mannered; he tries to "imitate in his walk the inflexible stiffness of some kind of automaton." This behavior stems, Sartre argues, from the fact that the waiter is "playing at being a waiter in a café" (59). Sartre lists other examples of bad faith, such as a "soldier at attention [who] makes himself into a soldier-thing with a look straight in front of him, which does not see at all"; he concludes, "There are many precautions to imprison a man in what he is, as if we lived in perpetual fear that he might escape from it" (59). Fleming might be like Sartre's waiter: he is playing at being a brave soldier, and all of his actions in the novel's final battle are made in bad faith, for he has imprisoned himself in a role that limits his natural freedom.

One could also take the opposite approach, arguing that while Fleming was in bad faith through much of the novel, his actions and his state of mind at the novel's conclusion are an example of what Sartre terms "authenticity" or "sincerity." Sartre has a great deal of difficulty defining these terms, for the attempt to be true to oneself inevitably calls on one first to define oneself—and hence to fall into bad faith. Acknowledging that bad faith and sincerity are closely aligned structures, Sartre argues that each involves "the same game of mirrors" of an individual both being and not being what he or she is (66). Bad faith aims "to put oneself out of reach; it is an escape," and sincerity can move toward the same goal (65). In trying to define the two terms, Sartre uses an example that is very apropos to Crane's novel: cowardice. He argues that "in order for me not to be cowardly, I must in some way also be cowardly" (66). The act of trying to determine one's own quality (e.g., cowardice or bravery) is itself an act of bad faith—even if it is undertaken in the spirit of sincerity. There is only one way to be sincere: "to dissociate oneself from oneself" and hence "to draw up a perpetual inventory of what one is" (65). This may be the closest Sartre comes to defining an existential virtue: the sincerity that may point the way to good faith. Understanding that the self, like the world, is always changing, the sincere individual becomes "no longer anything but a pure, free look" (65). Fleming may have achieved this by novel's end, gazing at his own past ideas and conceptions about bravery and cowardice as if they were objects belonging to a stranger. In the novel's final scene, Fleming has moved from self-consciousness to a subject-less contemplation of "tranquil skies, fresh meadows, cool brooks" (131). The novel might therefore be read as ending with its hero in a place of sincerity, where his own past selves are as much objects as are the natural elements around him.

There is a final Sartrean reading of Fleming's transformation, one that turns Sartre's work itself from subject to object. The great weakness of Sartrean existentialism has often been identified as its negative and negating quality. Sartre has a genius for identifying the problems inherent in consciousness and in the individual's conception of the self, but he is far less capable of providing solutions. In fact, it is a critical commonplace to note that although Sartre readily defines bad faith, he never really defines good faith. The closest he comes may be in his 1946 lecture *Existentialism Is a Humanism*, wherein he argues that good faith involves "free commitment," the recognition that one is free to choose one's actions and that one should act to preserve rather than deny this freedom. In this same essay, however, Sartre discusses how he was unable to advise a pupil who, during the Nazi occupation, was struggling to decide whether to join the Resistance or stay in Paris to take care of his mother. Even years later, Sartre's system of thought cannot provide a moral or ethical basis on which the young man might have made his decision. Existentialism can therefore be criticized as being devoid of moral judgment; it describes, ultimately, a relationship between consciousness and itself rather than between an individual and the world. Fleming has left the battlefield behind him, and as he marches away, he smiles, "for he saw that the world was a world for him" (131). Fleming's smile is ineffable, somehow, as is his reverie about his place in the world. Sartre's writings illuminate Fleming's crisis on the battlefield, but, in leaving the battlefield behind him, Fleming may pass beyond the limits of what existentialism can offer a man. In fact, the final scene of *The Red Badge of Courage* may demonstrate that some aspects of the human experience can be represented in literature but somehow escape philosophical inquiry. With an ineffable, unexplainable smile, Fleming shakes off the Sartrean worldview and moves toward the good faith that Sartre himself was never able to articulate.

Works Cited

Crane, Stephen. *The Red Badge of Courage*. 1895. New York: Bantam, 1983.

Hemingway, Ernest. *Men at War*. New York: Crown, 1942.

Homer. *The Iliad*. Trans. Robert Fagles. New York: Penguin, 1990.

Faulkner, William. *Selected Letters*. Ed. Joseph Blotner. New York: Random House, 1977.

Kazin, Alfred. Introduction. *The Red Badge of Courage*. 1895. By Stephen Crane. New York: Bantam, 1983. vii-xviii.

Nussbaum, Martha C. *Love's Knowledge: Essays on Philosophy and Literature*. New York: Oxford UP, 1990.

Sartre, Jean-Paul. *Being and Nothingness: An Essay in Phenomenological Ontology*. 1958. New York: Routledge, 2000.

_____. "Existentialism." *Basic Writings*. Ed. Stephen Priest. New York: Routledge, 2000.

_____. *Existentialism Is a Humanism*. 1946. New Haven, CT: Yale UP, 2007.

_____. *Nausea*. New York: New Directions, 1949.

_____. *The Transcendence of the Ego: An Existentialist Theory of Consciousness*. Trans. Forrest Williams and Robert Kirkpatrick. New York: Noonday Press, 1957.

The Unmistakable Stephen Crane_____

Stanley B. Greenfield

I

In a letter to a friend early in his brief writing career, Stephen Crane wrote, "I always want to be unmistakable"; and, at a later date, to another friend he explained retrospectively that "My chieftest [sic] desire was to write plainly and unmistakably, so that all men (and some women) might read and understand."[1] There is an irony in the critical fate that has befallen Crane's writings that perhaps that master ironist himself might have appreciated. For though the best criticism of his own time reveals a careful reading and understanding of his works, most recent criticism has seen Crane through a glass darkly.

I refer particularly to the body of commentary on Crane's war novel, *The Red Badge of Courage*, though the criticism of his other works is also lacking in clarity. An examination of the criticism of the novel reveals errors ranging from inadvertent though disturbing misstatements of fact to quotations out of context and gross distortion of sense. We find, for example, V. S. Pritchett avowing that Henry Fleming is never given a name, and Charles Walcutt, in the most recent study of the novel, completely forgetting the tattered man, saying that Henry deserts the dying Jim Conklin instead of this forlorn figure.[2] These are indisputably simple lapses of memory. But we read elsewhere, with more apprehension than comprehension, remarks to the effect that Henry has "a complete lack of appetite for glory," and that he deserts in protest "because war wrenches young people out of their path of life, thwarting their aspirations for work, education, love, marriage, family, self-development."[3] Such interpretations are not only patently wrong but too simple, for the human condition of the typical Crane character, as John Berryman has pointed out (p. 280), is a combination of pretentiousness and fear, as in the Swede of "The Blue Hotel," or the New York Kid of "The Five White Mice," or Henry Fleming, who throughout almost the entire novel is vainglorious and, when he deserts, scared stiff. In another analysis we find the novel as a whole regarded as defective because Henry's becoming a man "is largely a matter of accident, [and] lacks the authority of a consciously willed readiness to work out the hard way of salvation,"[4] a critical remark that suggests a confusion of ethics with aesthetics and, in the context of the whole article, a failure to perceive or understand irony. In still another article we find the author confidently proclaiming at the outset: "As one way of re-examining *The Red Badge of Courage*, we would want to read it as myth and symbolic action."[5] We may well wonder why we would or should.

I must examine at greater length the criticism of Crane by Robert Stallman. We are indebted to a great degree to Stallman for the revival of an interest in Crane. But his critical method and interpretation I find very disturbing. His symbolic reading of *The Red Badge of Courage*, with Jim Conklin emerging as Jesus Christ, appears in his edition of the novel for the Modern Library and, with some additional material, in his essay on Crane in *Critiques and Essays on Modern Fiction* (ed. John W. Aldridge), and in his *Stephen Crane: An Omnibus*; if I read aright the "For Members Only" section of *PMLA*, it is now appearing in a Greek edition of the novel. And this perseverance of the same argument and method of criticism has led to converts.[6]

As an example of Stallman's method in his analysis of the novel, we may look first at his purported objective summary of the action, which precedes the explicit formulation of his theory of salvation and redemption. In reviewing the sequence of events in the opening chapter, he describes the reception of Jim Conklin's rumor that the army is going into action the next day (italics, save for the word *tall*, are mine):

> But Jim Conklin's *prophecy* of hope meets with *disbelief*. "It's a lie!" shouts the loud soldier. "I don't believe this derned old army's ever going to move." No *disciples* rally round the red and gold flag of the herald. A furious altercation ensues; the *skeptics* think it just another *tall* tale. Mean-

while Henry in his but engages in a *spiritual* debate with himself: whether to believe or disbelieve the word of his friend, the *tall* soldier. It is the *gospel truth*, but Henry is one of the *doubting apostles.*[7]

There are several comments this account calls for. There is an error of fact that is *not* negligible: Jim Conklin's rumor is *not* the gospel truth, or any truth at all, for the first sentence of Chapter ii clearly states that "The next morning the youth discovered that his tall comrade had been the fast-flying messenger of a mistake."[8] Another error of fact: Henry is not debating, spiritually or otherwise, about believing or disbelieving his friend; he has a more serious concern, trying "to mathematically prove to himself that he [will] not run from battle." Finally, consider the words I have italicized in the above quotation: not one of them appears in the part of the novel Stallman is describing. In brief, there is not the faintest hint of a religious question of faith versus doubt. Religious phrasing unfortunately predisposes the reader toward an interpretation of spiritual redemption.

This is not the only instance of such distortion. Let us consider a passage describing the climax of the book, the end of Chapter ix, where Henry watches Jim Conklin die: "[Henry] curses the red sun pasted in the sky 'like a wafer.' Nature, we are told, 'had given him a sign.' Henry blasphemes against this emblem of his faith, the wafer-like red sun" (*Omnibus*, p. 223). First, the Crane quotation about Nature giving Henry a sign is not from this part of the novel at all: it is from Chapter vii, and is *Henry*'s reaction to the squirrel's running when he threw a pine cone at him—a phrase, in other words, that is to be construed ironically in its proper context! Moreover, the text of the novel at this point is as follows:

> The youth turned, with sudden, livid rage, toward the battlefield. He shook his fist. He seemed about to deliver a philippic.
>
> "Hell—"
>
> The red sun was pasted in the sky like a [fierce] wafer.

Surely an unbiased reading of this passage reveals that Henry is blaspheming against the battlefield, against war. The shift in point of view from Henry to an observer ("He seemed about . . .") suggests that Henry is not even aware of the sun.

Again, this time in connection with the last part of the novel, Stallman makes a statement about Henry's so-called spiritual change: "The brave new Henry, 'new bearer of the colors,' triumphs over the former one. The flag of the enemy is wrenched from the hands of 'the rival colorbearer,' the symbol of Henry's own other self, and as the rival colorbearer dies Henry is reborn." The implication in this passage is that Henry has done the wrenching; otherwise the comment is pointless. But it is Wilson who has actually grabbed the flag. The ambiguous passive voice ("is wrenched") is highly misleading.

Although there are many other points at which Stallman's theory about *The Red Badge of Courage* may be attacked,[9] I wish to consider briefly only one more instance of the weakness of his critical approach, this time in his salvation theory about "The Open Boat." This interpretation of the Crane short story appears in *Stephen Crane: Stories and Tales*, in *Stephen Crane: An Omnibus*, and in Aldridge's *Critiques and Essays on Modern Fiction*. The distortion here is again partially the result of misplaced quotation. For example, Stallman writes, "At the end 'they [the survivors] felt that they could *then* be interpreters.' Life—represented by the ritual of comfort bestowed on the saved men by the people on the beach—life now becomes 'sacred to their minds.'"[10] What is the context of the quoted phrase "sacred to their minds?" Crane writes, "It seemed that instantly the beach was populated with men . . . and women with coffee pots and all the remedies sacred to their minds." That is, sacred to the women's minds, and it is remedies that are sacred. Even more damning to Stallman's "salvation" is the following: "The rescue of the men from the sea has cost them 'a terrible grace'—the oiler lies face-downward in the shallows." Where does the "grace" quotation appear in the story? On the second page, in the following context: "There was a terrible grace in the move of the waves, and they came in silence, save for the snarling of the crests."[11]

"I always want to be unmistakable." Poor Crane.

II

I should like to suggest that a clearer understanding of Crane's art, especially of *The Red Badge of Courage*, may be achieved if we examine the novel in conjunction with Crane's two most famous short stories, "The Open Boat" and "The Blue Hotel."

For these three masterpieces have much in common, and their very differences are illuminating. For instance, all of them give prominence to Nature and to man's impressions of her benevolence or malevolence, though the role of Nature in each work varies: it is *the* antagonist in "The Open Boat"; it should be but isn't the antagonist in "The Blue Hotel"; and it is a fancied antagonist in *The Red Badge of Courage*. Further, all of them are concerned with man's inflated sense of his own importance, but Crane's attitude toward man's pretentiousness ranges from sympathy in "The Open Boat" to sarcasm or bitterness in "The Blue Hotel." All of them emphasize the need for understanding and interpreting; but in them, again, Crane makes somewhat different suggestions about the possibility of man's evaluating his experience. But what this novel and these stories most strikingly reveal is the Crane artistic formula at its most complex and richest. None of them gives an answer to the mystery of life and death: man's fate is shown as neither the result of deterministic or naturalistic forces nor as an achievable salvation. Instead, Crane maintains an aesthetic perspective on all the elements that contribute to man's destiny: circumstance, instinct, ethical motivation, ratiocination, chance; he refuses to guarantee validity to any of them.[12] This balance between the deterministic and volitional views of life and between a sense of destiny and the haphazard workings of chance is, it seems to me, the secret of Crane's mature art; and I hope to demonstrate in the following pages that the meaning of these works is involved in this balance.

I shall begin with "The Open Boat," chronologically the middle piece of the three. In this story we are shown four shipwrecked men— the captain, the cook, the oiler, and a correspondent—in a bathtub of a boat contending with the sea for their lives. This is a classic situation, man against the elements, and the men proceed to act in the classic heroic manner, for, as Crane says, "The ethics of their condition was decidedly against any open suggestion of hopelessness." That is, on one level of behavior the men are ethically motivated to act as they do in their struggle for survival. So they carefully work together in this crisis and feel born a comradeship and loyalty that "even at the time, the correspondent [the critical intelligence of the story] knew was the best experience of his life." The men are concerned for each other's welfare throughout the long ordeal, spelling each other at the oars and giving what solace they can. Even at the end of their journey, when they abandon their boat and swim through the breakers for the shore, this self-negation is prominent: the captain waves the rescuer to the other men; and the correspondent, indicating the still form of the oiler, cries, "Go!"

But the story is not a simple one of heroic behavior or of the value of a common bond for humanity. Its meaning is enriched, for one thing, by the quality of the men's antagonist. In the beginning Crane presents Nature, the sea, from the point of view of the men, to whom she is cruel, barbarous and unjust, and simultaneously from the point of view of an uninvolved observer, to whom she can even in a moment of crisis appear beautiful and graceful. The real character of this antagonist comes later as a revelation to the correspondent when the men are stalled in sight of land: Nature is neither malevolent nor benevolent— "she [is] indifferent, flatly indifferent," to man's fate.

This explicit recognition and statement of Nature's indifference raises a question, not only about the ultimate value of heroic behavior, but even about the possibility of its existence; and this question is pointed up by a deterministic strand of action, attitude, and symbol in the story. Survival, after all, is uppermost in the shipwrecked men's minds, and survival at its most elementary level demands not only safety but food and water. In an indifferent universe one must eat or be eaten, one must drink or be drunk down. So we find that as hunger assails the men in the boat, the cook dreams of pie and sandwiches. But his vision is mocked by a terrible fin that the correspondent sees swimming round and round the boat in the dark, waiting for its weakening prey. Similarly we see an ironic contrast between the water which threatens to drown the men and the water in the jug so necessary to sustain them. During the journey in the boat the jug rests significantly beneath the captain's head. Then toward the end, while the men are in the water and trying to swim to shore, the correspondent, in the grip of a deadly current, watches the water jar "bouncing gaily over the seas" while he thinks, "I am going to drown? Can it be possible?" However, the men, all but the oiler, survive to receive sustaining food and coffee provided by the people on the beach. (This eating and drinking concept has nothing to do with sacramental rites; the irony involved and its relevance to Crane's Naturalism simply preclude such an interpretation.)

There are thus two planes on which the action of the story moves: the heroic and the deterministic; and the question of their relative pertinence to man's behavior is posed by the end of the story. After the oiler's death, when the survivors hear the great voice of the sea at night, Crane comments, "they felt that they could then be interpreters." This is the final note, the possibility of understanding and of evaluating the experience. What interpretation *can* the men place on their experience, and what, for the reader, is the ultimate meaning of the story? The former Crane does not tell us explicitly, but the answer is clear enough. The correspondent at least has learned the narrowness of his earlier impressions about the benevolence and malevolence of Nature; he has learned that the bell that tolled for the soldier dying in Algiers (he remembers a poem about this soldier while he is suffering on the sea) also tolls for him; and he has found that the comradeship born of their desperate situation was the best experience of his life. But he has also learned that the race is not always to the swift, nor the battle to the strong. The oiler, Billie—and it is worthy of note that he is the only character given a name—was the strongest and the most heroic; in fact, he was ahead in the swim for the shore, yet he was the one to die. On the other hand, there was nothing "determined" about Billie's death; it was, in the circumstance, ironically gratuitous. Chance, pure and simple, was responsible for his death. So chance too, we see, enters as an element in man's destiny.

The meaning of the story for the reader is this, and more. Crane is suggesting that while men's actions seem to have some value in deciding their fate, they are still limited by operating in an indifferent universe where chance can single out victims. On one level, Crane is saying, one must survive, and his struggle is dictated by circumstances; on another, one must do the right thing (as Henry's mother, in *The Red Badge of Courage*, had cautioned Henry) demanded by the ethical consideration. But neither of these is the whole answer. One must and should do something to achieve his fate; and still . . . . In short, Crane is, philosophically, refusing to guarantee that either a biologically or ethically motivated attempt at survival will produce the desired result, though he admits the necessity for the former and admires the heroism of the latter. An after-the-fact understanding, an interpretation, is the best we can manage; yet, "they *felt* that they could then be interpreters," not "they *could*." The refusal to guarantee, which hints at man's pretentiousness in aspiring to even so limited a control of his destiny, extends to the possibility of understanding as well.

What is perhaps most remarkable about this story is that the balance between the forces that make for human fate has a counterpart in a balance between the skepticism of Crane's philosophy and the sense of artistic inevitability that Crane gives to his narrative. For though, as I have stated above, the oiler's death is "undetermined" and gratuitous, Crane certainly manages to suggest *aesthetically* that it is inevitable. The thinness of Billie's oar, the strong bond of comradeship established between Billie and the correspondent, the fact of the oiler's being the only character named, and finally Billie's being ahead in the swim to shore—all these suggest the effect, at least in retrospect, of a classical concept of fate. This interplay between death-by-chance in an indifferent universe and the aesthetically inevitable fate gives the story its ultimate richness and meaning.

"The Blue Hotel" is an even more complex story than "The Open Boat." It has accordingly been more subjected to mistaken critical analysis. Generally, interpretations of this story fall into two camps. One sees the story as the narrative of a man who wills and achieves his own destruction; the story proper, this camp feels, ends with the Swede's death, and the last section, in which the Easterner proclaims collective guilt for his death, is a "Naturalist tag" completely unjustified by what has happened. The other interpretation views the narrative whole, but sees it as Naturalistic in theme. Walcutt, for example, says that "Crane simply shows how a sequence of events takes place quite independently of the wills and judgments of the people involved. . . . The writer does not have to argue that he has proved anything about causation or determinism: he has absolutely shown that men's wills do not control their destinies" (pp. 74-75). Neither of these opinions, I suggest, does justice to the complexity of the story and the integrity of Crane's art.[13]

"The Blue Hotel," although it has a different emphasis from "The Open Boat," is similar in subject matter and artistic technique. Here too we find Nature at war, or seemingly so, with man, ethical motivation along with deterministic behavior, the element of chance, the attempt at understanding, and the ultimate refusal to guarantee anything about what a man "owes" his destiny to. There is a greater focus here, however, on man's pretentiousness and vaingloriousness. Heroism is decidedly absent. The story counterpoises the theme of man's arrogance in even existing, let alone in pretending to moral behavior and to understanding on this "space-lost bulb," and the idea that one must withal act morally and try to interpret his experience.

Man's pretentiousness is stressed from the very beginning. The blue hotel, in its garishness making "the dazzling winter landscape of Nebraska *seem* only a grey swampish hush," is symbolic of society's illusions about itself and its place in the universe. When old Scully leads his three captives from the train platform at Fort Romper into a small room in the hotel, the room *seems* "merely a proper temple for an enormous stove, which, in the center, [is] humming with godlike violence." Scully bustles importantly about, destroying a game of cards between his son and an old farmer and making his three guests feel that he is very benevolent: "He was conferring great favours upon them." This ironic presentation of the hotel owner as a godlike destroyer and bestower of favors further suggests man's presumption.[14] When Scully has to resort to giving the Swede whiskey to maintain his well-ordered and organized world wherein all accept his favors and his decisions, when the whiskey overshoots its mark, when Scully's son gets whipped and Scully himself ultimately has to admit that he is fed up with the Swede—his arrogance is revealed in its proper perspective.

At the other end—or almost the end—of the story is the saloon and *its* reflection of mankind's presumption in the world. Here man is not merely puffing up simple existence in the face of the elements; he has constructed an elaborate moral façade. The best townspeople are in the saloon, including the D.A.; and the gambler who kills the Swede is "in all matters that occur eternally and commonly between man and man . . . so generous, so just, so moral, that in a contest, he could have put to flight the consciences of nine-tenths of the citizens of Romper." Crane's irony in his presentation of the moral presumptions of this societal hearth neatly matches his earlier irony in depicting the hotel and its proprietor. And when the gambler, this seemingly moral man (outside his card-thieving profession, that is), plunges his knife into the Swede, and "this citadel of virtue, wisdom, power [is] pierced as easily as if it had been a melon," and when the leading citizens disappear as if by magic, we see the precariousness of the sources of man's ethical strength and understand that his moral code is as much a fabrication as his presumption in merely living is, to use Crane's word, cox-combry.

The image which Crane chose to describe the Swede's vulnerability, "as if it had been a melon," is interesting. The Swede was ripe for being eaten. We are reminded of the way food and drink in "The Open Boat" are a focus in the struggle for survival. In "The Blue Hotel," however, food and drink reinforce both the deterministic and volitional themes. Crane gives quite a bit of attention to the meals eaten in the hotel and, of course, to Scully's whiskey, which is a necessity for the Swede's survival if he is not, it would seem, to die of fear. In contrast is the dispensing of whiskey in the saloon, whiskey that is above and beyond the call of necessity. Ironically, it is the Swede's insistence on making this extra-necessital drinking necessary that is the immediate cause of his being "eaten." (There is an ironic parallel between the scene where Scully forces the Swede to drink and this scene of attempted forced drinking.) The last section of the story once again presents food in terms of the necessities of life: the cowboy is frying pork over an open fire during his dialogue with the Easterner, in which they attempt to evaluate the sequence of events.

The action between the arrival of the cowboy, the Easterner, and the Swede at the blue hotel and the Swede's death in the saloon is studded with presumptuous behavior. Not only old Scully, but Johnnie, the cowboy, and of course the Swede act with a foolish disdain for the reality of their situation. Johnnie foolishly cheats at cards in a game that is for fun. The cowboy is a "boardwhacker" who jumps up and down inconsequentially and who cannot even be sure that the Swede is a Swede and not a Dutchman. The Swede's early fear is the result of an assumption of a knowledge of the West that is palpably false (they even, Scully boasts, have electric cars!), and his later bellicosity is also unwarranted by the reality of the men's attitude toward him and the fun nature of the card game. But if the characters are presumptuous in their dealings with each other, they are even more so in their behavior toward Nature. Nature *should* be their antagonist. It is indifferent to their fate, even, paradoxically, malevolently indifferent: it whirls and swirls about them throughout the action. But they are fools enough to go out into the storm to stage their fist fight, where the wind, significantly, swallows up their meaningful words. Later, the Swede stumbles through the blizzard, is coxcomb enough not to die in it, and tells the bartender in his arrogance that this weather suits him fine!

Certainly in all this behavior one is made to feel that men are wilfully bringing about their own destinies. Thus, when the Swede's dead eyes rest on the legend on the cash-machine, "This registers the amount of your purchase," one almost believes that the Swede has willed his own destruction. Almost—because it is his dead eyes, not his dying ones, that seem to tell him what he owes. Almost—because chance has been an element in the tragedy: it was accidentally that the Swede had found the saloon at all, and "by chance [that] he laid his hand upon the shoulder of the gambler." Almost—because in the final section the Easterner presents a plausible theory that his death was the result of collective guilt.

But how are we to view the Easterner's final summation? How reconcile it with the "first ending"? Here is his speech:

> Johnnie was cheating. I saw him. I know it. I saw him. And I refused to stand up and be a man. I let the Swede fight it out alone. And you—you were simply puffing around the place and wanting to fight. And then old Scully himself! We are all in it! This poor gambler isn't even a noun. . . . Every sin is the result of a collaboration. We, five of us, have collaborated in the murder of this Swede. . . . you, I, Johnnie, old Scully; and that fool of an unfortunate gambler came merely as a culmination . . . and gets all the punishment.

Up to this point, Crane has very effectively demonstrated the folly of man's existence in this malevolently indifferent universe, and the folly of his moral pretensions. Here he shows man's fallibility in interpreting his experience, for the Easterner's speech is swelling with self-importance and half-truth. The card game was for fun. What could the Easterner have done by standing up for the Swede that the Swede had not done for himself by whipping Johnnie? If old Scully had not given the Swede whiskey and thus made him belligerent, fear might have led to the same end. The cowboy's puffing did nothing one way or the other—and if he had taken a hand, would the Swede have stayed at the hotel and not gone to his death? The gambler is neither unfortunate nor a mere culmination: why was he carrying a knife in a civilized town and in such moral company—and he such an honorable man—and why did he choose to use the knife under rather innocent circumstances? And what about the element of chance and the Swede's apparent death wish?

The final meaning of the Easterner's interpretation is that it is neither right nor wrong. It is pretentious, yes; but it has some force as a moral injunction. For if the "collaborators" had acted morally, who knows what the Swede's fate might have been? The men in "The Open Boat" had acted ethically, but that hadn't saved Billie; still . . . This ambiguity, this refusal to guarantee interpretation, paralleling the end of "The Open Boat," is ironically pointed up in the final paragraph: "The cowboy, injured and rebellious, cried out blindly into this fog of mysterious theory: 'Well, I didn't do anythin', did I?'" The Easterner's theory *is* foggy, but only to the cowboy, limited and blind in his injured rebelliousness. The cowboy hadn't done anything; he should have. Just as earlier, when the Swede makes his way through the storm, Crane balances his attack on man's pretensions to existence on this "space-lost bulb" with the statement that "the conceit of man was explained by this storm to be the very engine of life" (and thus essential), so here, at the end, he balances man's pretensions to moral behavior and interpretive ability with the theme that man must behave morally and try to understand his actions or inactions.

The counterpoint of meaning in "The Blue Hotel" is thus quite similar to that in "The Open Boat." But whereas the tone of the latter is sympathetic, that of the former is sardonic. This inversion in tone is even reflected in the fact that the "hero" of the sea tale is the only character given a name, while the only characters who don't have names in the "Western" are the man who "feared that he might find an assassin" and the one who found a victim. Still, even when Crane views people and the universe most darkly, as he seems to in this story, he suggests the possibility of and a rationale for heroism.

III

The nature of heroic behavior and the state of mind of the courageous man lie at the heart of *The Red Badge of Courage*. The majority of critics accept the point of view that the novel is a study in growth, whether that growth be spiritual, social, or philosophic. These critics "concede" that the novel, especially in its earlier parts, has a strong naturalistic bias which tends to vitiate, most of them feel, its aesthetic integrity, though Berryman, a believer in Henry's ultimate heroism, asserts that it is the end of the novel that is deficient, since it fails to sustain the irony (p. 107).[15] Two critics, notably, depart from this opinion. Shroeder sees evidence of growth but feels it is inconsequential: he complains that the novel fails because Henry's heroism is largely accidental and because the pretty picture at the end "smacks too strongly of the youth's early impressions of the haunted forest; Crane seems to have forgotten everything that has gone before in his own book" (p. 126). Walcutt, on the other hand, claims that Henry, at the end of the novel, is back where he started from, naturalistic man still swelling with his ignorant self-importance (pp. 81-82).[16] I submit that neither interpretation of the novel—the heroic, with or without qualifications, or the antiheroic—gives proper credit to Crane's aesthetic vision. For though earlier than "The Open Boat" and "The Blue Hotel," *The Red Badge of Courage* exhibits the same interplay of deterministic and volitional forces as the two short stories, and the same pervasive irony binding the heroic and the antiheroic themes. It reveals the same ultimate refusal to guarantee the effectiveness of moral behavior or the validity of man's interpretative processes, while simultaneously approving of the moral act and the attempt to gain insight into the meaning of experience.

To understand the novel, then, we must analyze Crane's handling of *behavior* and *attitude*. We may begin with the former. Its deterministic side has so often been commented on that a brief summary will suffice. It is enough to note that, like Scully's presumptuous behavior in "The Blue Hotel," Henry's presumption to patriotic motivation and ethical choice, in the guise of enlistment in the army, is ironically punctured by the circumstance of his enlistment, the "twisted news of a great battle"[17] to observe that Henry moves from tradition-conditioned behavior ("the moving box" of "tradition and law") to instinct-conditioned behavior as the atmosphere of battle overwhelms him; and to recall that Henry *awakes* to find himself a *knight* because he had gone on "loading and firing and cursing without the proper intermission," and had acted like "a barbarian, a beast."

The use of animal imagery to reinforce the determinism of the novel and to deflate man's pretensions to heroic conduct has also often been noted. The similar use of eating and drinking, both in deed and in imagery, has not, however, been given sufficient attention. What is most interesting is the variety of ways in which Crane stresses the survival theme by his handling of food and drink.

When Henry returns home with the news of his enlistment, his mother is milking the brindle cow, and when he departs, "she . . . doggedly [peels] potatoes." Here, food and drink are shown on the simple level of existence, as staples of life, and they point up by understatement the contrast between normality and the excited Henry's impressions of war. As the men march along, they shed all superfluous equipment: "'You can now eat and shoot,' said the tall soldier to the youth. 'That's all you want to do'." Here, war as an eat-or-be-eaten affair is stated explicitly. When Jim Conklin and Wilson dispute about the running of the army, the former eats sandwiches "as if taking poison in despair. But gradually, as he chewed, his face became again quiet and contented. He would not rage in fierce argument in the presence of such sandwiches. During his meals he always wore an air of blissful contemplation of the food he had swallowed. His spirit seemed then to be communing with the viands." This passage is almost pure comedy, with its emphasis on the power of food to condition man's frame of mind. In contrast is the tragedy in the description of Jim Conklin's death: "As the flap of the blue jacket fell away from the body, he [Henry] could see that the side looked as if it had been chewed by wolves." According to Stallman, this wound is supposed to be an unmistakable hint, among others, that Jim Conklin is Jesus Christ, but clearly it is part of the same eat-or-be-eaten concept that pervades "The Open Boat" and that we find in the melon image in the description of the Swede's death. Still another way in which food and drink contribute to meaning is found in the scene in which Henry and Wilson, at a significant lull in the battle after Henry has awakened a knight, go looking for water. Instead of finding the water, which is only an illusion on Wilson's part, they discover their own insignificance. Finally, at the end of the novel, Henry turns "with a lover's thirst" to images of peace. An evaluation of this image must be saved for later.

If Henry's and the other soldiers' behavior is conditioned by tradition and the instinct for survival, their fate, unlike Maggie's in Crane's earlier novel, is not the product of circumstance and the cumulative effect of other people's behavior. Their destiny involves other elements.[18]

For one thing, there is Nature or the Universe. Henry visualizes Nature as being most concerned with his fate. She sympathizes or is hostile according to his mood and circumstance; and this impressionism is part of the philosophy and aesthetic of the novel. But Nature's involvement in the affairs of man is really, as in the two stories, noninvolvement, though in *The Red Badge of Courage* she is not flatly indifferent as in "The Open Boat," or malevolently indifferent as in "The Blue Hotel," but cheerfully so. Regularly throughout the book Crane provides glimpses of this cheerful reality, so that the reader does not lose sight of the illusions and delusions of Henry's limited perspective. The reader of the novel will recall the surprising "fairy blue" of the sky and the references to Nature's "golden process" and "golden ray" of the sun.[19] Henry sees this indifference, but he does not understand it.

Another element is man's will. Jim Conklin, for one, demonstrates that man has and makes ethical choices. Before the battle, he states that he will probably act like the other soldiers; but when many of them run, he nonetheless stands his ground. Wilson, too, feeling as the battle joins that it will be his death, does not run. And there is a decided growth in Henry's moral behavior as the novel progresses. From running away and rationalizing his cowardice as superior insight, Henry moves through a series of actions in which he does the right thing. When he and Wilson, on their mistaken expedition for water, overhear the officer say that not many of the "mule-drivers" will get back, both keep the secret and do not hesitate to make the charge. When the two friends grab the flag from the dead colorbearer, Henry pushes Wilson away to declare "his willingness to further risk himself." And in the final charge, Henry "saw that to be firm soldiers they must go forward. It would be death to stay in the present place, and with all the circumstances to go backward would exalt too many others." Henry at these moments is more than an animal.

Ethical choice, then, is part of the novel's pattern: the moral act is admired. Yet Crane refuses to guarantee the effectiveness of moral behavior, even as he refuses in the two short stories. For there is the element of chance, finally, as in those stories, that makes the outcome unpredictable. Jim Conklin, for all his bravery, is killed. The tattered man, who watches with Henry Jim's death struggle and who is concerned over Henry's "wound," has acted morally, but he is dying and is, additionally, deserted for his pains. Wilson, on the other hand, who has also done the right thing, is rewarded by chance with life and praise; but Henry's immoral behavior, not only in running but later in lying about his head wound, is equally rewarded.

The complexity and withal the simplicity in the nature of man's behavior and its effect upon his destiny is crystallized, it seems to me, in the figure of the cheery soldier. This man, before whom obstacles melt away, guides Henry back to his regiment after Henry has received a "red badge" from the rifle butt of one of his own men. As they move along, he talks blithely of the mixup in the battle and of another's death; he comes out of nowhere but takes Henry "firmly by the arm"; and as he leaves, whistling audaciously, the youth realizes that he has not once seen his face. This disembodied jovial voice is, like Nature, cheerfully indifferent. His materialization out of the blue seems to be an element of chance. His bringing Henry back to his regiment willy-nilly suggests a deterministic pattern. Finally, he seems to represent Henry's own will, arriving as he does at that point in the action when Henry really desires to return to his regiment.

Man's behavior, then, as viewed in *The Red Badge of Courage*, is a combination of conditioned and volitional motivation. Man has a free-dom of choice, and it is proper for him to choose the right way; at the same time, much of his apparent choice is, in reality, conditioned. But even acting morally or immorally does not guarantee one's fate, for the Universe is indifferent and chance too has scope to operate. Crane is interested, however, in more than man's public deeds. He probes in ad-dition the state of mind of the heroic man and the possibility of his in-terpreting experience. Again, as in the short stories, the light of his irony plays over the presentation of man's attitude toward life.

The heroic attitude is given to us in the early part of the novel at a relatively simple level. Jim Conklin, the tall soldier, exhibits a serene faith in himself and his opinions, even when he is wrong. He will not run like Henry's squirrel. If the other soldiers stand firm, he will. Self-confidence, that is the keynote of the heroic temperament. The reader is made to admire Jim's attitude and subsequent bravery, to approve his calm acceptance of the incomprehensible movements of the army forc-ing him to build and then abandon three breastworks, "each of which had been an engineering feat worthy of being made sacred to the name of his grandmother." At the same time, however, as this last quotation reveals, Jim's self-confidence is slightly pretentious. We first see Jim developing virtues by washing a shirt, and he is "swelled with a tale he had heard from a reliable friend, who had heard it from a truthful cavalryman, who had heard it from his trustworthy brother." When this rumor is proved false the following morning, Jim feels called upon to beat severely a man from Chatfield Corners. And in a passage I have cited above, we see there is comic deflation in Jim's blissful and righteous eating of sandwiches.[20]

Wilson demonstrates this confidence in a somewhat different key. The loud soldier is brash, first in his optimism, then in his pessimism. But whether he is supremely confident that he will not be killed or, raising "his limp hand in a prophetic manner," that he will, his is the attitude of the hero. The bravura deflation involved in Wilson's switch from one kind of brashness to another is obvious. Even later, however, when Wilson has become nonassertive and more humbly and quietly confident, when we feel for him, as we did earlier for Jim, a warm approval, there is something a little too self-humiliating, at first, in his new relationship with Henry.

The tattered man furnishes a third glimpse of the heroic attitude. Although he has just seen Jim Conklin die, and he himself is badly wounded, he is very sure of his own destiny: "Oh, I'm not goin' t'die yit! There's too much dependin' on me fer me t'die yit. No sir! Nary die! I can't!" He is more concerned over Henry's "wound" than over his own. But his mind wanders and we know he is going to die as Henry deserts him in the fields. Again we find a mixture of admiration for and ironic puncturing of this state of mind, though the ultimate effect in this scene is one of pathos.

In these characters, however, we do not see development of attitude, and hence the possibility of understanding experience. Even Wilson, who undergoes a metamorphosis, is not developed; we are merely shown the results of his change. It is through Henry, of course, that Crane shows us growth. To see it, we have only to compare Chapter ii, where Henry fails to understand what a box of cigars has to do with war, with the "mule-driver" scene, where Henry overhears the officer speak of his regiment "as if he referred to a broom. Some part of the woods needed sweeping, perhaps, and he merely indicated a broom in a tone properly indifferent to its fate. It was war, no doubt, but it appeared strange." The word *properly* and the phrase "no doubt," which give us Henry's point of view, as well as Crane's explicit statement that Henry learns here that he is very insignificant, leave no room for doubt of the growth in Henry's insight and attitude. Indeed, by the time of this later scene, Henry is no longer worried about running away or pondering the question of death. Even when he reverts in the crises of action to illusions about himself and the nature of his accomplishments, his thoughts reveal the confidence that Jim, Wilson, and the tattered man had before him. To mention but one instance: when he is holding the colors, Henry resolves not to budge. "It was clear to him that his final and absolute revenge was to be achieved by his dead body lying, torn and glittering, upon the field. This was to be a poignant retaliation upon the officer who had said 'mule drivers,' and later 'mud diggers'." The fact that he does not recall Jim Conklin's torn body and that he has, in fact, only once thought about or alluded to Jim's death is not only ironic but an indication of self-confidence in the extreme.

There would seem to be, then, despite the naturalistic light in which Henry's behavior and attitude are bathed, growth and development on both counts. Most of the critics of this novel, as I have observed, note a fading away of the irony as the novel draws to an end. But Walcutt, in his dissenting theory, claims that if we take Henry's thoughts about his new manhood in the context of the whole novel, we see that his motives always have been and still are vain; that he "has never been able to evaluate his conduct," and he is still deluded about himself (pp. 81-82). There is irony in the end of the novel; in fact, if one examines the longer version in the earlier manuscript of *The Red Badge of Courage*, he can have no doubt that there is. For there are long passages there, later excised by Crane, which clearly reveal a delusion in Henry's thoughts. For example, a passage which Crane later omitted has Henry musing that "Fate had in truth been kind to him; she had stabbed him with benign purpose and diligently cudgelled him for his own sake"; another passage has Henry feeling that though he is insignificant, he is "not inconsequent to the sun. In the space-wide whirl of events no grain like him would be lost"; and a third reveals him thinking, "He had been to touch the great death, and found that, after all, it was but the great death, and was for others." In his revision of this last sentence, Crane excised the telltale "and was for others." These pretentious thoughts about his role in the universe, coupled with the image of Henry turning "with a lover's thirst [to] an existence of soft and eternal peace" and the enigmatic last sentence, "Over the river a golden ray of sun came through the hosts of leaden rain clouds," reveal an irony similar to that in the endings of "The Open Boat" and "The Blue Hotel."

But at what is this final irony directed? Not, as Walcutt would have it, at Henry's evaluation of his conduct, but at the presumption in his false impressions of Nature and the Universe; at his *philosophical* self-confidence. Just as earlier Jim Conklin's, Wilson's, and the tattered man's supreme confidence in themselves had been held up to ironic scrutiny, so here is Henry's, only on a befittingly larger scale. But even as the minor characters' confidence has its approbation from Crane, even as in "The Blue Hotel" man's conceit was shown to be the very engine of life, so has Henry's. It seems to me that what Crane was trying to do in his revision was to eliminate the too obvious irony and redress the tonal balance of the novel.

This tonal balance is seen in Crane's handling of Henry's final evaluation of his conduct. Shifting from the apparency of things to positive statement in Henry's recapitulation of his conduct, Crane abandons the word *seems*, so pervasive in the novel. "His mind was undergoing a subtle change. . . . Gradually his brain emerged from the clogged clouds, and at last he was enabled to more closely comprehend himself and circumstance." As Henry reviews his deeds, Crane writes: "From his present viewpoint he was enabled to look upon them in spectator fashion and to criticize them with some correctness, for his new condition had already defeated certain sympathies." No *seems* here; the tone is entirely sympathetic, though the refusal to guarantee interpretation is still here with "to more closely comprehend" and "with some correctness." There is no vain delusion about the past. As for the future—well, that is a different matter, highly ambiguous: "at last his eyes *seemed* to open to some new ways," and he "thirsts" for the obviously impossible, unchanging, "eternal peace." But however insecure the basis of Henry's thoughts about his future actions may be, Henry still has emerged from his experience with a new assurance of which Crane obviously approves: "He felt a quiet manhood, non-assertive but of sturdy and strong blood."[21]

The achievement of Crane in *The Red Badge of Courage* may be likened, it seems to me, to Chaucer's in *Troilus and Criseyde*, despite the lesser stature of the novel. Both works are infused with an irony which neatly balances two major views of human life—in *Troilus and Criseyde*, the value of courtly love versus heavenly love; in *The Red Badge of Courage*, ethical motivation and behavior versus deterministic and naturalistic actions. Both pose the problem, "Is there care in Heaven?" One is concerned with human values in a caring Universe, the other in an indifferent Universe. It is the age-old question of human values appearing in both, though the context varies. Too many critics of both works have suffered from an inability to see the validity of both of the conflicting sets of values. Chaucer shows us earthly love at its best. Alas that it is ephemeral against the backdrop of eternity and Christ's love for us and ours for Him: the perdurable quality of the poem that teases us out of our senses (and provokes so much critical commentary) is precisely the interplay throughout the poem of the two sets of values, so that even though Chaucer "guarantees" in his palinode that the love of "thou oon and two and three eterne on lyve" is ultimately more rewarding, the lovely though perishable quality of human love is not effaced. Crane's magnum opus shows up the nature and value of courage. The heroic ideal is not what it has been claimed to be: so largely is it the product of instinctive responses to biological and traditional forces. But man does have will, and he has the ability to reflect, and though these do not guarantee that he can effect his own destiny, they do enable him to become responsible to some degree for the honesty of his personal vision. It is this duality of view, like Chaucer's, that is the secret of the unmistakable Crane's art.

From *PMLA* 73, no. 5 (1958): 562-572. Copyright © 1958 by the Modern Language Association of America. Reprinted with permission of the Modern Language Association of America.

Notes

1. Cited by John Berryman, in *Stephen Crane* (New York, 1950), p. 99. In all fairness, it should be noted that Crane elsewhere expressed an artistic credo to the effect that the meaning of a story should not be made *too* plain. (See Robert Wooster Stallman, *Stephen Crane: An Omnibus*, New York, 1953, p. 218.)

2. *The Living Novel* (New York, 1947), p. 174; *American Literary Naturalism: A Divided Stream* (Minneapolis, 1956), p. 81.

3. George D. Snell, *Shapers of American Fiction* (New York, 1947), pp. 225-226; M. Solomon, "Stephen Crane: A Critical Study," *Masses and Mainstream*, ix (Jan. 1956), 38.

4. John W. Shroeder, "Stephen Crane Embattled," *UKCR*, xvii (1951), 126.

5. John E. Hart, "*The Red Badge of Courage* as Myth and Symbol," *UKCR*, xix (1953), 249.

6. See, e.g., James T. Cox, "Stephen Crane as Symbolic Naturalist: An Analysis of 'The Blue Hotel,'" *Modern Fiction Studies*, iii (Summer 1957), 147-158.

7. Pages xxiv-xxv of the Modern Lib. edition.

8. All quotations from Crane are from *The Red Badge of Courage and Selected Prose and Poetry*, ed. William M. Gibson, Rinehart Eds. (New York, 1956).

9. A few of these will be mentioned in the course of my analysis of the novel, but I should like to mention here the lengths to which Stallman's critical method forces him. For example, when Henry, discovering that the wounded 'spectral soldier' is none other than his friend, the tall soldier, exclaims, "Gawd! Jim Conklin," Stallman comments that this "suggests an identification of Jim Conklin with God" (*Omnibus*, p. 282, n. 2). Must even swearing lend itself as evidence of religious symbolism?

10. *Stories and Tales*, p. 212.

11. Critics who follow Stallman's method—and this applies to critics in other areas than American Literature—should acknowledge that Biblical phrasing in a work is not *necessarily* a sign that Christian symbolism or allegory is also present in the work. The phrasing may simply be part of the language of a particular period or a particular writer, and though it may give a religious flavor to the work in question, it may have no more specific significance. Further, those who seek symbolic meanings on the strength

of such phrasing are in danger of ignoring tone and context. As far as Crane's Biblical phraseology is concerned, we should remember that after all Crane was a minister's son.

12. Cf. Berryman, pp. 287-288.

13. A recent variation of the Naturalist position, in which men's failure to understand one another is emphasized as the sole cause of the Swede's death, is to be found in Joseph N. Satterwhite's article, "The Blue Hotel," *Modern Fiction Studies*, ii (Winter 1956-57), 238-242.

14. Although critics have noted the "religious" description of the room and of Scully's behavior, they have failed to see the irony in Crane's handling of the scene.

15. Berryman's interpretation of Crane as a whole is vitiated by his peculiar psychoanalytical view of Crane.

16. It is interesting to observe that Stallman, after examining the earlier manuscripts of *The Red Badge of Courage*, seems to have had a change of mind about Henry's "salvation." He sees the "images of tranquil skies" at the end of the novel as flatly sentimental and feels that they are given an ironic turn by the sun-through-clouds image: "[Henry] has undergone no change, no real spiritual development" (*Omnibus*, p. 221). I'm not sure where this "conversion" leaves the rest of Stallman's theory about Henry's rebirth when the rival colorbearer dies, but he himself has let it stand.

17. Cf. Walcutt, pp. 76-77.

18. That Crane developed and matured in his art from *Maggie* to "The Five White Mice" is, I think, indisputable, but a demonstration of this maturation is beyond the scope of this paper.

19. As for the hotly-debated wafer image, although it cannot be said to be cheerful, it seems to me that Scott C. Osborn is perfectly right when he suggests that it is the seal of Nature's indifference to Jim's (and man's) fate ("Stephen Crane's Imagery: Pasted like a Wafer," *AL*, xxiii, 1951, 362). I believe it was to insure this meaning that Crane deleted the "fierce" from his final revision of this passage.

20. Stallman sees this shirt washing as a sign of the right way to achieve spiritual salvation, by immersion in the flux of things; but surely the context renders this interpretation invalid. Crane's ironic attitude toward Jim Conklin in the instances I have cited certainly militates against our seeing him as a Christ figure.

21. I must dispute Walcutt's interpretation of this famous passage: "With all these facts [the juxtaposition of courage, ignorance, vainglory, etc.] in mind we can examine the Henry Fleming who emerges from the battle and sets about marshaling all his acts. He is gleeful over his courage. Remembering his desertion of the wounded Jim Conklin, he is ashamed of the possible disgrace, but, as Crane tells with supreme irony, 'gradually he mustered force to put the sin at a distance,' and to dwell upon his 'quiet manhood'" (p. 81). The mistaken identification of character is negligible. But two points are, I think, crucial: Henry is not gleeful about his courage, but "He was gleeful when he discovered that he now despised [the brass and bombast] of his earlier gospels." And Henry doesn't *dwell* upon his quiet manhood (the word is, I feel, prejudicial): "He felt a quiet manhood . . . ."

CRITICAL
READINGS

The Red Badge of Courage:
The Purity of War_____

James M. Cox

As I write this essay on *The Red Badge of Courage*,[1] we are once again at war. It is the fourth war in my lifetime in which this country has engaged in major conflict. I do not of course count the Spanish Civil War in which Americans sent significant volunteer units; nor do I count such recent paltry rehearsals for the present war in Iraq—Grenada, Libya, Panama—in which instant success was inevitable. Our last major war was in Viet Nam—the longest though far from bloodiest war we have ever fought—and the reaction to it was so negative that one would have thought we would never fight a war again. Yet only a bit more than fifteen years later we are again at war, and many who opposed the Viet Nam war almost to the death now find themselves dusting off theories of just wars by way of explaining their approval of what in their youth appalled them. To review this history with a slight detachment (even I was in World War II) is to know how great a title Hemingway had for his first collection of short stories. *In Our Time* he named it, quoting from the Book of Common Prayer, yet with an irony that must strike any reader as little short of savage when considered in relation to the contents of those remarkable chapters that lie between the stories forming the interchapters. The irony is even greater when the title is considered in relation to this now dying century, which seems to have given us more war than peace in our time. Not only that. We might as well realize that war, if it is not necessary, is nonetheless inevitable—that we can't do without it, that we need it, that somewhere and somehow as human beings we want it. Like hate and love, killing and birthing, living and dying, peace and war are a binary axis in the mind and heart of humanity as well as in its language. Hard pressed as we might be to define war, we know what it is. We know that far from being merely savage, it is nothing if not civilized, the civilized form of at once channeling and releasing the instincts of aggression that reside in the heart and soul—yes, the soul—of humanity. Milton was well on target when he put his pure war not on earth but in heaven. Seeing war as the process of civilizing aggression is as essential as seeing the family as the civilizing form for the control and release of sexual energy. No wonder the craft of war—the discipline, the codes of conduct, the making of arms—is as much art as science. Any visitor to West Point has to be struck by the evidence on every hand that the institution wants to think of military art as much as it wishes to emphasize military science.

Being both civilized and instinctual, both science and art, war is at once dynamic and inertial. It carries with it all the acceleration at the command of civilization to discover new and more powerful forms of weaponry just as it forever retains the possibility of hand-to-hand combat. The very word "arms" evokes the development from club through gunpowder to rifle to bomb at the same time that it refers to the aggressive upper limbs of the body. The combination of acceleration and inertia works through the emotions attending war. War is after all a hastening toward death; it is for the young, who, whether eager for it or forced into it, whether reckless or afraid, whether angry or appalled, find themselves both rushing and rushed toward an end that by the logic of peace ought to be further in their future. Given such acceleration, wonder that the emotions of fear and anger, the twin expressions of helplessness, are forever at play beneath the soldier's burden of facing death in the form of an enemy.

Given this form, a science and art at the heart and soul of civilization, we should not be surprised at the fierce reality it holds for our imagination. Since its essence is mortal conflict, it fatally attracts narration. We may deplore the narration we get—the censored presentations from the Pentagon, the lies and shameless exaggerations, the bureaucratic masking of violence, the banal human interest stories, the gamelike accounts of missiles hitting their targets—yet we are both galvanized and magnetized by these reports and wish to read and hear and see more and more of them. Indeed, the technology of communication is equal in its acceleration to the technology of weaponry, as if the processes of war and narration were one vast symbiosis. Here if ever is proof that the technology of language itself is equal to the technology of war—so much so, that we well could wonder whether the technology of language may have preceded the technology of war, whether the origin of language may have been a curse, whether the mouth itself were the prefiguration of the caves our ancestors once occupied. We always come out to such an uncertainty between the primacy of word or world.

There is a reason that the acceleration of both communication and weaponry have brought us increasingly disappointing accounts. Even with reporters near the front to relay stories and images *instantly* to us of soldiers in their trenches, or planes roaring off a runway, or antiaircraft explosions making a thousand points of light over Baghdad, we seem as far as ever from what we know is the truth of war, and so we settle for the observation, now proverbial, that truth is the first casualty of war. Thinking of that truth, we know that it must have at its heart fear, excitement, recklessness, hate, rage, horror, and death. Melville's lines are apt here. In a poem, "The Coming Storm," after claiming that Sanford Gifford's painting of that name served as a prefiguration of the Civil War, he concluded by relating both picture and war to the primary language of Shakespeare:

> No utter surprise can come to him
>   Who reaches Shakespeare's core;
> That which we seek and shun is there—
>   Man's final lore.

Surely, reflecting on the dynamic and inertial nature of war, we might well brood, in this last decade before the millennium, on the fact that the United States, claiming that it possesses the most advanced civilization and the accelerating technological weapons that accompany it, is bombing Baghdad, located at the confluence of the Tigris and Euphrates rivers—the very place that we learned in our earliest schooling was the Cradle of Civilization. Beyond that, there is the first great image of the war disclosing the incinerated bodies being pulled from the rubble of an air raid shelter in Baghdad—a building that the Pentagon insists was a command and communications center. Such reflections could lead us to a larger fact: that the Middle East, which sustained the birth of three of the world's great religions, has held beneath its surface the richest oil wells in the world. Facing such a fact we know that the burning bush did indeed burn. As the dynamic force of religion has faded, or been converted, into the secular force of science, the inertial force of oil has been discovered to fuel the "advanced" nations.

All of which brings us to the Civil War—the one war that, for all its horror, has come down to us as a just war. Even Bob Dylan in his anti-war song of the Viet Nam era significantly omitted it from the list of wars which were brutally conducted with "God on our side." That war, far more than any of our others, was surely fought with God on our side. Beside every other war, even World War II, it has to seem to the majority of Americans a just war. At the same time it was the most total and bloody war in our history; its 700,000 dead would be in relation to our current population fifteen million. It was also a modern war, replete with great advances in weaponry and communications. If railroads, ironclads, submarines, and breechloading carbines came into use, so did the telegraph, observation balloons, and hordes of reporters to file their stories. Both during and after the war it was the most *written* war that had ever been fought anywhere. There were the day-to-day accounts in hundreds of newspapers, there were the letters home; then came the endless postwar accounts by participants, the 128 volumes of Official Records published by the United States Government, the countless histories of the war that continue to be written, and finally the innumerable fictive efforts to capture the "reality" of the war.

Of all the fictions, *The Red Badge of Courage* is without question preeminent. In the almost one hundred years since its publication in 1895 it has incontrovertibly established itself as the greatest Civil War novel and one of the great war novels of world literature. It still seems miraculous that the novel could have been written by a twenty-four-year-old author who had not even been born until six years after Appomattox. From almost the moment of its publication, its striking power seemed to be grounded on two contradictory categories of life: experience and youth. Since it immediately brought Crane both popularity and notoriety, the compressed authority of its representation of battle experience was belied by the youth and art of its author. If the book brought Crane forward in this country as a Bohemian writer, it brought him recognition, particularly in England (when it was published there in 1896), from the literary establishment. A writer as strong as the young Conrad and a critic as acute as Edward Garnett immediately recognized that the element that resolved the contradiction between experience and youth was nothing less than the remarkable art of Crane's narrative. The art, in a word, was what made the book new, or we could say young, at the same time that it reorganized the vision of war, one of the oldest subjects to attract the narrative efforts of humanity. After all, what we consider Homer's oldest epic was *The Iliad*.

Those who focussed on the youth of the author found themselves at pains to provide a literary precursor from whom Crane had descended, an effort that has continued down the years. Was it Tolstoy, or Zola, or Stendhal? Was it, among American authors, J. W. DeForest (*Miss Ravenal's Conversion*) or Wilbur Hinman (*Corporal Si Klegg and His Pard*)? Or was it *Battles and Leaders of the Civil War*, a series of articles by former commanders published in the *Century* magazine? Or could it have been the monumental *Official Records*? Although these questions, in the form of scholarly claims and contention, have been put forth throughout the century, the stark originality of *The Red Badge* continues to remain by far the most striking aspect of the book. The originality is, after all, at once the experience of the narrative. Small wonder that it would be classed as a work of realism, since it seemed true to what we now imagine is the reality of war. Or that it would be seen as naturalistic, since that classification places it in an up-to-date relationship with the sequence of literary movements that followed realism. Or that it would be called impressionistic, since that designation places it in graphic relation to the art of its time.

These efforts to locate the book either in relation to its author or in relation to its literary origins or to literary history are but an index to the manner of its originality. What no one would or could doubt is its identity; as a war novel—and a war novel not just about any war but about the Civil War. We feel that we would know that much even if its subtitle were not *An Episode of the American Civil War.* As a matter of fact, the subtitle is usually absent in most editions of the novel. Yet here again, the hunger for more specific references has led to many speculations as to what particular battle of the war is being represented. Of the many interpretive forays in this direction, the battle of Chancellorsville has been the leading candidate, yet the book itself is utterly mute in the matter of naming either battle or state where the action takes place.

To see, in what we never doubt is a Civil War novel, just how little there is of what we traditionally associate with the historical Civil War, may not tell us what the novel is, but will at least impress us with what it is not. Not only are there no actual place names; there are no fictive place names. If there is topography in the form of a small river or an open field or a forest, it remains utterly generalized. There is exactly one mention of Richmond and Washington. There is no Grant or Lee or Hooker or Jackson or Meade or A. P. Hill. There is not even a North or a South. Even the terms "Yankee" and "Rebel" appear only once or twice as "yank" and "reb." There is no fight for the union or against slavery. There is not a mention of Abraham Lincoln or Jefferson Davis. There is not a hint of states' rights or the protective tariff. Even the characters themselves are barely named; they are a tall soldier, a loud soldier, and a youth before they are Jim Conklin or George Wilson or Henry Fleming. A tattered soldier and a cheery soldier, although they play significant roles in the book, have no names at all. Beyond all this absence, there is no real sense of the technology of war. We know that Henry Fleming has a rifle, that he moves through a world of bullets and exploding artillery shells, that there are horses and wagons and gun carriages, but we get no particular or detailed identity of any of the machinery. We get no mention of supply depots or howitzers. Finally, there is no romance in the book—no real girl left behind or met—no letters from home, no sense of a society behind or outside the society of the battlefield. True there is Henry's mother and a girl schoolmate Henry believes is looking at him as he readies for departure (this all stated in a few paragraphs in the first chapter), but they are left behind as completely as Aunt Charity in *Moby Dick* when the *Pequod* makes its plunge into the lone Atlantic.

To see what is left out—or better, cut away—is to see how Crane achieved both reduction and concentration of his vision to the field of battle and to the single consciousness of a *private* soldier. He emerged with an incredibly short novel—shorter even than *The Scarlet Letter*—whose twenty-four short chapters stand at once as reminders of the twenty-four books of *The Iliad* and as a line of sentinels marking the violently abrupt sequence of war. The very first paragraph of the book sets the scene:

The cold passed reluctantly from the earth, and the retiring fogs revealed an army stretched out on the hills, resting. As the landscape changed from brown to green, the army awakened, and began to tremble with eagerness at the noise of rumors. It cast its eyes upon the roads, which were growing from long troughs of liquid mud to proper thoroughfares. A river, amber-tinted in the shadow of its banks, purled at the army's feet; and at night, when the stream had become of a sorrowful blackness, one could see across it the red, eyelike gleam of hostile camp-fires set in the low brows of distant hills.

So much is done here. First there is the pathetic fallacy hard at work throughout the passage: the cold *reluctantly* passing, the fogs *retiring*, the river *purling* by day and *sorrowful* at night. Nature itself is being personified as if it had a human will, and at the end of the paragraph it has become an animated form containing the eyelike gleam of hostile campfires set in the *brows* of distant hills. Even more important, the natural process *reveals* the army stretched out and resting, awakening, and trembling at the noise of rumors. Yet if nature is sufficiently animated by the repertorial narration to reveal the scene, it nonetheless must be invested with the power. In such an exchange we can see at the very outset that the book is neither fully naturalistic nor impressionistic, neither deterministic nor subjective but involved in both worlds even as it is subjected to a reportorial narration that implicates both forces, glaringly mixing them together.

Naturalism and impressionism are not the only literary registers brought into focus in the text. There is also realism. No wonder W. D. Howells saw in Crane's early work—he was less enthusiastic about *The Red Badge*—a writer who was extending the range of realism into the urban streets. In *The Red Badge*, Crane extends realism down into the society of soldiers. They are invariably middle class soldiers, speaking an American vernacular that could be either urban or rural. The narration is clearly committed to erasing any distinction that could be made between the two. Crane, who had written *Maggie, a Girl of the Streets*, could clearly have made such a distinction, but here he wants merely to mime an informal language characterized by its deviation from formally "correct" speech yet not individuated to city or region. More important, the language is not discriminated in terms of character. The youth, the tall soldier, the loud soldier all speak alike. If they are privates they nonetheless speak a "general" vernacular—a representative language of their society—an ungrammatical, slightly deviant, and unschooled language, yet not one to evoke sympathy so much as to express a unity, directness, and informal simplicity of background. Just as their designation as tall soldier, loud soldier, and youth takes precedence over their individual names, their language designates their identity as soldiers rather than individuals.

For all that they are soldiers, their world is not in any strict sense military. True, they are subject to orders from the officers, but there is nothing in this beginning that stresses the abuse, repression, and rigorous discipline so familiar in narratives of military life. Indeed these private soldiers seem wonderfully free in their informality. Instead of being called to attention or suffering under highhanded officers, they are subject to the vanity, skepticism, and restiveness that come from the boredom of waiting for action. When the tall soldier, whose name is later revealed to be Jim Conklin, brings a new rumor of a military action, he "swells" with the importance of his narration but is greeted with such scoffing disbelief by a loud soldier that their exchange threatens to descend into anger. Then a corporal begins to swear at the thought of moving from the comfortable quarters he has constructed for himself. Finally the company joins in a "spirited debate" replete with arguments about strategy. The entire discussion resembles nothing so much as a small town cracker barrel discussion. What is uppermost in the representation is the *ordinariness* of the participants. They have no real distinction, yet if their foolishness and pretensions are exposed by the narration, they are not belittled. The informal, unschooled ordinariness of these soldiers is the very stamp of Crane's realism.

From this introductory scene and action, accomplished in less than two pages, the narration moves to a "youthful private" who is listening to the "words of the tall soldier," and we are brought abruptly in relation to the consciousness of the central figure of the book. The relation between the narration and Henry Fleming's consciousness is not so much one of invasion as it is of concentrated attachment. The consciousness of Henry Fleming is, after all, his *private* thoughts. The thoughts of the privates we first see are their public thoughts—what they can say to each other.

Upon hearing them, Private Fleming retires through an "intricate hole" into the privacy of his hut—it is not a tent—"to be alone with some new thoughts that had lately come to him." The narrative rarely leaves that consciousness but reports it in such a way that there is always detachment in its attachment. Thus there is always a gap between the report and the thoughts, sensations, and responses of this youth.

The essential nature of the gap is one of irony, an irony that results in exposure as much as disclosure. If we see what Henry is thinking and feeling, we also see the illusory nature of his thoughts in relation to the field of battle in which he finds himself. The great force of the narrative rests in its capacity to render the reality of his experience as well as the external nature of battle. His experience of course colors the battle, but the battle colors his experience. His thoughts always at war with each other, he is himself embattled; at the same time, he is in a battle. To see so much is to see both the nature and violence of civil war.

The best way to see that violence is to sketch the action from the moment the narrative attaches itself to the consciousness of this youth. First of all there is the fact that Henry had "of course dreamed of battles all his life" and had enlisted in the army. If he had dreamed of war, his waking consciousness had feared that wars, the "crimson splotches on the pages of the past," were the vividly red moments of history that were now as bygone as crowns and castles. "Secular and religious education had effaced the throat-grappling instinct or else firm finance held in check the passions." Disappointed at his mother's objections to, rather than her support of, his enlistment, he had nonetheless volunteered, had then felt a pang at his mother's helpless assent to his departure and her gift of blackberry jam, and had even felt shame at looking back at her tear-stained face as she knelt among the potato parings; but he had felt a thrill of self-importance in the village as he thought he saw a feminine schoolmate looking upon him as he and his company assembled.

The narrative gives but the briefest moment to this recapitulation of his boyish fantasies of Homeric battles—as an inner life they are every bit as ordinary as the public language of the soldiers—before launching its report of the move into battle. Throughout the brief march toward the conflict, replete with the soldiers' inveterate complaints and their continuing arguments about strategy, Henry remains silent with his own continuing doubts. Afraid to reveal them, he is astonished when, at the threshold of battle, Wilson, the outwardly brave and loud soldier, sobbingly announces his belief that he is to die and gives Henry a packet of letters to be sent home. In the ensuing battle, Henry manages to stand his ground against the first attack, forgetting himself in the rage of action; but while he is in the very throes of luxuriating in his accomplishment the enemy attacks again. Seeing men beside him waver and run, Henry joins in a flight as blind as his battle stand had been. His flight brings him to a point behind the lines from which, watching artillerymen mechanically serve their battery, he discovers that the blue line has held. Afflicted with this new knowledge, he feels like a criminal and, rationalizing his behavior, begins to justify his flight as an instinctive effort at self-preservation. This line of thought results in his full retirement from the field, and he finds himself in the isolated depths of a forest where "the high, arching boughs made a chapel." Pushing the boughs aside and entering, he confronts the eyes of a rotting corpse.

Recoiling from this ultimate reach of his retreat, he stumbles into a column of wounded soldiers making their way to the rear amid the rush of horse teams bringing reinforcements to the front. Two figures, a spectral soldier and a tattered soldier, galvanize his attention, and, in a true shock of recognition, he realizes the spectral soldier to be Jim Conklin. Stricken with anguish, he listens to Jim's supplications for protection and then watches him spectacularly die. When the wounded tattered soldier, who has reappeared to watch Conklin die, renews his queries about where Henry is wounded (queries which had made Henry try to escape him), Henry feels his questions like knife thrusts. Fearing that he is about to witness another death and distraught at the tattered soldier's delirium, he tears himself away from such a gruesome possibility.

He then finds himself rounding a little hillock, from which he can see retreating soldiers coming from the front in disarray and being met by another column advancing toward the front. That scene, an objective correlative of his conflicted state of mind, mirrors his wish that the army will be defeated so as to hide his cowardice as well as his shame at his own flight. When the advancing column suddenly bursts upon him in full retreat, he accosts a fleeing soldier with the all but inarticulate question of "Why—why—" only to be smashed in the head with the impetuous soldier's gun. Stunned and bloodied, he struggles through the littered battlefield in confusion until a cheery soldier, whose face he never sees, miraculously leads him back to his regiment.

Reunited with his company, he is treated with great solicitation by Wilson, who, after a time, sheepishly asks for his bundle of letters. If Wilson's kindness lacerates the inner sore beneath Henry's wound, his shamed request for the letters gives Henry a privileged stance of superiority. The battle continuing on the following day, he and Wilson—both goaded to rage at an officer's referring to the company as mule drivers—perform with distinction not only in a first but also in a second engagement. So the battle ends on a successful note for Henry Fleming, and he once again indulgently luxuriates in his achievements.

This brief summary of the action provides what we might call a dead line along which to chart the sequence of Henry's emotions. Out of the most basic adolescent fantasies that bring him to the ground of battle, there are first the private doubts that isolate him, then the helpless rage of battle, then the pride of having survived without fleeing, then abject fear and flight, then a shame that produces defensive rationalizing, then the recoil from the ultimate horror of death (the images of the rotting dead soldier and the dying Jim Conklin), then more rationalization combining fear, shame, doubt; then the blow, the wound—both false and true—reducing him to a hopeless, helpless, and lost wanderer whose one instinct is to keep on his feet; then the reunion with his company bringing with it a mixture of relief and guilt; then Wilson's shamefaced request for a return of the letters, producing a triumphant superiority and aggression; then the rage of battle once more and a fuller sense of triumph when his actions receive praise, and finally a self-satisfied pride in accomplishment resting yet uneasily on the lie of his wound, his red badge of courage.

This abrupt sequence of emotions forms the ground of Henry's action, determining his behavior more than the orders of his officers. Crane's achievement is to displace the technology of war, its accelerating machinery, with an acceleration of emotions running between the poles of fear and rage. Fear is flight from death, rage the assault upon it. Death is, of course, the enemy, at once the feared and fated end of the natural process of living, and, in battle, the hated and feared living enemy determined to kill. It is no accident that the word "courage"—designating the chief virtue of the soldier—contains within it the word "rage," the aggression of the heart and mind. Both fear and rage are all but blind, instinctual, and both generate the lines of energy that society—in this instance civilian society at war with itself—transforms into shame and honor, cowardice and courage, with all the feelings that attend them. Henry Fleming's inner civil war is his violent experience of these emotions at war within himself. Crowded together in the closest proximity, they are always at the point of conflict and collision.

But there is the outer war, whose external reality we never doubt. If it is an expression of Henry's inner conflicts, he is equally an expression of its intensity. It is, as I have noted, the objective correlative of his inner turbulence, but the point is that it *is* objective. Its essential nature is violent *civil* disorder—a melee of discordant sounds, as if civil society and speech were themselves dissolving into roars and curses even as the machinery of war assumes the role of civil discussion. Thus artillery opens with a "furious debate," musketry "sputters," cannons "enter the dispute," guns "argue with abrupt violence," shells hurtle overhead in "long wild screams," cannon are engaged in a "stupendous wrangle," artillery "assembles as if for a conference." At the same time the speech of soldiers increasingly descends into incoherence, emanating in curses, oaths, screams, bellowing, yells, roars. Chapter XI concludes with this description of Henry Fleming: "He was a slang phrase." Battle utterances are characterized by incompleteness. A good example—one among many—occurs late in the book when the lieutenant rallies his men:

As they halted thus the lieutenant again began to bellow profanely. Regardless of the vindictive threats of the bullets, he went about coaxing, berating, and bedamning. His lips, that were habitually in a soft and childlike curve, were now writhed into unholy contortions. He swore by all possible deities.

Once he grabbed the youth by the arm. "Come on, yeh lunkhead!" he roared. "Come on! We'll all git killed if we stay here. We've on'y got t' go across that lot. An' then"—the remainder of his idea disappeared in a blue haze of curses.

That blue haze of curses brings us to the matter of color. Just as Crane's sounds of war veer always between curses and roars, his colors are boldly primary. The brown and green of the opening paragraph set the tone. There we see the process of nature revealed not in gradual but bold change. And we see that process again startlingly shown in the description of the dead soldier in the green forest chapel:

He was being looked at by a dead man who was seated with his back against a columnlike tree. The corpse was dressed in a uniform that once had been blue, but was now faded to a melancholy shade of green. The eyes, staring at the youth, had changed to the dull hue to be seen on the side of a dead fish. The mouth was open. Its red had changed to an appalling yellow. Over the gray skin of the face ran little ants. One was trundling some sort of a bundle along the upper lip.

The strength of the passage gives the corpse a life of its own, which indeed it has, since it is still in the process of nature's change; the youth is the one who is arrested in the face of those staring eyes.

But the more memorable presence of color comes about when Crane seems to have almost violently asserted it by abruptly and visibly thrusting it on objects. A sort of index to the process is disclosed in the final battle sequence when Henry, resting on the laurels he feels he has won, recalls "bits of color that in the flurry had stamped themselves unawares upon his engaged senses." This stamping of color is evident in the very title of the book. Even more telling are the "crimson splotches" that, in Henry's mind, constitute the wars on the pages of history. Then there is the red god of battle. Rage, like new blood, is red, though like old blood it can also be black. Flames of musketry are seen as yellow tongues. This flash and splash of color is seen in the red badge itself that Henry wishes for when he enters the column of wounded men; and later, angry at being called a mule driver, he pictures "red letters of revenge" to be written to the insulting officer. Though a search for color will disclose that sound is actually much more present in the prose, the instances of color have a vivid force. The title of the book has its own finality, reminding us almost helplessly of those other American titles, *The Scarlet Letter* and "The Masque of the Red Death," and reminding us too that Poe and Hawthorne are deeply inscribed in this book. Given other Crane titles—"The Blue Hotel," "The Bride Comes to Yellow Sky," *Black Riders*, and *The Third Violet*—possibilities of color begin to haunt the mind. It is possible, of course, to pursue these colors into patterns of meaning and symbolism, yet such pursuits inevitably evade the much more important fact that the violent presence of color abruptly converts meaning into vivid images that annihilate prior symbolic reference. Henry Fleming is both enacting and fulfilling this instantaneous process of conversion when, in his triumphant red rage of charging the enemy lines, he becomes the color bearer of his company.

Finally there is the primary quality of form itself. The images in *The Red Badge* violently assert deformity. Corpses are twisted, bodies writhe, faces are contorted, dead soldiers lie upon the field as if they have been dumped from the sky, a dying soldier is seen "thrashing about in the grass, twisting his shuddering body into many strange postures," soldiers in battle are stretched on the ground or on their knees "as if they had been stricken by bolts from the sky." All the qualities of sound, color, and deformity are concentrated, at almost the exact center of the book, in the description of Jim Conklin's death:

His spare figure was erect; his bloody hands were quietly at his side. He was waiting with patience for something that he had come, to meet. He was at the rendezvous. They [Henry and the tattered soldier] paused and stood, expectant.

There was a silence.

Finally, the chest of the doomed soldier began to heave with a strained motion. It increased in violence until it was as if an animal was within and was kicking and tumbling furiously to be free.

This spectacle of gradual strangulation made the youth writhe, and once as his friend rolled his eyes, he saw something in them that made him sink wailing to the ground. He raised his voice in a last supreme call.

"Jim—Jim—Jim——"

The tall soldier opened his lips and spoke. He made a gesture. "Leave me be—don't tech me—leave me be—"

There was another silence while he waited.

Suddenly, his form stiffened and straightened. Then it was shaken by a prolonged ague. He stared into space. To the two watchers there was a curious and profound dignity in the firm lines of his awful face.

He was invaded by a creeping strangeness that slowly enveloped him. For a moment the tremor of his legs caused him to dance a sort of hideous hornpipe. His arms beat wildly about his head in expression of implike enthusiasm.

His tall figure stretched itself to its full height. There was a slight rending sound. Then it began to swing forward, slow and straight, in the manner of a falling tree. A swift muscular contortion made the left shoulder strike the ground first.

The body seemed to bounce a little way from the earth. "God!" said the tattered soldier.

The youth had watched, spellbound, this ceremony at the place of meeting. His face had been twisted into an expression of every agony he had imagined for his friend.

He now sprang to his feet and, going closer, gazed upon the pastelike face. The mouth was open and the teeth showed in a laugh.

As the flap of the blue jacket fell away from the body, he could see that the side looked as if it had been chewed by wolves.

The youth turned, with sudden, livid rage, toward the battlefield. He shook his fist. He seemed about to deliver a philippic.

"Hell——"

The red sun was pasted in the sky like a wafer.

There it all is. The violent heaving, the strained motion, the animal action, Henry's sinking wail and unfinished supreme call, the muscular contortion, the pastelike face fixed in a frozen laugh, the wolf-like wound, the truncated philippic, and the final sentence sealing the passage in the color of the red sun.

It is hardly surprising that the striking final sentence of this passage has arrested critics in search of meaning. Robert Wooster Stallman took the wafer to refer to communion and Jim Conklin—with his initials, his wound in the side, and the tattered soldier's accompanying passionate cry, "God"—to be the Christ. Stallman has been sufficiently flogged for his interpretation, so I shall not join the host of his detractors other than to note that he, like those seeking for literary precursors, actual battle sites, and color symbolism as literary, historical and symbolic subtexts of the narrative, was yearning for a religious subtext. The point is that all these subtexts have been blown away by the violence of battle. Henry's philippic breaks off with but one word—"hell." Hell in this text has utterly lost its theological sense; it, like all the other curses, is but the expression of present rage springing from the annihilation of traditional religious meaning. The wafer of the final sentence is, as others have seen, like the molten wafer of wax used to seal a letter. Whether it comes from Kipling's *The Light that Failed*, which Crane had surely read, is beside the point. Just as a wax wafer is pasted on a letter to seal it, so is the sun, as if it had been passed over Conklin's pastelike dead face, pasted in the sky.

The force that pastes the sun in the sky is of course the sentence itself. The entire passage shows just how, even as Henry's voice is unable to complete sentences, the narrative does nothing but complete them. Sentences in this book are the units of force effacing and displacing the author behind them with their own authority. They both report and execute the action. They literally sentence Henry Fleming to the war he has dreamed of all his life. They boldly and visibly stand forth, in the manner that Emerson spoke of his own sentences, as infinitely repellent particles. They all but annihilate paragraphs in their determination to stand alone. Of course they are in sequence, but they expose the discontinuity as much as the continuity of sequence. Their conclusiveness has sufficient finality to transform the silence between them into an abrupt gap of stillness as astonishing as the grotesque images they assert. That astonishment is really the ultimate emotion of battle—more violent than mere surprise. It is an emotion that *excessively* fulfills the anxiety and curiosity of suspense, those emotions on which novelistic narration so much depends.

That is why these sentences not only threaten to annihilate paragraphs, they threaten the plot and suspense of traditional novelistic narrative. They are as determined to conclude action as they are to continue it. All but equal to each other in their declarative brevity, they have a genuinely democratic order, transforming turning points and climaxes of narrative into a continuum of violent intensity and at the same time annihilating the distinctions of military hierarchy and rank. The officers speak the same informal, ordinary, and violent language as the privates; Henry and the lieutenant are utterly equal in their united bellowing appeals for the men to charge. Higher battle strategy, like the battle lines that dissolve in the violence of battle, disintegrates into the soldiers' arguments about strategy.

Still, this book is a narrative, and the conventions of narrative, like all the traditional meaning and symbols of history and religion are, like the enemy, threatening a counterattack. That threat, indicating that there is also a civil war in the very form of the book, is very much evident in the concluding movement of the novel. In the midst of Henry's heroic charge when men, "punched by bullets, fell in grotesque agonies," and the regiment "left a coherent trail of bodies," we are given this passage:

> It seemed to the youth that he saw everything. Each blade of the green grass was bold and clear. He thought that he was aware of every change in the thin, transparent vapor that floated idly in sheets. The brown or gray trunks of the trees showed each roughness of their surfaces. And the men of the regiment, with their starting eyes and sweating faces, running madly, or falling, as if thrown headlong, to queer, heaped-up corpses—all were comprehended. His mind took a mechanical but firm impression, so that afterward everything was pictured and explained to him, save why he himself was there.
>
> But there was a frenzy made from this furious rush. The men, pitching forward insanely, had burst into cheerings, moblike and barbaric, but tuned in strange keys that can arouse the dullard and the stoic. It made a mad enthusiasm that, it seemed, would be incapable of checking itself before granite and brass. There was the delirium that encounters despair and death, and is heedless and blind to the odds. It is a temporary but sublime absence of selfishness. And because it was of this order was the reason, perhaps, why the youth wondered, afterward, what reasons he could have had for being there.

The delirium that encounters despair and death is, then, the sublime absence of selfishness. Here the novel hovers at the threshold of ennobling Henry's "heroism" and we might well be lulled into seeing the narrative, which is so much in the convention of the *bildungsroman*, as a register of Henry Fleming's moral growth toward maturity. The book's conclusion, with the regiment retiring from the battlefield and Henry once more luxuriating in a feeling of accomplishment, can be seen to reinforce such a vision of growth. Nearing its end, the narrative boldly asserts, "He was a man."

Yet to conclude moral growth and maturity from this sentence is to displace the irony of the narrative with blatant sentimentality. Although Crane cut some passages from the concluding chapter which expose the same complacent self-satisfaction, there is sufficient irony remaining to indicate that his asserted manhood is no more secured than it was after his first battle when the narrative asserted the same thing. He is really no better or worse than he was then nor is there evidence that he is better or worse than all the men who were killed or who survived. He could just as well have been killed, but that end would truly have made the book sentimental. Crane did better to keep him alive, letting all that selfishness, which had been for a moment sublimely absent, return in the form of pride.

This does not mean that there was nothing to Henry's bravery. He did fight as blindly as he ran, and presumably he killed some of the enemy when he kept blindly firing after his company had retreated, though we are spared actually seeing him in the act of killing. His distinction in battle comes from the excessive rage that is within him if it comes from anything. He had *of course* dreamed of battles all his life, and he just as arbitrarily of course fought out of the rage and dream that was in him. If war is an expression of death and grotesque disorder, it is nonetheless the sentence of existence, as near as the rage and dream that are always in us. The sentence of war was always in Crane, evident in the violence of *Maggie* with its opening on a street fight and in *George's Mother* opening with a woman battling with pots and pans in a kitchen. In *The Red Badge* he made it fully and exclusively *present*, so present that he could do little afterward except pursue it over the world as a reporter.

Grotesque and terrible as war may be, Crane does not write *against* war; he writes through it. His sentences, flattening perspective in their bold and visible presence, have the strength of line and form that we see in a Cézanne painting. They possess the "curious and profound dignity in the firm lines of [Jim Conklin's] awful face." If George Wyndham, who reviewed the book when it appeared in England and who had himself been a soldier, felt that it perfectly expressed his past experience of battle action, Ford Madox Ford, who fought in World

War I, felt that it perfectly foretold the experience of that war, too. It retains to this day a remarkable modernity.

Joseph Conrad was good, in his memoir of Crane, to leave us his remembered image of Crane sitting at a table with a half-empty glass of beer gone flat, writing by hand in steady deliberation. No one who reads *The Red Badge* can doubt that that hand—the inertial hand that writes writing about the hand that fights—was possessed of true courage.

From *Southern Humanities Review* 25, no. 4 (1991): 305-320. Copyright © 1991 by *Southern Humanities Review*. Reprinted with permission of *Southern Humanities Review*.

Note

1. Stephen Crane, *The Red Badge of Courage: An Annotated Text, Backgrounds and Sources, Essays in Criticism*. Edited by Sculley Bradley et al. New York: W. W. Norton and Company, 1962.

"That Was at Chancellorsville":
The Factual Framework of
The Red Badge of Courage

Harold R. Hungerford

The name of the battle in which Henry Fleming achieved his manhood is never given in *The Red Badge of Courage*. Scholars have not agreed that the battle even ought to have a name; some have implied that it is a potpourri of episodes from a number of battles.[1] Yet an examination of the evidence leads to the conclusion that the battle does have a name—Chancellorsville. Throughout the book, it can be demonstrated, Crane consistently used the time, the place, and the actions of Chancellorsville as a factual framework within which to represent the perplexities of his young hero.[2]

I

Evidence of two sorts makes the initial hypothesis that Crane used Chancellorsville probable. In the first place, Crane said so in his short story "The Veteran," which was published less than a year after *The Red Badge*. In this story he represented an elderly Henry Fleming as telling about his fear and flight in his first battle. "That was at Chancellorsville," Henry said. His brief account is consistent in every respect with the more extended account in *The Red Badge*; old Henry's motives for flight were those of the young Henry, and he referred to Jim Conklin in a way which made it clear that Jim was long since dead.

This brief reference in "The Veteran" is, so far as I know, the only direct indication Crane ever gave that the battle in *The Red Badge* was Chancellorsville. He appears never to have mentioned the matter in his letters, and his biographers recount no references to it. Such evidence as that cited above must be used with discretion; Crane might conceivably have changed his mind. But there is no good reason why he should have done so; and in any case, the clue given us by "The Veteran" can be thoroughly corroborated by a second kind of evidence, that of time and place.

No one questions that *The Red Badge* is about the Civil War; the references to Yanks and Johnnies, to blue uniforms on one side and to gray and butternut on the other clearly establish this fact. If we turn now to military history, we find that the evidence of place and time points directly to Chancellorsville.

Only three actual place-names are used in the book: Washington, Richmond, and the Rappahannock River.[3] Henry Fleming and his fellow-soldiers had come through Washington to their winter quarters near the Rappahannock River, and their army was close enough to Richmond that cavalry could move against that city. Such a combination points to northern Virginia, through which the Rappahannock flows, to which Union soldiers would come through Washington, and from which Richmond would be readily accessible. Chancellorsville was fought in northern Virginia.

Furthermore, the battle was the first major engagement of the year, occurring when the spring rains were nearly over. The year cannot be 1861; the war began in April, and soldiers would not have spent the winter in camp. Nor can it be 1862; the first eastern battle of 1862, part of McClellan's Peninsular Campaign, in no way resembled that in the book and was far removed from the Rappahannock. It cannot be 1864; the Battle of the Wilderness was fought near the Rappahannock but did not end in a Union defeat. Its strategy was in any case significantly different from that of the battle in *The Red Badge*. Finally, 1865 is ruled out; Lee had surrendered by the time the spring rains ended.

If we are to select any actual conflict at all, a *reductio ad absurdum* indicates the first eastern battle of 1863, and that battle was Chancellorsville. Moreover, 1863 marked the turning-point in the Union fortunes; before Gettysburg the South had, as Wilson remarked in *The Red Badge*, licked the North "about every clip" (p. 255). After Gettysburg no Union soldier would have been likely to make such a statement; and Gettysburg was the next major battle after Chancellorsville.

Like the evidence of "The Veteran," the evidence of time and place points to Chancellorsville, and it is therefore at least a tenable hypothesis that Chancellorsville and *The Red Badge* are closely connected. In the next three sections I shall present independent proof of that hypothesis by showing that the battle in Crane's novel is closely and continuously parallel to the historical Chancellorsville.[4]

II

The events preceding the battle occupy the first two chapters and part of the third (pp. 238-258). The opening chapter establishes the situation of the Union army. As winter passed into spring, that army was resting in winter camp across a river from a Confederate army. It had been there for some time—long enough for soldiers to build huts with chimneys, long enough for a new recruit to have been encamped for some months without seeing action. ". . . there had come months of monotonous life in a camp. . . . since his regiment had come to the field the army had done little but sit still and try to keep warm" (p. 244). Such was the situation of the Army of the Potomac in April, 1863; it had spent a cold, wet winter encamped at Falmouth, Virginia, on the north bank of the Rappahannock River opposite the Confederate army. The army had been inactive since mid-December; its men had dug themselves into just such huts, covered with folded tents and furnished with clay chimneys, as Crane describes (p. 240). Furthermore, the arrival of a new Union commander, General Joseph Hooker, had meant hour after hour of drill and review for the soldiers; and Henry was "drilled and drilled and reviewed, and drilled and drilled and reviewed" (p. 245).

To this monotony the "tall soldier"—Jim Conklin—brought the news that "The cavalry started this morning. . . . They say there ain't hardly any cavalry left in camp. They're going to Richmond, or some place, while we fight all the Johnnies. It's some dodge like that" (p. 247). He had earlier announced, "We're goin' t' move t'-morrah—sure. . . .

We're goin' 'way up th' river, cut across, an' come around in behint 'em" (p. 238). Of course Jim was "the fast-flying messenger of a mistake," but the mistake was solely one of dates; the infantry did not move at once. Many soldiers at Falmouth jumped to Jim's conclusion when eleven thousand cavalrymen left camp April 13 for a raid on the Confederate railroad lines near Richmond. No one in the book denied that the cavalry had left; and Jim's analysis of the flank movement was to be confirmed at the end of the book when another soldier said, "Didn't I tell yeh we'd come aroun' in behint 'em? Didn't I tell yeh so?" (p. 373). The strategy Jim had predicted was precisely that of Chancellorsville.

The Union army at Falmouth did not leave camp for two weeks after the departure of the cavalry, and such a period accords with the time represented in the book; "for days" after the cavalry left, Henry fretted about whether or not he would run (p. 249).

Finally Henry's regiment, the 304th New York, was assembled, and it began to march before dawn. When the sun rose, "the river was not in view" (p. 252). Since the rising sun was at the backs of the marching men, they were going west. The eager soldiers "expressed commiseration for that part of the army which had been left upon the river bank" (p. 253). That night the regiment encamped; tents were pitched and fires lighted. "When another night came" (p. 257), the men crossed a river on *two* pontoon bridges and continued unmolested to a camping place.

This description fits aptly the march of the Second Corps. Many of its regiments were mustered before dawn on April 28, and then marched west and away from the Rappahannock. The Second, unlike the other corps marching to Chancellorsville, was ordered not to make any special secret of its whereabouts and was allowed fires when it camped. The Second crossed the Rappahannock on *two* pontoon bridges the evening of April 30 and camped safely near Chancellorsville that night; all the other corps had to ford at least one river, without the convenience of bridges. Furthermore, by no means all of the army moved at once; two full corps and one division of the Second Corps were left behind at Falmouth to conduct a holding action against Lee.

It is clear from the text that at least one day intervened between the evening on which Henry's regiment crossed the bridges and the morning of its first day of fighting (pp. 257-258). If Crane was following the chronology of Chancellorsville, this intervening day of pensive rest was May 1, on which only the Fifth and Twelfth Corps saw fighting.

III

Action began early for Henry's regiment the next day, the events of which parallel those at Chancellorsville on May 2. The statements (pp. 258-279) about what Henry and his regiment did are clear enough. He was rudely awakened at dawn, ran down a wood road, and crossed a little stream. His regiment was moved three times before the noon meal, and then moved again; one of these movements took Henry and his companions back, for in the afternoon they proceeded over the same ground they had taken that morning and then into new territory. By early afternoon, then, Henry had seen no fighting. At last a brigade ahead of them went into action; it was routed and fled, leaving the reserves, of which Henry's regiment was a part, to withstand the enemy. The regiment successfully resisted the first charge, but when the enemy re-attacked, Henry fled.

It might seem that tracing the path of Henry and his regiment before his flight would not be impossible, but it has proved to be so. The regimental movements which Crane describes loosely parallel the movements of many regiments at Chancellorsville; they directly parallel the movements of none.[5] Nevertheless, broad parallels do exist. Many regiments of the Second Corps moved southeast from Chancellorsville on May 2; many of them first encountered the enemy in midafternoon.

Furthermore, it can be demonstrated that the 304th, like the regiments of the Second Corps, was near the center of the Union line. In the first place, the "cheery man" tells Henry, and us, so (p. 312). His testimony deserves some credence; anyone who can so unerringly find a regiment in the dark should know what he is talking about. Moreover, the conversation of the soldiers before the assault (pp. 266-267) makes it clear that they were not facing the rebel right, which would have been opposite the Union left. Nor were they far to the Union right, as I shall show later.

The evidence given us by the terrain Henry crossed also points to a position at about the center of the Union line. During the morning and early afternoon he crossed several streams and passed into and out of cleared fields and dense woods. The land was gently rolling; there were occasional fences and now and then a house. Such topographical features, in 1863, characterized the area south and east of Chancellorsville itself. Further east, in the area held by the Union left, the terrain opened up and the dense second-growth forest thinned out; further west the forest was very thick indeed, with few fields or other open areas. But southeast of Chancellorsville, where the Union center was located, the land was cultivated to a degree; fields had been cleared and cut off from the forest by fences. Topography so conditioned action at Chancellorsville that every historian of the battle perforce described the terrain; if Crane knew the battle as well as I suggest he did, he must have known its topography.

Topography also gives us our only clue to the untraceable path of Henry's flight. At one point he "found himself almost into a swamp. He was obliged to walk upon bog tufts, and watch his feet to keep from the oily water" (p. 285). A man fleeing west from the center of the Union line would have encountered swamps after a few miles of flight. The detail is perhaps minor, but it corroborates the path Henry had to follow to reach the place where he received his "red badge of courage." He went west, toward the Union right held by the Eleventh Corps.

Henry's flight led him to the path of the retreating wounded soldiers, among them Jim Conklin. The scene of Jim's death (pp. 289-301) contains no localizing evidence, for Crane was concentrating upon the men, not their surroundings. Nevertheless, it is appropriate to Chancellorsville; the roads leading to the river were clogged with retreating Union wounded in the late afternoon of May 2. There were no ambulances near the battle lines, and many wounded men died as they walked.

By contrast, the scene of Henry's wound can be readily fixed. He received it in the middle of the most-discussed single action of the battle, an action which cost Stonewall Jackson his life and a major general his command, almost surely won the battle for Lee, and generated thirty-five years of acrimonious debate. Even today, to mention Chancellorsville is inevitably to bring up the rout of the Eleventh Corps.

About sunset on May 2, 1863, Stonewall Jackson's crack troops attacked the predominantly German Eleventh Corps. The Eleventh, which was on the extreme right of the Union line and far from the fighting, was taken wholly by surprise, and many soldiers turned and ran in terrified disorder. The result was near-catastrophe for the Union; now that Jackson's men had turned the flank, the path lay open for an assault on the entire unprotected rear of the Union army.

Appropriately enough for such a battle, Jackson's men were halted by one of history's more extraordinary military maneuvers. For in a battle in which hardly any cavalry were used, a small detachment of cavalrymen held Jackson's corps off long enough to enable artillery to be dragged into place and charged with canister. The cavalrymen could do so because the dense woods confined Jackson's men to the road. The small detachment was the Eighth Pennsylvania Cavalry; the time was between 6:30 and 7 P.M. Theirs was the only cavalry charge at Chancellorsville, and it became famous not only because it had saved the Union army—perhaps even the Union—but also because no two observers could agree on its details; any historian is therefore obliged to give the charge considerable attention.

All these elements fit the time and place of Henry's wounding. Night was falling fast after his long afternoon of flight; "landmarks had vanished into the gathered gloom" (p. 308). All about Henry "very burly men" were fleeing from the enemy. "They sometimes gabbled insanely. One huge man was asking of the sky, 'Say, where de plank road? Where de plank road?'" A popular stereotype holds that all Germans are burly, and an unsympathetic listener could regard rapidly-spoken German as "gabbling." Certainly the replacement of *th* by *d* fits the pattern of Germans; Crane's Swede in "The Veteran" also lacks *th*. These might be vulgar errors, but they identified a German pretty readily in the heyday of dialect stories. Furthermore, plank roads were rare in northern Virginia; but a plank road ran through the Union lines toward the Rappahannock.

One of these fleeing Germans hit Henry on the head; and after he received his wound, while he was still dazed, Henry saw the arrival of the cavalry and of the artillery:

> Around him he could hear the grumble of jolted cannon as the scurrying horses were lashed toward the front. . . . He turned and watched the mass of guns, men, and horses sweeping in a wide curve toward a gap in a fence. . . . Into the unspeakable jumble in the roadway rode a squadron of cavalry. The faded yellow of their facings shone bravely. There was a mighty altercation. (pp. 309-310)

As Henry fled the scene, he could hear the guns fire and the opposing infantry fire back. "There seemed to be a great ruck of men and munitions spread about in the forest and in the fields" (p. 310).

Every element of the scene is consistent with contemporary descriptions of the rout of the Eleventh Corps. The time is appropriate; May 2 was the first real day of battle at Chancellorsville as it was the first day for Henry. The place is appropriate; if Henry had begun the day in the Union center and then had fled west through the swamps, he would have come toward the right of the Union line, where the men of the Eleventh Corps were fleeing in rout. The conclusion is unavoidable: Crane's use of the factual framework of Chancellorsville led him to place his hero in the middle of that battle's most important single action.

The first day of battle in *The Red Badge* ended at last when the cheery man found Henry, dazed and wandering, and led him back to his regiment by complicated and untraceable paths.

IV

The second day of battle, like the first, began early. Henry's regiment was sent out "to relieve a command that had lain long in some damp trenches" (p. 328). From these trenches could be heard the noise of skirmishers in the woods to the front and left, and the din of battle to the right was tremendous. Again, such a location fits well enough the notion of a center regiment; the din on the right, in the small hours of May 3, would have come from Jackson's men trying to re-establish their connection with the main body of Lee's army.

Soon, however, Henry's regiment was withdrawn and began to retreat from an exultant enemy; Hooker began such a withdrawal about 7:30 A.M. on May 3. Finally the retreat stopped and almost immediately thereafter Henry's regiment was sent on a suicidal charge designed to prevent the enemy from breaking the Union lines. This charge significantly resembles that of the 124th New York, a regiment raised principally in the county which contains Port Jervis, Crane's hometown; and the time of this charge of the 124th—about 8:30 A.M.—fits the time-scheme of *The Red Badge* perfectly.[6]

The next episode (pp. 360-362) can be very precisely located; Crane's description is almost photographically accurate. Henry was about a quarter of a mile south of Fairview, the "slope on the left" from which the "long row of guns, gruff and maddened, denounc[ed] the enemy" (p. 360). Moreover, "in the rear of this row of guns stood a house, calm and white, amid bursting shells. A congregation of horses, tied to a railing, were tugging frenziedly at their bridles. Men were running hither and thither" (p. 361). This is a good impression of the Chancellor House, which was used as the commanding general's headquarters and which alone, in a battle at which almost no cavalry were present, had many horses belonging to the officers and orderlies tied near it.

The second charge of the 304th, just before the general retreat was ordered, is as untraceable as the first. It has, however, its parallel at Chancellorsville: several regiments of the Second Corps were ordered to charge the enemy about 10 A.M. on May 3 to give the main body of the army time to withdraw the artillery and to begin its retreat.

The two days of battle came to an end for Henry Fleming when his regiment was ordered to "retrace its way" and rejoined first its brigade and then its division on the way back toward the river. Such a retreat, in good order and relatively free from harassment by an exhausted enemy, began at Chancellorsville about 10 A.M. on May 3. Heavy rains again were beginning to make the roads into bogs; these rains prevented the Union soldiers from actually recrossing the river for two days, for the water was up to the level of several of the bridges. "It rained" in the penultimate paragraph of *The Red Badge*; and the battle was over for Henry Fleming as for thousands of Union soldiers at Chancellorsville.

V

This long recitation of parallels, I believe, demonstrates that Crane used Chancellorsville as a factual framework for his novel. We have reliable external evidence that Crane studied *Battles and Leaders of the Civil War* in preparation for *The Red Badge* because he was concerned with the accuracy of his novel.[7] He could have found in the ninety pages *Battles and Leaders* devotes to Chancellorsville all the information he needed on strategy, tactics, and topography. A substantial part of these ninety pages is devoted to the rout of the Eleventh Corps and the charge of the Eighth Pennsylvania Cavalry. These pages also contain what someone so visually minded as Crane could hardly have overlooked: numerous illustrations, many from battlefield sketches. The illustrations depict, among other subjects, the huts at Falmouth;

men marching in two parallel columns;[8] pontoon bridges; the Chancellor House during and after the battle; and the rout of the Eleventh. With these Crane could have buttressed the unemotional but authoritative reports of Union and Confederate officers which he found in *Battles and Leaders*.

If it is unfashionable to regard Crane as a man concerned with facts, we ought to remember that late in his life he wrote *Great Battles of the World*[9]—hack work, to be sure, but scrupulously accurate in its selection of incident and detail and in its analysis of strategy. One can do far worse than to learn about Bunker Hill from Crane.

VI

Two questions remain unanswered. First, why did Crane not identify the battle in *The Red Badge* as he did in "The Veteran"? One answer is fairly simple: no one called the battle Chancellorsville in the book because no one would have known it was Chancellorsville. No impression is more powerful to the reader of Civil War reports and memoirs than that officers and men seldom knew where they were. They did not know the names of hills, of streams, or even of villages. Probably not more than a few hundred of the 130,000 Union men at Chancellorsville knew until long afterwards the name of the four corners around which the battle raged. A private soldier knew his own experiences, but not names or strategy; we have been able to reconstruct the strategy and the name because Crane used a factual framework for his novel; and the anonymity of the battle is the result of that framework.

Of course the anonymity is part of Crane's artistic technique as well. We do not learn Henry Fleming's full name until Chapter ii; we never learn Wilson's first name. Crane sought to give only so much detail as was necessary to the integrity of the book. He was not, like Zola and Tolstoi, concerned with the panorama of history and the fate of nations, but with the mind and actions of a youth unaccustomed to war. For such purposes, the name of the battle, like the names of men, did not matter; in fact, if Crane had named the battle he might have evoked in the minds of his readers reactions irrelevant to his purpose, reactions which might have set the battle in its larger social and historical frame-work. It would have been a loss of control.

Why, with the whole Civil War available, should Crane have chosen Chancellorsville? Surely, in the first place, because he knew a good deal about it. Perhaps he had learned from his brother, "an expert in the strategy of Gettysburg and Chancellorsville" (Beer, p. 47). More prob-ably he had heard old soldiers talk about their war experiences while he was growing up. Many middle-aged men in Port Jervis had served in the 124th New York; Chancellorsville had been their first battle, and first impressions are likely to be the most vivid. It is hard to believe that men in an isolated small town could have resisted telling a hero-worshiping small boy about a great adventure in their lives.

Moreover, Chancellorsville surely appealed to Crane's sense of the ironic and the colorful. The battle's great charges, its moments of hero-ism, went only to salvage a losing cause; the South lost the war and gained only time from Chancellorsville; the North, through an incredi-ble series of blunders, lost a battle it had no business losing. The dead, as always, lost the most. And when the battle ended, North and South were just where they had been when it began. There is a tragic futil-ity about Chancellorsville just as there is a tragic futility to *The Red Badge*.

Finally, Chancellorsville served Crane's artistic purposes. It was the first battle of the year and the first battle for many regiments. It was therefore an appropriate introduction to war for a green soldier in an untried regiment.

The evidence of this study surely indicates that Crane was not merely a dreamer spinning fantasies out of his imagination; on the con-trary, he was capable of using real events for his own fictional purposes with controlled sureness. Knowledge of the ways in which he did so is, I should think, useful to criticism. For various cogent reasons, Crane chose Chancellorsville as a factual framework within which to represent the dilemma of young Henry Fleming. Many details of the novel are clearly drawn from that battle; none are inconsistent with it. Old Henry Fleming was a truthful man: "that was at Chancellorsville."

From *American Literature* 34, no. 4 (1963): 520-531. Copyright © 1963 by Duke University Press. All rights reserved. Used by permission of the publisher.

Notes

1. Lyndon Upson Pratt, in "A Possible Source for *The Red Badge of Courage*," *American Literature*, XI, 1-10 (March, 1939), suggests that the battle is partially based upon Antietam. Lars Åhnebrink denies his arguments and favors elements from Tolstoi and Zola in *The Beginnings of Naturalism in American Fiction*, "Upsala Essays and Studies in American Language and Literature," IX (Upsala, 1950). Both argue from a handful of parallel incidents of the sort which seem to me the common property of any war; neither makes any pretense of accounting for all the realistic framework of the novel.

2. This study developed from a class project in English 208 at the University of California (Berkeley) in the spring of 1958 and 1959. I am grateful to those who worked with Crane in these courses; and I am particularly grateful to George R. Stewart, who was unfailingly helpful to me in many ways and to whose scholarly acumen and knowledge of the Civil War I am deeply indebted.

3. All references to the novel are to *The Red Badge of Courage and Selected Prose and Poetry*, ed. William M. Gibson, Rinehart Editions (New York, 1956); page references will be included in the text. Although this edition contains the manuscript passages excised from the first edition, I have based no conclusions upon them. For Washington, see p. 244; for Richmond, p. 247; for the Rappahannock, p. 329. Henry's reference to the Rappahannock may be an ironic twist on a journalist's cliché, but the twist itself—the original was Potomac—seems to me to be the result of conscious intent on Crane's part.

4. The literature on Chancellorsville is substantial. The most useful short study is Edward J. Stackpole, *Chancellorsville: Lee's Greatest Battle* (Harrisburg, Pa., 1958). The definitive analysis is John Bigelow, Jr., *The Campaign of Chancellorsville: A Strategic and Tactical Study* (New Haven, 1910). Orders, correspondence, and reports are available in *The War of the Rebellion: A Compilation of the Official Records of the Union and Confederate Armies*, ser. I, vol. XXV, parts 1 and 2 (Washington, D. C., 1889). See also *Battles and Leaders of the Civil War* (New York, 1884), III, 152-243. The parallels presented below are drawn from these; all are in substantial agreement.

5. So flat a statement deserves explanation. I have read with great care all of the 307 reports of unit commanders in the *Official Records*. I have also studied more than a

dozen histories of regiments which first saw action at Chancellorsville. Many show general parallels; none show parallels with the novel which I consider close enough to be satisfactory.

6. See Cornelius Weygandt, *History of the 124th New York* (Newburgh, N.Y., 1877).

7. Thomas Beer, *Stephen Crane* (New York, 1923), pp. 97-98. Corwin Knapp Linson, *My Stephen Crane*, ed. Edwin H. Cady (Syracuse, 1959), pp. 37-38 corroborates Beer's account.

8. Here the illustration seems to explain the otherwise inexplicable description in the novel (p. 252); Civil War soldiers rarely marched thus.

9. Philadelphia, 1901. *Great Battles* is not in the collected edition, *The Work of Stephen Crane*, 12 vols. (New York, 1925-1926), and apparently has never been discussed by scholars. It includes no Civil War battles, although Crane at one time considered an article on Fredericksburg, the battle immediately preceding Chancellorsville; see *Stephen Crane: Letters*, ed. R. W. Stallman and Lillian Gilkes (New York, 1960), p. 98.

Content and Style in
*The Red Badge of Courage*_____
Robert C. Albrecht

Several critics have identified irony as the distinctive characteristic of Stephen Crane's prose in *The Red Badge of Courage*.[1] Though the word is not wholly accurate, it does suggest the doubleness which is the mark of Crane's style and which dominates the themes in this work. Greenfield has written of the "duality of view" in Crane's work, emphasizing in *The Red Badge of Courage* the theme of man's will, on the one hand, and deterministic forces, on the other; on "ethical motivation and behavior versus deterministic and naturalistic actions."[2] While focusing on this duality (and its variants), Greenfield touches on the doubleness which stylistically reflects such thematic statements. My intention is to examine some other varieties of doubleness which function in this fashion and become part of the virtual substance of the novel. These include metaphors and other figures which are not decoration or embellishment but constitute the essence of a style which is artistically appropriate to its counterpart of content. The shifting point of view and the almost excessive reminders that reality is apparent stylistically support Crane's view of men at war and of reality itself. Reflecting reality and suggesting its deceptiveness, doubleness forms the heart of the style and content.

Crane relies chiefly on two techniques for presenting reality, each reinforcing the other to make it more distinct and effective. In the traditional technique of revealing patterned reality to the reader, one view of a scene or action is given unambiguously. The following paragraph illustrates this familiar technique:

> He came to a fence and clambered over it. On the far side, the ground was littered with clothes and guns. A newspaper, folded up, lay in the dirt. A dead soldier was stretched with his face hidden in his arm. Farther off there was a group of four or five corpses keeping mournful company. A hot sun blazed upon the spot.[3]

Such scenes of selected and patterned reality are what the novelist chooses to present through the eyes of an observer. Crane does not attempt to hide his observer. The words "littered" and "mournful" imply interpretation, and the notions of the soldier's "face hidden in his arm" and the group of "corpses keeping mournful company" are even more revealing of a point of view. Most noticeable is the life given to the dead men. They are described as objects having acted to hide or to find company. This is patterned reality without ambiguity, but it is also a scene presented by an active intelligence which infuses meaning into the reality. The reader is presented not with a photograph but with an essay which distinguishes men from objects.

Crane uses variants of this technique in which the presence of the narrator is even more obvious. The sentence, "The regiment bled extravagantly," is an example of such commentary (p. 102). The personification of a body of men is a descriptive device, but the word "extravagantly" is the observer's judgment that it lost more blood than it could afford. Both the unit and the individuals in it bled. Sometimes the doubleness is more explicit, as in this description: "A mounted officer displayed the furious anger of a spoiled child. He raged with his head, his arms, and his legs" (p. 28). The metaphor is completely carried out; the officer displays his rage in just the manner of a child—with his whole body. The difference between the verbal rage of an officer and a child is carefully omitted to strengthen the metaphor. Pursuing the way of doubleness Crane often robbed his characters of such qualities. In the familiar animal imagery of *The Red Badge of Courage*, the men and the units they compose lose their human characteristics. "It [the regiment] was now like one of those moving monsters wending with many feet. The air was heavy, and cold with dew. A mass of wet grass, marched upon, rustled like silk" (p. 16). There is no human sound, sight or feeling; the regiment has lost human quality. Ironically, the doubleness which enriches the passage impoverishes the object.[4]

Crane's employment of the basic technique of patterned reality, which is by no means unsophisticated, is made unusual and effective through the continual manipulation of the observers. This implies a view of relative reality, since it suggests that reality depends upon the observer. When Crane wished Fleming's perspective to be obvious, he usually employed pronouns to indicate it. "At times he regarded the wounded soldiers in an envious way. He conceived persons with torn bodies to be peculiarly happy" (p. 47). The first irony is that Fleming did envy the wounded; that anyone would envy the maimed is absurd. But the second irony—further doubleness and a grotesque joke on the reader—is that Fleming correctly judges the wounded to have won the right to leave the field and therefore to be "peculiarly happy." In this instance the reader who refuses to follow Fleming's logic is rejecting Crane's. Crane frees the reader to follow the reasoning of Henry Fleming, but he is not always to agree with the youth. At one point the narrator begins, "As the horseman wheeled his animal and galloped away he turned to shout over his shoulder, 'Don't forget that box of cigars!' The colonel mumbled in reply." Then Fleming. "The youth wondered what a box of cigars had to do with war" (p. 15). The reader's reaction may be a chuckle, followed by the impression that Fleming's mystification is justified. Finally he may realize that this time Crane has used an incident to emphasize Fleming's battlefield isolation from normal life. The battlefield is one part of man's activities but need not exclude all else. Such manipulation can only draw the reader into more careful consideration of the meanings which Crane gives to characters and events through his forms of doubleness.

Crane handles the shifting of the point of view between the narrator and Fleming[5] with such skill that the doubleness of observers scarcely intrudes on the movement of the work. Sometimes the observer is concealed. In a paragraph apparently related by the narrator, the colonel is introduced, "In the eastern sky there was a yellow patch like a rug laid for the feet of the coming sun; and against it, black and patternlike, loomed the gigantic figure of the colonel on a gigantic horse." Two paragraphs later the point of view is clear. "He [Fleming] turned toward the colonel and saw him lift his gigantic arm and calmly stroke his mustache" (p. 15). But the reader need not decide who is speaking in the earlier sentence. He need only follow the picture and reflect that the giant who can be compared to the sun is only a man who can stroke his mustache. The doubleness does not necessarily rest on two observers.

Another example may suggest why the identity of the observer is not always important. "Once he saw a tiny battery go dashing along the line of the horizon. The tiny riders were beating the tiny horses" (p. 34). Clearly the point of view is Fleming's. If the reader could put himself in Fleming's position, the battery and riders would appear in the distance and therefore tiny. Nevertheless, the characteristic doubleness is here. The implications of Lilliputians at war persuades the reader of a further meaning which Fleming does not see. The reader is invited to share Fleming's view of the scene but Crane's view of men at war. Though this passage functions in further revealing Fleming's character, it significantly conveys Crane's views. Reality not only depends on the perception of the observer but on his perceptiveness as well. Through the metaphors, images, similes, appearances and explanations, the reader is convinced of the deceptiveness of reality, since Crane so often suggests alternative views.

Common metaphors in the novel include those of men and animals, men and machines, battlefield and home. In these latter figures, complex household imagery in which the battlefield actions and scenes are explained by home and farm images is used. These metaphors quite appropriately give the battlefield another dimension, since the battlefield, though a distinct aspect of life, is a counterpart of home life—men perform all the functions here which they might perform on a farm. It is a life rather than an occupation. Neither life at home nor life on a battlefield is fantasy; both are real. "'I didn't come here to walk. I could 'ave walked to home—'round an' 'round the barn, if I jest wanted to walk'" (p. 25), says the soldier. So he could. The implied metaphor describes the actions of the regiment, the attitude of the soldier and is a comment on war and armies.

A significant example of this type of doubleness is found in two parallel examples, one near the beginning and one toward the end of the novel. First, "From his home his youthful eyes had looked upon the war in his own country with distrust. It must be some sort of play affair" (p. 7). In the second, the soldier says of the general, "He must think we went out there an' played marbles! I never see sech a man!" (p. 97). The doubleness of reality is presented through the images. War is a play affair in the sense of its proximity to games and the procedures of games. For all that it accomplished, the regiment might as well have gone "out there an' played marbles." War is and is not a game; the realities are equivalent, though the point of view can be crucial.

Crane constructs similes with such words as "seemed," "appeared," "looked" and "as if" to establish doubleness. The following sentences illustrate the "as if" construction: "The greater part of the men, discouraged, their spirits worn by the turmoil, acted as if stunned" (p. 91); "It was as if he [the lieutenant] planned to drag the youth by the ear on to the assault" (p. 89); "It was as if he had hit his fingers with a tack hammer at home" (p. 28).

The remarkable aspect of these is their quality of near reality. Rather than being remote similes, they are quite close to the experience being explained. In the second, for example, the lieutenant probably would have dragged Fleming by the ear if he could. Crane uses the same construction for less concrete similes. For example, in the early dead soldier scene, this sentence appears: "And it was as if fate had betrayed the soldier" (p. 22). Crane's use of the "as if" construction in such sentences encourages the reader to think that here too the quality of near reality is present, encourages him to think that perhaps fate had betrayed the man. It depends on one's view of reality.

The use of the word "seemed" is a more obvious suggestion of dual reality. "The youth stared at the land in front of him. Its foliages now seemed to veil powers and horrors" (p. 86). There are two "true" images: the land with its features, and, to the youth, the forces which are as real as the land. Another example of this construction appears when the regiment retreats, when "There seemed to be mobs all about them"

(p. 91). Though the hint of dramatic irony is here—some readers almost know the regiment is not surrounded by the enemy—the choice is presented but not made by character, observer, or author. Near the end of a skirmish Fleming thinks, "They [the enemy] seemed moving toward the blue regiment, step by step" (p. 94). But a few lines later it is apparent that the skirmish is over and that perhaps the enemy was not moving closer. Again the reader cannot be certain. Fleming may be an unreliable observer, but perhaps no other observer could have been certain.

The word "appeared" frequently suggests similar uncertainty. Near the beginning of a battle the men "appeared dazed and stupid" (p. 88). The narrator does not correct this view but soon relates that the lieutenant succeeds in arousing his men. Later in this skirmish, from Fleming comes the view that there "appeared to be many" enemy soldiers (p. 94). Again, certainty is not achieved. Crane does not hesitate to use the same device figuratively. "It appeared that the swift wings of their desires would have shattered against the iron gates of the impossible" (pp. 103-104). In this battle the unit succeeds, and they accomplish "the impossible." The doubleness in such a presentation involves both the reality of what seemed to be true—the inability to accomplish the task—and the reality of what the regiment finally does. The doubleness is not between the real and the unreal but between one reality and another. Crane is not attempting to deceive but to reveal the deceptiveness of reality.

The fourth type of construction under discussion is the use of "looked." "They [bodies of dead men] looked to be dumped out upon the ground from the sky" (p. 33) seems only a metaphoric explanation; however, it suggests not only physical appearance but cause. The reader may accept as much of the image as he wishes. Fleming's view of a pastoral scene is that "It looked to be a wrong place for a battlefield" (p. 22); but it is a battlefield as he crosses with a line of skirmishers. Much later we are told that Fleming "looked to be an insane soldier" (p. 86). This is the type of doubleness which should momentarily confuse the reader. He can believe Fleming to be temporarily insane or not, but the choice is his.

Even the paragraphing is used to reinforce the presentation of doubleness. Early in the novel is this passage:

> He scrambled up the bank with a speed that could not be exceeded by a bloodthirsty man.
>
> He expected a battle scene.
>
> There were some little fields girted and squeezed by a forest. Spread over the grass and in among the tree trunks, he could see knots and waving lines of skirmishers who were running hither and thither and firing at the landscape. A dark battle line lay upon a sunstruck clearing that gleamed orange color. A flag fluttered. (p 22)

Instead of using "but" or "seemed" Crane uses paragraphing to establish the contrast. At the end of the first paragraph the youth is climbing a hill. The next sentence slows the pace and gives the expectation. The following slows the action further and contrasts with the expectation. But the reader is caught short, for the pace of the action is increased ("lines of skirmishers who were running hither and thither and firing"), and then slowed again, and almost stopped. The reader is with Fleming in this passage. Not only is the reader virtually told that he shares the youth's experience, the prose buttresses the tempo of the experience and the impressions. Beyond this, however, the reader is aware, as Henry Fleming could not be, of the scene and action outside Fleming's experience. The phrase, "he expected," keeps the reader at a distance. This contradiction of putting the reader with the character while separating them creates an artistic tension while suggesting doubleness.

All these devices would be of less interest were they not intimately related to other aspects of the novel. This relation can be seen in part in the following paragraph:

Off a short way he saw two regiments fighting a little separate battle with two other regiments. It was in a cleared space, wearing a set-apart look. They were blazing as if upon a wager, giving and taking tremendous blows. The firings were incredibly fierce and rapid. These intent regiments apparently were oblivious of all larger purposes of war, and were slugging each other as if at a matched game. (p. 99)

The typical similes are here as Fleming's point of view is presented. But by this point in the work (Chapter 22), Fleming has matured. He can see some of the ironies of war as he could not in the early chapters. One of the major uses of the shifting point of view and other forms of doubleness is to underscore the changes in Fleming from an untrustworthy observer (as contrasted with the narrator), unable to cope with the ironies of war and his own situation, to one almost as reliable as the narrator. The doubleness is not eliminated; the youth still speaks as one human observer with a limited view of reality. Henry Fleming has matured, but as Crane shows in the last chapter Fleming, like all men, can be deceived by apparent reality. The incredible frequency of "seemed," "as if," and "appeared" virtually cause a reader to supply them to Fleming's comments in that chapter, so that he "seems" to perceive his own and the regiment's situation. The doubleness is used to emphasize the development of Fleming and to convey the elusiveness of reality.

Another use of doubleness in the style is to support its occurrence in the themes such as that of determinism and volition which Greenfield has examined. The red badge itself seems to reflect the youth's courage but shows his cowardice since he received it while running from the enemy, and yet it leads to courage. The twenty-four chapters can be neatly halved at the point where Henry Fleming returns to his regiment. The doubleness of nature as seen by Fleming, and the many contrasting pairs such as courage and fear, life and death, action and inaction which Crane exploits in the novel are some of the elements which doubleness in the prose style is intended to buttress. The final paragraphs, I have suggested, are almost exclusively devoted to Fleming's point of view. If we have been made sensitive to the importance of this in the foregoing chapters, we must realize that Fleming's is not the only point of view, that much of the time his vision has been limited and that there is another, often deeper, perception of events. The apparent triumph is Fleming's view; the regiment is retreating to fight another battle elsewhere. "He had been an animal blistered and sweating in the heat and pain of war" (p. 110). But a reply echoes from the rest of the novel that he may again be such an animal. Fleming dreams of peace he has no right to expect.

The shifting point of view which Crane carefully uses throughout the work has several advantages. It allows him to exploit the relation with his readers, permitting them occasionally to see more than the character or more than the narrator. Fleming and the narrator can be used to suggest different views of reality while neither can speak with final authority. The device frees Crane from explaining his own views of war in some didactic fashion and from using one character to present his views. He could exploit his own colorful vision of the war he never saw without adhering to what a Henry Fleming necessarily saw. The characters, the narrator, the audience and even the author share the problems of perceiving reality.

To relate Crane's style to the general development of American prose or the American novel is beyond the scope of this paper. However, it should be noted that Crane grew up and wrote in that period in which the faith in absolutes was crumbling rapidly for many. Perhaps the war itself had propelled the decline of simple faith in absolutes; certainly for Crane to manifest his belief in the doubleness of reality in a novel about that war is most appropriate. Whether the examination of reality which accompanied the movement towards Progressivism is a real cause of Crane's style we shall never know. But Crane's use of style to inform meaning is a significant achievement seldom matched by recent novelists.

From *College English* 27, no. 6 (1966): 487-492. Originally published by the National Council of Teachers of English.

Notes

1. See, for example, John Berryman, *Stephen Crane* (New York, 1950), pp. 277ff; and Mordecai Marcus, "The Unity of *The Red Badge of Courage*," in Richard Lettis, Robert F. McDonnell, William E. Morris, *Stephen Crane's The Red Badge of Courage: Text and Criticism* (New York, 1960), pp. 189-195.

2. Stanley B. Greenfield, "The Unmistakable Stephen Crane," *PMLA*, 73 (December 1958), 571.

3. Stephen Crane, *The Red Badge of Courage*, ed. Sculley Bradley, Richmond Croom Beatty, E. Hudson Long (New York, 1962), p. 44. (Hereafter cited in the text.)

4. The curious reference to silk works in at least two ways. It is a reference to the sound of moving silk but also an allusion to the silkworm which is appropriate to the metaphor of the centipede.

5. These two passages illustrate this difference: "At nightfall the column broke into regimental pieces, and the fragments went into the fields to camp. Tents sprang up like strange plants. Camp fires, like red, peculiar blossoms, dotted the night" (p. 17). "He lay down on the grass. The blades pressed tenderly against his cheek. The moon had been lighted and was hung in a treetop. The liquid stillness of the night enveloping him made him feel vast pity for himself" (p. 17). In the second, the impressions are clearly Henry Fleming's; in the first, the point of view is the narrator's.

Epistemological Uncertainty in
*The Red Badge of Courage*_____

Thomas L. Kent

From our historical angle of vision, Stephen Crane's ties to traditional nineteenth-century fiction and especially to naturalism seem more aesthetical than metaphysical or ideological. From the naturalistic tradition best represented by Zola, Crane borrows the techniques of close, detailed observation, detached narrative point of view, and irony. But in combination with these devices, Crane also employs a highly charged symbolism that goes beyond the technical formulations elaborated by naturalistic theorists like Zola and Garland about what constitutes an artistic narrative.[1] Crane seems to be at once a symbolist and a naturalist, and the uncertainty about how to read his fiction—about how to distinguish a symbol from the real thing—becomes part of the subject matter of his stories. This kind of aesthetic uncertainty is not the same as the uncertainty generally associated with blind chance, one of the forces like heredity or environment that animates existence in a deterministic universe; rather, the uncertainty encountered in Crane's most successful fiction is epistemological in nature. Commenting about "The Open Boat," Donna Gerstenberger maintains that the tale "may best be viewed as a story with an epistemological emphasis, one which constantly reminds its readers of the impossibility of man's *knowing* anything, even that which he experiences."[2] The "epistemological emphasis" Gerstenberger discovers in "The Open Boat" may be detected as well in *The Red Badge of Courage*. In *The Red Badge of Courage*, Crane confronts a distinctly twentieth-century problem, man's limited ability to know the meaning of existence, and he refuses to endorse without serious reservations any metaphysical precept, any moral or ethical value structure, including determinism.

In *The Red Badge of Courage*, epistemological uncertainty may be seen to function on two levels: on the narrative level within the text where characters and events are interwoven and on the extratextual level, or audience level, where judgments must be made by the reader about the meaning of the text. On the narrative level, the characters who populate *The Red Badge of Courage* are uncertain about their existential condition; they seek continually to know the meaning of events going on around them. On the extratextual level, the reader is uncertain about how to interpret the meaning of the narrative; he continually seeks to know how to "read" the story. In this way, Crane constructs a text that creates epistemological difficulties for the reader on the extratextual level while, at the same time, transforming epistemology on the narrative level into the subject matter of the text. So, in a sense, Crane manages to transform the very structure of the text into its own subject matter. In addition to the epistemological uncertainty that is treated overtly on the narrative and extratextual levels, Crane compounds the reader's difficulty by employing a subtle, mystifying narrator who revels in producing ironic commentary and ambiguous conceits.[3] By suggesting different meanings for events and by manufacturing conceits—like the wafer simile—that have multiple associations and many possible interpretations, the narrator helps increase the reader's uncertainty and perplexity until, finally, this uncertainty and perplexity become, paradoxically, the real "meaning" of the texts.

In *The Red Badge of Courage*, epistemological uncertainty is generated on the extratextual level by the defeat of certain reader expectations, and, in much the same fashion, epistemological uncertainty on the narrative level is created by the defeat of certain character expectations. On the narrative level, the characters vacillate between certain and uncertain knowledge about events going on around them, and the pattern formed by this vacillation gives structure to the text.[4] The novel, on the narrative level, may be regarded as a series of episodes that depict Henry Fleming's attempt to know his universe.

The first chapters firmly establish a pattern of vacillation between the characters' certain and uncertain knowledge and perception of events, and this pattern is continued throughout the narrative. Jim Conklin begins the pattern by delivering a bit of news about which he is certain: "We're goin' t' move t'morrah—sure. . . . We're goin' 'way up the river, cut across, an' come around in behint 'em."[5] Later, Jim's certain information proves to be false—he "had been the fast-flying messenger of a mistake" (*Works*, p. 13)—and he endures the ridicule of his comrades. The narrative begins with Jim's misapprehension, his faulty perception of troop deployment, and misapprehension, the inability to interpret correctly the meaning of events, soon engulfs every character. Henry's perceptions and expectations about the grandeur of warfare prove to be false, and although "he had privately primed himself for a beautiful scene" (*Works*, p. 6), even the news of his enlistment had not been at all what he had expected. His mother "had disappointed him by saying nothing whatever about returning with his shield or on it. . . . her words destroyed his plans" (*Works*, p. 6). After leaving his mother, Henry sadly discovers that the campaign cannot match the high adventure he had anticipated: "He had had the belief that real war was a series of death struggles with small time in between for sleep and meals; but since his regiment had come to the field the army had done little but sit still and try to keep warm" (*Works*, p. 8). The first chapter concludes with a discussion about courage, and courage in the face of possible death is, on the narrative level, one of the central issues that must be resolved as the text progresses. According to Jim, a man cannot know what his behavior will be in battle, and he maintains that "if a hull lot 'a boys started an' run, why, I s'pose I'd start an' run. . . . But if everybody was a-standin' and a-fightin', why, I'd stand an' fight" (*Works*, p. 12). After Jim confesses that he might run if the situation called for it, Henry "was, in a measure, reassured" (*Works*, p. 12); and the chapter ends on a promising note. But the promises and expectations suggested by the first chapter are rapidly dispelled in the second. At the conclusion of the second chapter, another discussion occurs about the possibility of running from battle, and this exchange does not conclude with Henry being reassured: "In the darkness he saw visions of a thousand-tongued fear that would babble at his back and cause him to flee, while others were going coolly about their country's business"

(*Works*, p. 20). Henry is certain about his courage at one moment and uncertain at the next; his expectations are continually defeated. Just when Henry concludes that the army will remain forever a "blue demonstration," his regiment moves out, but not to fight. During this futile, enigmatic march, Henry witnesses a horseman approach the commander of his regiment: "As the horseman wheeled his animal and galloped away he turned to shout over his shoulder, 'Don't forget that box of cigars!' The colonel mumbled in reply. The youth wondered what a box of cigars had to do with war" (*Works*, p. 15). Henry understands neither the behavior of his commanders nor his situation; in his perplexity, he finds the meaning of his experience incomprehensible.

The pattern of movement from certainty to uncertainty and back again that is established early in the opening chapters is the ordering principle of the text. Each of the major episodes in the narrative somehow contradicts Henry's expectations and perceptions. He misapprehends character; the loud, confident soldier is actually afraid. After he flees from what he perceives to be a slaughter, Henry discovers that "they had won after all! The imbecile line had remained and become victors" (*Works*, p. 45). After receiving a wound from an unexpected source, Henry returns to his regiment, where he expects that he will "soon feel in his sore heart the barbed missiles of ridicule" (*Works*, p. 75), but instead he is welcomed as a hero. When he finally experiences his first real test in battle, Henry fights like an unconscious beast only to discover that the general considers him and his comrades "a lot'a mule drivers" (*Works*, p. 101). Later, Henry inadvertently learns that his regiment is to be sacrificed as a diversion for the primary attack force; but unexpectedly the "mule drivers" fight gallantly—Henry seizes the flag and urges the men forward—and they seem to be victorious when they should have been destroyed. But their momentary exaltation turns to despair when the men learn that they "stopped about a hundred feet this side of a very pretty success!" (*Works*, p. 118). The regiment fights bravely during the climactic battle, and Henry's friend captures the enemy flag. But, again, their euphoria turns to consternation when they are ordered to relinquish the territory they gained. The narrative concludes in a flurry of uncertainty. Henry "saw that he was good. He recalled with a thrill of joy the respectful comments of his fellows upon his conduct" (*Works*, p. 134). But Henry's joy changes almost instantaneously to guilt: ". . . the pursuing recollection of the tattered man took all elation from the youth's veins. He saw his vivid error, and he was afraid that it would stand before him all his life" (*Works*, p. 135). Once again Henry's perception and interpretation of events flip-flops, and the fear of his "vivid error" subsides; he becomes confident and assured:

> Yet gradually he mustered force to put the sin at a distance. And at last his eyes seemed to open to some new ways. He found that he could look back upon the brass and bombast of his earlier gospels and see them truly. . . .
>
> With this conviction came a store of assurance. He felt a quiet manhood, nonassertive but of sturdy and strong blood. . . . He was a man. (*Works*, p. 135)

Henry's wavering evaluation of his conduct ends on this promising note, but nothing in the narrative indicates that Henry's current assessment of reality is any more accurate than his previous assessments. We suspect that Henry's certainty and new-found assurance soon will be reversed.

Henry's understanding and evaluation of the events occurring around him must be separated from the reader's understanding and evaluation of these same events; the characters' experience is not, of course, the same as the reader's. The reader comprehends the pattern of events formed by the characters' experience on the narrative level, the swing between certainty and uncertainty that the characters find incomprehensible. Because he watches the characters' vacillation, because he knows that the characters' perception of events within the text is continually undermined, the reader grows to expect what the characters regard as unexpected. In this context, the reader "understands" more than the characters, and for the reader it is no surprise that the narrative concludes with Henry's scars "faded as flowers" (*Works*, p. 135). The reader understands that Henry's final self-satisfied musings are transitory. On the narrative level, Henry's inability to know and to understand his condition and situation, Henry's epistemological uncertainty, is not the uncertainty experienced by the reader. Epistemological uncertainty on the extratextual level is generated by Crane's mixture of symbolic and naturalistic narrative elements that creates contradictory and unfulfilled reader expectations. The reader is placed in a situation where he must choose among many possible and contradictory meanings for the text, and his inability to make a satisfactory choice, his uncertainty about what to expect from the text, how to know it or to "read" it, is the source of his epistemological uncertainty.

By suggesting an almost transcendental meaning for the events in the narrative, the tropes that are employed liberally throughout *The Red Badge of Courage* lure the reader away from a purely naturalistic interpretation of the tale. Crane's manipulation of symbolism, metaphor, and irony imbues *The Red Badge of Courage* with ritualistic, mythic associations which imply that the narrative is more than a simple depiction of determinism. But the nature of this "more," what the text means beyond a straightforward depiction of naturalism, is never clearly revealed, and the resultant ambiguity about how the text is supposed to be read and what it is supposed to mean—beyond its naturalistic surface meaning—creates reader uncertainty. Formulated another way, we may say that reader uncertainty is caused by the contradiction between what the text seems *literally* to mean and what it seems *figuratively* to mean. The events in the text, the pattern of vacillation between certainty and uncertainty that the characters display, suggest a naturalistic universe where man in his confusion thinks he knows and controls the world around him when, in reality, he is governed by chance or environmental and hereditary forces beyond his control. The reader watches this naturalistic pattern unfold, and as he begins to perceive what the text is about—a deterministic universe—the tropological devices begin subtly to undermine his certainty of perception by suggesting alternative interpretations for events. The text in effect creates twin, antagonistic impulses. One impulse makes the reader want to interpret the text deterministically as a story about man's subservience to forces beyond his control; the second makes the reader want to interpret the text idealistically as a story about man's regeneration and dignity in a time of crisis. Because they point toward contradictory meanings for the narrative, these impulses generate uncertainty about the "correct" interpretation of the text.

Another way to view this difficulty is to see *The Red Badge of Courage* as a hybrid genre that mixes generic conventions. When the text is read with conventional "naturalistic" generic expectations or, stated another way, when the text is read with expectations that have been conditioned by reading novels written by writers like Howells and Norris, *The Red Badge of Courage* will consistently mystify the careful reader. Because of its uncharacteristic optimism, the resolution is especially bewildering when read with conventional "naturalistic novel" expectations. To be interpreted naturalistically, the last few paragraphs of the text must be apprehended ironically; Henry is supremely self-deluded, his regeneration a sham. Also, reading the text with purely naturalistic response to the tale requires the reader to ignore the tropes that would have us interpret the novel as a story about regeneration and growth. If, on the other hand, the text is read only as a symbolic novel, as a Christian allegory, or as a story about a child's rite of passage, then the naturalistic details intrude. When interpreted symbolically, the resolution becomes a positive statement about a boy's progress toward manhood or everyman's successful journey toward redemption, and this interpretation obviously disregards the naturalistic pattern established on the narrative level by Henry's uncertainty and ambivalence. *The Red Badge of Courage* may be read as neither a naturalistic nor symbolic novel, and it is the uncertainty about how to know the text and interpret the textual universe that creates most of the reader's epistemological difficulties.

Although epistemological uncertainty is evident throughout the text, I would like to concentrate on three episodes, at the beginning, middle, and end of the story, in an attempt to describe more carefully how uncertainty is manufactured on the extratextual level. The narrative begins with a metaphor:

> The cold passed reluctantly from the earth and the retiring fogs revealed an army stretched out on the hills, resting. As the landscape changed from brown to green the army awakened and began to tremble with eagerness at the noise of rumors. It cast its eyes upon the roads which were growing from long troughs of liquid mud to proper thoroughfares. A river, amber-tinted in the shadow of its banks, purled at the army's feet and at night when the stream had become of a sorrowful blackness one could see, across, the red eye-like gleam of hostile camp-fires set in the low brows of distant hills. (*Works*, p. 3)

More than personification is employed in this passage; the metaphors suggest a being—perhaps human, perhaps animal—of gigantic proportions. Across the "sorrowful blackness" of a river, which conjures up the Styx, a red-eyed monster waits in a hellish glow. The two almost mythic creatures seem destined to participate in a momentous, earth-shaking battle, but this initial promise of imminent and deadly action goes unfulfilled. From the Olympian heights of impending battle, we plummet precipitously to earth:

> Once, a certain tall soldier developed virtues and went resolutely to wash a shirt. He came flying back from a brook waving his garment, banner-like. He was swelled with a tale he had heard from a reliable friend who had heard it from a truthful cavalryman who had heard it from his trust-worthy brother, one of the orderlies at division head-quarters. He adopted the important air of a herald in red and gold. (*Works*, p. 3)

Following the epic opening paragraph is this mock-epic description of Jim Conklin. There is nothing heroic in Jim's demeanor, and he certainly appears insignificant, even pathetic, when compared to the creature described in the preceding paragraph. Jim has been washing a shirt—evidently a ritual he seldom practices—and in this epic parody his garment becomes the banner of a mistaken messenger. Jim is "swelled with a tale" that is false, and Crane is careful to show Jim's arrogance. Verbal irony is employed to reveal that the sources for Jim's information are not "reliable," "truthful," or "trust-worthy"; he is a caricature of "a herald in red and gold." Jim is simply a poor, gullible soldier who misinterprets the meaning of events occurring around him. In the two opening paragraphs of the tale, two contradictory expectations are established. From the first description comes the expectation that the tale will possess epic and mythic dimensions; from the second comes the expectation that the tale will be ironic, realistic, perhaps satiric, but certainly not epic or mythic. Established also by these contrary descriptions is the expectation that one of these modes will displace the other: that is, we naturally anticipate that either the mythic/symbolic mode or the realistic/ironic mode will ascend to dominance. But, of course, this expectation is defeated.

In the much discussed ninth chapter, the symbolic aura surrounding Jim Conklin's death conflicts with the graphic and brutal description of the event. The question "In what mode is the text to be read?" that confronted the reader at the very beginning of the text is still unanswered in the middle. Because the text may be read in two different modes, the reader has at least two possible and contradictory interpretations for Jim's death. The death may be interpreted as a mythic/symbolic event that marks the beginning of Henry's regeneration, or it may be interpreted as a realistic/ironic event that reveals the horrible reality of war and the apathy of nature. Because they are inherently contradictory, both interpretations may not be held at once, yet both are possible. Thriving on this kind of paradox and uncertainty is the wafer simile that concludes chapter nine: "The red sun was pasted in the sky like a wafer" (*Works*, p. 58). This complex conceit is an excellent example of Crane's penchant for metaphors and symbols with multiple associations. The meanings we attach to "wafer," "pasted," and "red sun" depend on our interpretation of the story, and more than one interpretation is possible. In a mythic/symbolic story about Henry's regeneration, the wafer may be interpreted as a "communion wafer,"[6] or in a realistic/ironic story about Henry's victimization by his environment and heredity, the wafer may be interpreted as "canon primer."[7] Both interpretations are feasible; both are coherent depending on the mode in which the story is read. Because the text permits at least two different, contradictory interpretations, no single meaning given to the wafer simile is finally correct. The wafer image becomes a kind of touchstone in that the uncertainty produced about the meaning of this one figure reflects the reader's greater uncertainty about the meaning of the entire text.

Extratextual uncertainty about the proper interpretation of the tale reaches its zenith at the conclusion. Recalling the opening paragraphs, the reader discovers that the final paragraphs give a mythic and universal significance to Henry's new understanding of the world. Throughout the tale the men have been described metonymically as the "youth" or "tall soldier" or "tattered soldier," and these labels give a note of universality to the men. The final chapter seems, in part, to address the experience of everyman, and even the cadences of biblical language, complete with biblical allusions, are employed to emphasize the importance and universal significance of Henry's culminating vision:

> So it came to pass that as he trudged from the place of blood and wrath, his soul changed. He came from hot-ploughshares to prospects of clover tranquility and it was as if hot-ploughshares were not. Scars faded as flowers. (*Works*, p. 135)

Henry comes to understand that:

... the world was a world for him though many discovered it to be made of oaths and walking-sticks. He had rid himself of the red sickness of battle. The sultry nightmare was in the past. He had been an animal blistered and sweating in the heat and pain of war. He turned now with a lover's thirst, to images of tranquil skies, fresh meadows, cool brooks; an existence of soft and eternal peace. (*Works*, p. 135)

If this passage is interpreted in the mythic/symbolic mode, there can be no mistake about the outcome of Henry's suffering; he is a young pilgrim who has truly progressed. But we must remember that this single interpretation is feasible only if the reader ignores the pattern of undulation between certain and uncertain perception that has been established on the narrative level. The reader's uncertainty and indecision culminate in the final, controversial image which is identical in effect to the wafer image: "Over the river a golden ray of sun came through the hosts of leaden rain clouds" (*Works*, p. 135). Our interpretation of this statement—like all the other tropes—is dependent directly upon our interpretation of the text, and because more than one interpretation is possible, actually because more than one interpretation is encouraged, the image has more than one "correct" meaning. The image as symbol could refer to regeneration—the golden light of man's heroic potential overcoming his leaden, mundane existence—or the image as irony could refer to one more example of man's self-delusion.

Concerned more with epistemology than metaphysics, *The Red Badge of Courage*, in a sense, casts the reader into the role of one of its characters. Henry, on the narrative level, struggles to comprehend events that never coincide with his expectations; and, like Henry, the reader, on the extratextual level, struggles to comprehend a polysemous text that rejects traditional interpretations. Although Henry comes to what seems to be a reconciliation with his universe, the reader cannot know with certainty that Henry's final peace is the real thing; he cannot know any final extratextual meaning, and he is confronted with the disturbing possibility that a knowable, interpretable universe may well be nonexistent. Because it confronts on both the narrative and extratextual levels the difficulties of knowing and understanding the events that constitute our experience, *The Red Badge of Courage* does not fit easily into any traditional generic category of naturalism, romanticism, or symbolism, and it might be better classified an "epistemological text." In this kind of text, the ability to know meaning is the ultimate issue. Metaphysical and theological questions are secondary, and Stephen Crane, in his most acclaimed fiction, presents the unsettling suggestion that the universe is more than apathetic or even antagonistic: it is unknowable.

From *Modern Fiction Studies* 27, no. 4 (1981-1982): 621-628. Copyright © 1982 by Purdue Research Foundation. Reprinted with permission of the Johns Hopkins University Press.

Notes

1. In 1924 Joseph Hergesheimer was one of the first critics to recognize that Stephen Crane's narratives are more than naturalistic tales in the Howells and Norris tradition. In his "Introduction" to *The Red Badge of Courage*, Volume I of *The Work of Stephen Crane*, ed. Wilson Follet (New York: Knopf, 1924), p. xvii, Hergesheimer tells us that *"The Red Badge of Courage* is both a novel and a narrative; since the difference between realism and romance has never been defined it may, as well, be both romantic and realistic. At once, I mean. I have an idea, too, that it is poetry, lyrical as well as epic; no one, certainly, can deny that it is completely classic in its movement, its pace and return." Today, Hergesheimer's observation is a critical commonplace. Writing about "The Blue Hotel," James T. Cox in "Stephen Crane as Symbolic Naturalist: An Analysis of 'The Blue Hotel,'" *Modern Fiction Studies*, 3 (1957), 148, tells us that Crane "carefully selects his details not as pieces of evidence in a one-dimensional report on man but as connotatively associated parts of an elaborately contrived symbolic substructure." Crane is, according to Cox, a "symbolic naturalist." Eric Solomon in "The Structure of *The Red Badge of Courage*," *Modern Fiction Studies*, Stephen Crane Special Number, 5 (1959), 263, tells us that *"The Red Badge of Courage* should be called an impressionistic-naturalistic novel—or vice-versa." Hugh N. Maclean in "The Two Worlds of 'The Blue Hotel,'" *Modern Fiction Studies*, Stephen Crane Special Number, 5 (1959) sees "The Blue Hotel" reflecting two different "worlds," one symbolic, the other naturalistic.

2. Donna Gerstenberger, "'The Open Boat': Additional Perspective," *Modern Fiction Studies*, 17 (1971-72), 560. Two other studies that regard Crane's fiction as epistemological in nature are Frank Bergon's *Stephen Crane's Artistry* (New York: Co-

lumbia University Press, 1975) and James B. Colvert's "Introduction" to *Great Short Works of Stephen Crane* (New York: Harper & Row, 1979).

3. I am making a distinction here between the author and the narrator or "implied author," but no harm is done to the argument, I believe, if "narrator" is replaced with "Crane."

4. Robert Wooster Stallman in "Introduction" to *Stephen Crane: An Omnibus* (New York: Knopf, 1952), p. xxiv, makes a similar observation although he calls the vacillation "repetitive alternations of contradictory moods."

5. Stephen Crane, *The Red Badge of Courage*, Volume III of *The University of Virginia Edition of The Works of Stephen Crane*, ed. Fredson Bowers (Charlottesville: The University of Virginia Press, 1975), p. 3. All subsequent references to Crane's fiction will be from this edition.

6. Stallman, p. xxxiv.

7. Jean G. Marlowe, "Crane's Wafer Image: Reference to an Artillery Primer?", *American Literature*, 43 (1972), 645-647.

Subjectivism and *The Red Badge of Courage*_____
Eric Carl Link

J. C. Levenson writes: "Crane believed that, despite man's readiness to project ideas of order—and even attitudes toward himself—upon external nature, the universe is only a neutral backdrop to human activity." Without the aid of firsthand knowledge of either William James or Chauncey Wright, Levenson argues, Crane "was reduced to showing how, reacting to his own changeable situation, a man might regard nature in various ways."[1] The indirect connection Levenson notices between James and Crane has recently been explored at length by Patrick Dooley, who examines the compatibilities of Jamesian thought with the philosophy of Stephen Crane. Dooley demonstrates that, like James, Crane was a philosophical pluralist who used conflicting observer/participant/reader perceptions to expose both the multiplicity of reality and the corollary fact that "truth" changes depending upon one's viewpoint. Crane is not "skeptical about humanity's ability to know the world," writes Dooley; however, "no single world exists. Accordingly, no single record of it can claim truth. On the contrary, because a multitude of worlds can be experienced, a plurality of true descriptions is both a realistic goal and a reasonable expectation." But the "search for relatively true accounts of the worlds of experience does not amount to a surrender to subjectivism because equal value is not attributed to every interpretative report."[2]

Dooley seems to use the term "subjectivism" in this passage to mean a relativism in which no one point of view can be judged better or worse than another. Indeed, Crane often points out in his fiction that certain subjective perceptions provide a false impression of reality. In chapter 6 of *Red Badge*, for example, Fleming's perception that the regiment is doomed is proven false when upon approaching the general he discovers that the regiment has won the battle after all. In this passage the general's perspective on the battle was superior to Henry Fleming's.

But James makes a related but special use of the term "subjectivism" in "The Dilemma of Determinism." As we have seen, the dilemma of determinism, in James's view, is that it leads either to pessimism or subjectivism. Subjectivism, we recall, posits that one must stop viewing good and evil objectively and begin to view them as indifferent materials useful for the production of scientific and ethical consciousness in humankind. One of the better illustrations of James's concept of subjectivism can be found in Stephen Crane's *The Red Badge of Courage*. In order to avoid a pessimistic interpretation of nature based upon a conviction of the fundamental absurdity of war and human behavior, Henry Fleming retreats into subjectivism: his shifting perspectives on nature are grounded in a belief that the sensory data provided by nature are there to teach him how to interpret the meaning of his apparent cowardice. Thus, Fleming becomes a symbolist of sorts, seeking to interpret the signs presented to him by nature; yet, these attempts are veiled in what we might call a pervasive romantic irony, for the very signs Fleming attempts to decipher are, in part, products of the youth's subjective imagination.

The book begins by emphasizing Fleming's shifting perspectives on war. He had "dreamed of battles all his life—of vague and bloody conflicts that had thrilled him with their sweep and fire. In visions he had seen himself in many struggles. . . . But awake he had regarded battles as crimson blotches on the pages of the past. He had put them as things of the bygone with his thought-images of heavy crowns and high castles" (4-5).[3] With youthful eyes he "had long despaired of witnessing a Greeklike struggle" (5). His "busy mind had drawn for him large pictures extravagant in color, lurid with breathless deeds" (5). These great expectations are left unfulfilled. After enlisting he finds that his regiment does little but "sit still and try to keep warm" (7). He grows to regard himself merely "as part of a vast blue demonstration" (7).

The general inactivity of the regiment gives Fleming considerable time for self-analysis. He tries to "mathematically prove to himself that he would not run from a battle" (8). Such proofs do not present themselves to him, however, and he "was forced to admit that as far as war was concerned he knew nothing of himself" (8). In this crisis he finds "his laws of life were useless. Whatever he had learned of himself was here of no avail. He was an unknown quantity" (8). As a result, he concludes that he will have to perform an "experiment" and "accumulate information on himself" (8). The rest of the book concerns his "experiment." The problem for Fleming is that he has trouble interpreting the results.

Having set up the plot of the book and introduced its major theme in the first chapter, Crane uses the rest of the narrative to dramatize Fleming's experiment and to explore how he tries to integrate the information he collects into his perspectives on self, nature, and experience. The book, then, is built around shifting participant/observer perspectives. While conducting his "experiment," his perspective is that of a participant. When trying to interpret the results, his perspective is that of observer. Fleming thus shifts between an active and participatory "self in action" and a passive and observational "self in reflection." These two selves are mutually exclusive: he cannot both act and reflect at the same time. For instance, when early in the narrative the regiment, hearing gunfire, begins to run, he "was bewildered. As he ran with his comrades he strenuously tried to think, but all he knew was that if he fell down those coming behind would tread upon him. All his faculties seemed to be needed to guide him over and past obstructions" (17).

When Fleming does find time for self-analysis and reflection, he oscillates between deterministic and indeterministic interpretations of nature and experience. Fleming's shifting interpretations are linked to whether he perceives himself to have acted heroically or cowardly. In order to compensate for the guilt he feels for his cowardly acts, he turns toward determinism. But when he believes himself to have acted courageously, he shifts toward indeterminism. This pattern emerges shortly after the regiment's run in chapter 3. Here, realizing that his "experiment" is about to happen, and believing himself imprisoned in the mob of soldiers, he feels the first pangs of cowardice (17). In order to justify his apprehension, he formulates a deterministic interpretation of his position in the regiment.

> But he instantly saw that it would be impossible for him to escape from the regiment. It inclosed him. And there were iron laws of tradition and law on four sides. He was in a moving box.
>
> As he perceived this fact it occurred to him that he had never wished to come to the war. He had not enlisted of his free will. He had been dragged by the merciless government. And now they were taking him out to be slaughtered. (18)

Despite these apprehensions, "the ardor which the youth had acquired" during the march fades when the regiment lapses into inaction again (19). If an "intense scene had caught him with its wild swing as he came to the top of the bank, he might have gone roaring on" (19). But this "advance upon Nature was too calm" and it provided him with "opportunity to reflect" (19). In his reflections "absurd ideas" took hold of him: he "thought that he did not relish the landscape. It threatened him" (19). Soon he comes to the conclusion that the "generals did not know what they were about" and that the regiment was "going to be sacrificed" (19).

Although anxious over how he will react when the attack finally occurs, Fleming steadies himself by recalling that he "had been taught that a man became another thing in a battle. He saw his salvation in such a change" (20). When the first skirmish takes place, he does, in a sense, become "another thing," changing from observer/reflector to participant/actor.

> He got the one glance at the foe-swarming field in front of him, and instantly ceased to debate the question of his piece being loaded. Before he was ready to begin—before he had announced to himself that he was about to fight—he threw the obedient, well-balanced rifle into position and fired a first wild shot. Directly he was working at his weapon like an automatic affair.
>
> He suddenly lost concern for himself, and forgot to look at a menacing fate. He became not a man but a member. (26)

When the skirmish ended, he "awakened slowly" and "came gradually back to a position from which he could regard himself" (29). The initial experiment concluded, he regards himself as a hero whose "supreme trial had been passed. The red, formidable difficulties of war had been vanquished" (30). Believing himself courageous, he turns from his prior deterministic outlook to one that asserts individual agency. He sees his courage arising from the fact that he is a heroic man. Delighted with this estimation of himself, he "went into an ecstasy of self-satisfaction. . . . Standing as if apart from himself, he viewed the last scene. He perceived that the man who had fought thus was magnificent" (30).

Fleming's self-satisfaction is short-lived, for the gray army quickly renews their attack. Awed by the apparent "valor" of these "machines of steel," he turns and runs like the "proverbial chicken" (31). In order to justify his desertion, he interprets his flight as the deliberate act of a man with a superior sense of perception. Those who stayed to fight were "methodical idiots" and "machine-like fools," and he "pitied them as he ran" (32). Coming upon a general, whom he considers "unable to comprehend chaos," he contemplates telling him that the regiment was doomed (33). Before he does so, however, he overhears the general declare that the regiment has not been crushed, but has actually held the line (34).

His cowardice and misapprehension exposed, Fleming "cringed as if discovered in a crime" (34). Chapter 7 of *Red Badge* explores how he tries to reconcile himself with his guilt. He does so by turning back to a deterministic interpretation of Nature and experience. The chapter begins with his attempt to hold on to his sense of manhood and agency by arguing that, despite the fact that the line had held, he had run because of his "superior perceptions and knowledge," and he knew it could be proved that his comrades "had been fools" to stay and fight (35). This argument he knows is flawed, and he soon begins to "pity himself acutely," feeling himself "ill used" and "trodden beneath the feet of an iron injustice" (35). Then, "seeking dark and intricate places," he flees farther into the woods (35). Throwing a pine-cone at a squirrel, he watches the frightened animal scurry up a tree. He uses this event to construct a deterministic interpretation of Nature that helps rationalize away his feelings of cowardice and guilt.

> The youth felt triumphant at this exhibition. There was the law, he said. Nature had given him a sign. The squirrel, immediately upon recognizing danger, had taken to his legs without ado. He did not stand stolidly baring his furry belly to the missile, and die with an upward glance at the sympathetic heavens. On the contrary, he had fled as fast as his legs could carry him; and he was but an ordinary squirrel, too—doubtless no philosopher of his race. The youth wended, feeling that Nature was of his mind. She reenforced his argument with proofs that lived where the sun shone. (35-36)

Fleming's deterministic reassurance does not last long, however. Wandering near a swamp, he sees "a small animal pounce in and emerge directly with a gleaming fish" (36). Then, passing from "obscurity into promises of a greater obscurity," he comes upon a place where the "high, arching boughs made a chapel" (36). Pushing open the "green doors" of the chapel and stepping into the "religious half light," he finds himself staring at a dead man seated against a tree (36). The man's eyes had the dull hue of a "dead fish" and ants were crawling across the face (36). The detail of the dead-fish eyes connects the chapel scene with the preceding scene in which the animal catches a fish in the swamp. This connection suggests a different law of nature: life feeds or exists on death. This observation regarding the inherent violence in nature contrasts with the youth's earlier observation that nature itself—as exemplified in the squirrel's flight—abhors violence. A comparison of these two different interpretations of the law of nature shows that the first privileges (and justifies) his flight; the other privileges the battle, and is another argument for Fleming's cowardice.[4]

The next several chapters of the book detail Fleming's further attempts to reconcile himself with his feelings of guilt and cowardice, and in so doing continue the process of interpreting the results of his earlier experiments with war. The difficulty of this interpretive process is compounded by the fact that Fleming's varying perspectives on nature and experience are driven by his subjectivism. What one observes repeatedly is that nature is described in a way that mirrors Fleming's own internal struggles. Nature acts as a backdrop upon which he projects his shifting perceptions. Fleeing from the chapel in the forest, for instance, he feels that the trees begin to "softly sing a hymn of twilight" and that the insects are bowing their beaks and "making a devotional pause" (37). When his legs get caught in some brambles as he walks toward the battlefield, he interprets this to mean that "Nature could not be quite ready to kill him" (38). As he gets within sight of the battle, he sees it as an "immense and terrible machine" and he wishes to get closer and "see it produce corpses" (38). Soon he comes across some wounded soldiers. Here, the innocent probings of the tattered soldier remind him once again of his cowardice. He comes to believe that "his shame could be viewed. He was continually casting sidelong glances to see if the men were contemplating the letters of guilt he felt burned into his brow" (40-41). Because of his shame Fleming wishes that "he, too, had a wound, a red badge of courage"; such a wound would give him an alibi to cover his guilt (41). He does have a wounded conscience, however, and the tattered soldier points out that internal wounds are sometimes the worst (46).

The "simple questions" of the tattered man were "knife thrusts" to Fleming, and he perceives them as evidence of a "society that probes pitilessly at secrets until all is apparent" (47). So powerful are these probing forces that he believes he will be unable to keep buried "those things which are willed to be forever hidden. He admitted that he could not defend himself against this agency" (47). As a result of this renewed fear that his guilt will eventually be exposed, he tries to construct yet another deterministic interpretation of nature to help assuage his conscience. Feeling that he will never join the ranks of the heroic and courageous, he "searched about in his mind for an adequate malediction for the indefinite cause, the thing upon which men turn the words of final blame. It—whatever it was—was responsible for him, he said. There lay the fault" (48).

Fleming's reflections shortly come to an end. In chapter 12 the "dragons" of the rebel army advance and the blue soldiers begin to retreat en masse (51-52). At the sight of soldiers running past him he becomes "horror-stricken" (52). Caught up in the midst of the activity, he shifts from observer to participant, from the reflective self to the active self. He "forgot that he was engaged in combating the universe. He threw aside his mental pamphlets on the philosophy of the retreated and rules for the guidance of the damned" (52). In the midst of this flurry of activity he is unable to formulate whole sentences and is reduced to asking fleeing soldiers "why—why—what—what's th' matter?" (52). It is here, in the middle of the book, that Fleming receives his red badge (52-53). With this wound and the help of the cheery soldier, he is able to return to his regiment, where he is nursed by Wilson and his "disordered mind" interprets the "hall of the forest as a charnel place" (60).

Enabled to rejoin the regiment without having his guilt exposed, Fleming is able to formulate a new theory of nature. This newest experience teaches him that "many obligations of a life were easily avoided. The lessons of yesterday had been that retribution was a laggard and blind" (65). He need not fear battles to come; instead he could "leave much to chance" (65). Besides, "a faith in himself had secretly blossomed. There was a little flower of confidence growing within him. He was now a man of experience" (65). The "dragons" of war were "not so hideous as he had imagined them," and they were "inaccurate; they did not sting with precision" (65). Furthermore, "how could they kill him who was the chosen of gods and doomed to greatness?" (65). While others had fled the battlefield like "weak mortals," Fleming believes himself to have "fled with discretion and dignity" (65). Thinking he has escaped detection from his peers, Fleming is thus able to reinterpret nature as governed by a "soft" determinism: "chance" is a law of nature, but it is "laggard" and therefore allows for those, like himself, with superior perceptions to act with "discretion."

When the time finally comes to prove himself in battle, Fleming's perspective shifts back to that of participant. He fights without thinking, so unconscious of his surroundings that when a lull comes in the fighting he continues to fire his weapon for some time (71-72). When he does stop firing, he interprets his actions: "It was revealed to him that he had been a barbarian, a beast. He had fought like a pagan who defends his religion. Regarding it, he saw that it was fine, wild, and, in some ways, easy. He had been a tremendous figure, no doubt. . . . he was now what he called a hero. And he had not been aware of the process. He had slept and, awakening, found himself a knight" (72). Unfortunately, his high regard for himself is not corroborated by an officer who claims that the regiment not only fights like "a lot 'a mule drivers,'" but also is his most dispensable unit (75). These overheard remarks give him "new eyes," and he learns "suddenly that he was very insignificant" (75). The information that the 304th is to charge the rebels presents him with a new mystery. He had proven that he could maintain a line, but actually charging the enemy was a different matter. As a result, he perceives "powers and horrors" in the foliage ahead of him (76). He is able to see his surroundings, but is unsure of their meaning, particularly as they relate to himself. His "mind took a mechanical but firm impression, so that afterward everything was pictured and explained to him, save why he himself was there" (77). The signs are there, but they elude interpretation.

The skirmish won, Fleming and other members of the 304th, feeling themselves heroic again, return to an indeterminate theory of nature.

It had begun to seem to them that events were trying to prove that they were impotent. These little battles had evidently endeavored to demonstrate that the men could not fight well. When on the verge of submission to these opinions, the small duel had showed them that the proportions were not impossible, and by it they had revenged themselves upon their misgivings and upon the foe.
. . . And they were men. (84)

As men they have the ability to stand up against "events" and prove themselves heroic (despite grand master/novice odds). They gain further evidence for this interpretation when the battle resumes and the 304th, with Fleming acting as color-bearer and Wilson capturing the enemy flag, wins yet another skirmish.

The book's final chapter is dedicated to self-analysis and reflection. This process of reflection begins when Fleming shifts back into the observational mode: "For a time the youth was obliged to reflect in a puzzled and uncertain way. His mind was undergoing a subtle change. It took moments for it to cast off its battleful ways and resume its accustomed course of thought. Gradually his brain emerged from the clogged clouds, and at last he was enabled to more closely comprehend himself and circumstance" (96). Having thus engaged his "machines of reflection" Fleming struggles to "marshall all his acts," but "at last they marched before him clearly. From this present view point he was enabled to look upon them in spectator fashion and to criticize them with some correctness, for his new condition had already defeated certain sympathies" (96). He sees "that he was good" (96), but in the midst of this goodness "the light of his soul flickered with shame" at the memory of deserting the tattered soldier in the field (97). As with his original desertion, he fears that "he might be detected in the thing" (97), and this fear darkens an otherwise "purple and gold" view of himself (97). One final time, then, he must adjust his interpretation of nature in order to accommodate "his vivid error":

> Yet gradually he mustered force to put the sin at a distance. And at last his eyes seemed to open to some new ways. He found that he could look back upon the brass and bombast of his earlier gospels and see them truly. He was gleeful when he discovered that he now despised them.
>
> With this conviction came a store of assurance. He felt a quiet manhood, nonassertive but of sturdy and strong blood. . . .
>
> So it came to pass that as he trudged from the place of blood and wrath his soul changed. He came from hot plowshares to prospects of clover tranquility. (97-98)

Fleming reconciles himself to his "sin," thus, by reading the events of the past two days as a redemption story. He may have "sinned," but that sin opened his eyes to the falseness of his "earlier gospels." This revelation changes his "soul" Now, having "rid himself of the red sickness of battle," he can look forward to "an existence of soft and eternal peace" (98). As a symbol of this newfound redemption, "over the river a golden ray of sun came through the hosts of leaden rain clouds" (98).

Fleming's deterministic interpretations of nature are at varying times natural and supernatural. On some occasions he interprets experiences by appealing to the scientific "laws" of nature, such as instinct, as in the case of the fleeing squirrel. On other occasions, combined with these scientific "laws" are supernatural and religious elements, some of which point toward a providential determinism. Fleming often turns toward religious imagery and language.[5] He is one of the "damned" and longs to prove himself one of the "chosen" or elect (see 48, 52, 64). He finally reconciles himself to his "sin" by turning to what amounts to a type of *felix culpa* argument: God allowed him to sin, for it ultimately led to the purification of his soul. That Fleming turns to this type of argument at the end of the book is made even more explicit in one of the uncancelled but unpublished passages in the manuscript version: "He was emerged from his struggles, with a large sympathy for the machinery of the universe. With his new eyes, he could see that the secret and open blows which were being dealt about the world with such heavenly lavishness were in truth blessings. It was a deity laying about him with the bludgeon of correction" (105).[6] Although Crane's irony does undercut attempts to read *Red Badge* as a positive redemption story, he does provide enough language within the text to at least legitimize *Fleming*'s various religious interpretations of nature. There is a "chapel" in the forest. The walk with the cheery soldier suggests the Emmaus road. Fleming divides the courageous and the cowardly into the "chosen" and the "damned."Fleming sees his desertions as "sins." When his "soul" changes at the end of the book, Fleming sets aside his "former gospels."

The irony of the ending does not arise so much from the reader's assumption (based presumably on a knowledge of the mind of Crane) that *Crane* believes there is no power in redemption, but rather it stems from the realization that Fleming's latest interpretation of nature is a product of his "machines of reflection." Once again he justifies his feelings of guilt by constructing a theory of nature that helps separate him from responsibility for his "sin." This irony was emphasized by Crane in another unpublished passage from the manuscript. After the line "Yet gradually he mustered force to put the sin at a distance," Crane had originally written:

> And then he regarded it with what he thought to be great calmness. At last, he concluded that he saw in it quaint uses. He exclaimed that its importance in the aftertime would be great to him if it even succeeded in hindering the workings of his egotism. It would make a sobering balance. It would become a good part of him. He would have upon him often the consciousness of a great mistake. . . .
>
> This plan for the utilization of a sin did not give him complete joy but it was the best sentiment he could formulate under the circumstances. (104-05)

Leaving out this and the "bludgeon of correction" passages takes the bluntness out of Crane's irony, but does not change the fact that Fleming's conviction of redemption is the product of subjective reflection.[7]

In the end, William James would reject the subjectivist approach to nature illustrated in the oscillating perspective on nature taken by Crane's Fleming. In "The Dilemma of Determinism" James quotes a passage from Carlyle, who wrote: "Hang your sensibilities! Stop your snivelling [*sic*] complaints, and your equally snivelling raptures! Leave off your general emotional tomfoolery, and get to WORK like men!" (174). Adopting such a position, argues James, requires a complete break with the subjectivist perspective, for it claims conduct, not perception, is the basis of value in the universe. And so James openly opposes his "romantic rival"—the subjectivism of soft determinism—

by positing what he refers to as the "philosophy of objective conduct" (174). James describes his philosophy in this manner: "It is the recognition of limits, foreign and opaque to our understanding. It is the willingness, after bringing about some external good, to feel at peace; for our responsibility ends with the performance of that duty, and the burden of the rest we may lay on higher powers" (174-75). The distinction drawn here between a philosophy of objective conduct and the subjectivism of soft determinism is important for illustrating a key difference between realism and romanticism. Positing metaphysical and epistemological speculation so central to romanticism as subsidiary to the pragmatic action valorized by James goes far toward explaining the shift in the realistic novel away from the abstract speculation of the romance and toward an examination of social behavior and conduct.

Beyond illustrating this difference in realism and romanticism, James's discussion of the dilemma of determinism is remarkable for a number of reasons. First, predating Norris's "Zola as a Romantic Writer" by a dozen years, James adds his weight to Norris's claims by positioning Zola as a writer of romances, and of viewing the soft determinism so vital to American literary naturalism as a type of romanticism. Furthermore, James's observation that soft determinism often invites a fatalistic orientation generally confirms speculations raised earlier in this chapter about the intermingling of fatalism with scientific and providential determinism in American naturalist narratives.

But even more importantly, James makes some significant linkages among epistemology, perception, romanticism, and soft determinism that help open up the texts of American literary naturalism. Neither the antebellum romancers nor the later literary naturalists in America would have been satisfied with James's philosophy of objective conduct. They generally were not satisfied with the "recognition of limits, foreign and opaque to our understanding." On the contrary, writers like Brown, Poe, Melville, Hawthorne, Crane, Norris, and London attempted to push beyond these limits—and it is one of the chief characteristics of negative romanticism/naturalism that these attempts either failed, revealed further limits, or only served to open up more questions. Sometimes they achieved a brief glimpse of supernal beauty or a quick flashing forth of the axis of reality, but they just as often ran up against the inscrutable pasteboard mask of nature. They were left, like Crane's youth, walking around and around a dead soldier, trying "to read in dead eyes the answer to the Question."[8]

From *The Vast and Terrible Drama: American Literary Naturalism in the Late Nineteenth Century* (2004), pp. 129-140. Copyright © 2004 by The University of Alabama Press. Reprinted with permission of The University of Alabama Press.

Notes

1. J. C. Levenson, introduction, *The Works of Stephen Crane*, vol. 2. *The Red Badge of Courage*, ed. Fredson Bowers (Charlottesville: UP of Virginia, 1975), lvi-lvii.

2. Patrick K. Dooley, *The Pluralistic Philosophy of Stephen Crane* (Urbana: U of Illinois P, 1993), 29-30.

3. All page references are to *The Red Badge of Courage*, ed. Donald Pizer (New York: W. W. Norton, 1994).

4. In one of the manuscript versions of *Red Badge*, Crane was more explicit about the juxtaposition of these two conflicting laws of nature. In a passage that originally followed Fleming's confrontation with death in the chapel, Crane wrote: Fleming "thought as he remembered the small animal capturing the fish and the greedy ants feeding upon the flesh of the dead soldier, that there was given another law which far-over-topped it—all life existing upon death, eating ravenously, stuffing itself with the hopes of the dead" (qtd. in Levenson, lviii). The effect of removing this passage from the final draft is to leave the question open as to which law of nature was the greater.

5. There have been many attempts to interpret the religious imagery and language in *Red Badge*. Ever since Stallman in 1951 suggested that *Red Badge* could be interpreted as a positive redemption story, critics have argued about whether Fleming's "redemption" at the end is ironic or not. Some have even argued that there is no substantial religious component to *Red Badge* at all. One of the main questions stems from asking if the author of *The Black Riders* would also write a narrative that concludes with a positive redemptive vision. It seems to me that the answer lies in the realization that it is not Crane who turns to the hope of redemption at the end of *Red Badge*, but Henry Fleming. The answer, therefore, lies in Fleming's subjectivism. Regardless, virtually every study concerned with the religious imagery in the novel includes a discussion of the symbolism (or lack thereof) in the novel.

For a sample of some of the more important essays that tackle this problem see the following: R. W. Stallman, "Notes Toward an Analysis of *The Red Badge of Courage*," in *Stephen Crane: A Collection of Critical Essays*, ed. Maurice Bassan (Englewood Cliffs, NJ.: Prentice-Hall, 1967), 128-40; the articles by Isaac Rosenfeld, John E. Hart, Edward Stone, and James B. Colvert reprinted in *Stephen Crane's The Red Badge of Courage: Text and Criticism*, eds. Richard Lettis, Robert F. McDonnell, and William E. Morris (New York: Harcourt, Brace, 1959); Scott C. Osborn, "Stephen Crane's Imagery: 'Pasted Like a Wafer,'" in *The Red Badge of Courage*, eds. Sculley Bradley, Richmond Croom Beatty, E. Hudson Long (New York: W. W. Norton, 1962), 163-64; R. W. Stallman, "The Scholar's Net: Literary Sources," *College English* 17 (1955): 20-27; James Trammell Cox, "The Imagery of 'The Red Badge of Courage,'" *Modern Fiction Studies* 5 (1959): 209-19; James W. Tuttleton, "The Imagery of *The Red Badge of Courage*," *Modern Fiction Studies* 8 (1963): 410-15; Marston LaFrance, "Stephen Crane's Private Fleming: His Various Battles," in *Patterns of Commitment in American Literature*, ed. Marston LaFrance (Toronto: U of Toronto P, 1967), 113-33; and Ben Satterfield, "From Romance to Reality: The Accomplishment of Private Fleming," *CLA Journal* 24 (1980-1981): 451-64.

Curiously, in his introduction to *The Red Badge of Courage and Other Writings* (Boston: Houghton Mifflin, 1960), Richard Chase claims that Crane is not a symbolist and that *Red Badge* does not have a "symbolic center," but if it did, the chapel scene in chapter 7 would certainly be it (see xi and xvi).

6. The uncancelled but unpublished passages from the manuscript version of *Red Badge* are printed in an appendix to the Norton Critical Edition.

7. There is a further irony to be found in the ending of *Red Badge*. As John E. Curran Jr. points out, Fleming's feelings of glory are incongruous with the fact that the battle of Chancellorsville was one of the single worst defeats of the Union Army during the entire Civil War. See Curran's article "'Nobody seems to know where we go': Uncertainty, History, and Irony in *The Red Badge of Courage*," *American Literary Realism* 26.1 (fall 1993): 1-12.

8. Stephen Crane, *The Red Badge of Courage* (New York: Signet, 1980), 31.

From Romance to Reality:
The Accomplishment of Private Fleming_____
Ben Satterfield

To offer yet another contribution to the interpretation of "so notori-
ously overanalyzed a novel"[1] as *The Red Badge of Courage* is to invite
the charge of performing a dispensable act. But just the opposite is
true: a coherent and uncontradictory reading is necessary. This short
novel by Stephen Crane has engendered critical and expository
schisms of so profound a nature that there is not even common agreement as to what the book is about; in form, it is generally labeled a
novel of initiation, a *Bildungsroman*, but in content, it has been called
everything from a negative and dehumanized portrait of pessimistic-
deterministic philosophy to an inspiring religious allegory.[2] In fact,
The Red Badge, while neither plotless nor obscure, remains something
of an enigma on any level other than that of a war story, in spite of its
having been pored over by myriad critics. My intention here is to present a tenable analysis that views the book as a consistent and unified
work of art that is neither allegorical nor naturalistic, but essentially affirmative and humanistic in scope.

The controlling premises of this paper are: one, the work of any
good writer merits continual reinterpretation and reappraisal, the dy-
namics of which are a certain testimony to the vitality of the work itself; two, an artist knows what he is doing and he should be understood
on his own terms, not the reader's; three, Crane is an artist (this is apo-
dictic, and I see no reason to say more than that it is understood); four,
any interpretation in harmony with the most or all parts of the work is
not only likely to be the best but also closest to the intent of the author.

Since Crane relies so heavily upon it, imagery will be stressed as a
key to meaning, with particular emphasis on animal imagery, the abun-
dance of which makes it impossible to read the novel without being
constantly aware of it. Although this imagery has been repeatedly
cited, its dominance is not yet apparent to all. In the Stephen Crane is-

sue of the *University of Minnesota Pamphlets on American Writers*, Jean Cazemajou's insistence is that "religious imagery prevails" in *The Red Badge of Courage*. Following this declaration, a few examples are quoted, including "the ghost of his flight," "columnlike," and "the tattered man." These meager and dubious examples are then subsequently and inaccurately referred to as a "procession of religious images."[3]

Most of the images in this novel are not religious in any recognizable sense; indeed, one would have to expand the definition of "religious" beyond credible limits to include "a specter of reproach" and "the creed of soldiers" as phrases appropriate to its meaning. The animal imagery, however, is not doubtful and permeates the novel. The first definite allusions occur in chapter one where the recruits are referred to as "prey" and "fresh fish," and the same type of imagery persists through the final chapter where one particular officer is described as a "whale"—an image that recalls the "fish" of chapter one. But despite the fact that over seventy comparisons of the men to animals have been counted[4] in *The Red Badge of Courage* and one article has been written solely about animal imagery (in which is stated: "Excluding all the numerous sunken metaphors which imply animal-like action, this short novel contains at least 80 figures of speech employing animals or their characteristics"[5]), this imagery has not been adequately explained nor its coherence demonstrated. The often noted (and I believe mistaken) interpretation of the animal imagery is that it reinforces Crane's "naturalism." As Eric Solomon phrases it:

> War seems so brutally deterministic to Crane that it robs man of the free will and intelligence that differentiate him from the animals. For this reason the use of animal imagery is fitting for the naturalistic interpretation of war.[6]

The prevailing assumption seems to be that Crane's "naturalistic tendency" is to portray "men as sheep" in order to present his determin-

---

istic viewpoint that "man's life is shaped by forces beyond his comprehension or control."[7] Regardless of its widespread acceptance, I disagree with a naturalistic interpretation of *The Red Badge*, and I dissent because the novel itself, as I will illustrate, denies the claim and violates the definition of naturalism.[8] As indicated above, the prevalence of animal imagery has been cited as supporting evidence of naturalism; I will use the same imagery to demonstrate that naturalism plays no part.

Initially, Henry has a romantic vision of war as a "sort of a play affair," and he despairs "of witnessing a Greeklike struggle,"[9] fearing that the throat-grappling instinct has been effaced; in short, Henry has a callow and unreal view of war. If war is a metaphor (and I doubt that many would argue against the statement that it usually is in fiction), it represents a unique confrontation, not only between men but between a man and himself, and it provides an atmosphere in which one confronts the animal in one's self. I think *The Red Badge* offers sufficient indications to support the claim that Henry Fleming does just that. He flees from battle with the animal instinct of self-preservation and he seeks succor in Nature, the habitat of all animals. Chapter seven contains an often quoted passage in which Henry throws a pine cone at a squirrel and watches it run "with chattering fear":

> The youth felt triumphant at this exhibition. There was the law, he said. Nature had given him a sign. The squirrel, immediately upon recognizing danger, had taken to his legs without ado. He did not stand stolidly baring his furry belly to the missile, and die with an upward glance at the sympathetic heavens. On the contrary, he had fled as fast as his legs could carry him: and he was but an ordinary squirrel, too—doubtless no philosopher of his race. The youth wended, feeling that Nature was of his mind. She reenforced his argument with proofs that lived where the sun shone. (p. 274)

The "proofs" Henry sees are valid only if man, too, is merely an animal; Nature is of his mind if he wants only to be an animal and live in an animal world. But Henry is in the process of learning that he is a man and that man is not just another animal; he goes deeper into the forest, into the heart of Nature, seeking solace—but finding a corpse. Donald Gibson makes the following observation about this encounter:

> In the very heart of the forest Henry finds not safety, escape from death, comfort, succor, peace, but death, death at the very center of nature. . . . There is no choice but to come to terms with the possibility of his own destruction.[10]

Surely no one would quarrel with that statement; but it is Gibson's thesis that Henry is here reborn:

> After his experience in the forest the youth is in a position to achieve the goal of his quest by having in large measure severed his ties with nature, becoming dependent upon his own resources. . . . We should expect that when he is strong enough to face the possibility of his own destruction, he will no longer identify with nature, will not see nature as an antagonistic force because he will have freed himself from nature's domain. Such is indeed the case.[11]

I think just the opposite is true. Henry comes to terms with his own animal nature and learns to use it for his benefit as a man and as a member of the community to which he belongs by fact and by choice: he accepts his animality just as he comes to accept death. Professor Gibson points out that prior to the scene in the forest, Henry "had been awed more by the idea of death than by death itself."[12] This is unquestionably true, and Henry learns that once death is accepted, then life can be accepted; the romantic illusions can be cast off and he can become a man in reality. Only by reconciling himself with reality can he put an end to romantic thoughts of dying "with an upward glance at the sympathetic heavens." Of course the woods can offer no solace because death is an ineluctable part of Nature. There is no place to run in real life and Henry knows it now, just as he knows the "signs" Nature gives are not to be trusted, because Nature is uncognizant—as is so clearly indicated throughout the novel, a point I will return to shortly.

Critics have unanimously suggested that the combat background in general stands "for such abstractions as the harsh reality of life or the difficulty of survival,"[13] asserting in particular "that life is a battle is a Crane commonplace,"[14] and that Crane "equates war with life, and makes the reality of battle parallel the reality of human existence."[15] If life is equated with battle, then running from the battle is tantamount to running from life. Although he makes an attempt to escape, Henry comes to accept life (his animal nature, the harshness of existence, and the indifference of Nature) and to assert his own humanity by a moral comprehension of his responsibilities, something a mere animal cannot do. He returns to the battlefield *of his own volition*—that is, by making a moral choice—and fights animalistically, but this time with a human, self-chosen motive. His attitude is becoming more realistic now; he no longer romanticizes his situation or feels persecuted by malevolent forces as he had previously: "Yesterday, when he had imagined the universe to be against him, he had hated it, little gods and big gods; to-day he hated the army of the foe with the same great hatred" (p. 328). Henry had previously "imagined" the universe to be against him, just as he had imagined, before facing his first battle, that the mood of Nature was one of "sympathy for him in his distress" (p. 243). But he is now incontrovertibly dealing with reality: the army of the foe is Henry's enemy and his emotions are now focussed on the real; his actions, therefore, are very responsible and have no connection with naturalistic motivation. That the indifference of Nature and the universe creates the necessity for Henry's human responsibility in combat seems clear, but critical disagreement covers the full spectrum of possibility in interpreting this behavior:

Although Henry does show courage, there is decisive evidence that it is motivated chiefly by animal fierceness and competitive pride.[16]

Afterward, the youth shows himself worthy of his reward, for he shows an increasing ability to perform consciously in opposition to his animal self, which urges him to follow the dictates of his body.[17]

Note that in chapter seventeen Henry continues fighting "like a dog" (p. 330) even after the enemy has retreated. He is certainly not "in opposition to his animal self," but is acting most in union with and response to animal reactions, not "rational" ones. However, this is not an indication of naturalism: as contradictory as it may sound, I contend that Henry is here a whole person, a man who has come to terms with the facts of existence, who realizes he is animal in nature and yet something more than animal because he can make moral choices and commitments that might involve the giving up of life itself. When he returns to the battle Henry assumes responsibility for his position, whereas earlier he complained he had been put there against his will. Only man can choose as Henry does. Only man can make such decisions—decisions which are the measure of true heroism. In battle Henry loses his sense of individuality. He overcomes his animal instinct for self-preservation because he has dedicated himself. He has made a human commitment, and he uses all the animal strength within him to satisfy that commitment. He is now more than an animal; he is, as Crane says, a man: "And to be a man in Crane's world is to perceive fulfilling the commitments such a perception demands of the human situation as it is, accept it, and remain honest in fulfilling the commitments such a perception demands of the individual."[18]

I think Crane sees the whole person as a human being well integrated with his animality rather than at odds with it—which is one reason why I reject a religious reading of *The Red Badge*, since religion and animality are in conflict.[19] R. W. Stallman, however, interprets the novel as a Christian allegory, with Jim Conklin at the center as Christ.[20]

Other critics—for various reasons—disagree: one believes "the implications of Mr. Stallman's claim for religious symbolism leads [sic] away . . . from the core of Crane's true meaning,"[21] and another states: "In the ironic resemblances of Conklin to Christ, Crane is perhaps naively, but clearly and powerfully saying that in this red world Jesus Christ is a grim joke."[22] When Henry, returning to the war, sees the wounded Jim Conklin, he starts "as if bitten" (p. 282), and the dying man tells what he fears: "'I'm 'fraid I'll fall down—an' then yeh know—them damned artillery wagons—they like as not 'll run over me. That's what I'm 'fraid of—'" (p. 283). What Jim fears, obviously, is that he will die like an animal and be treated like an animal. His death throes are described "as if an animal was within and was kicking and tumbling furiously to be free" (p. 286). Using "animal" as a simile for the soul hardly seems appropriate—except ironically. To further demonstrate the polarity of opinion: "Here is a negation of the Christian conversion, in which one sees the light and is enrolled among the saints. Yet from this negation, the boy will take strength. . . . He has no prop but himself."[23]

Confusion arises because there is biblical language and religious imagery in the novel, but also a great deal of irony.[24] That the irony undercuts the religious elements cannot be manifested to the reader who imputes religious significance to the line, "The red sun was pasted in the sky like a wafer" (p. 287). But the imagery itself is two-dimensional, implying a heaven without depth, and hence any religious implications would have to be ironic. Contrary to Professor Stallman's assertion, the wafer is an image of passivity, and I agree with the suggestion that it is the seal of Nature's indifference[25] rather than a symbol of salvation or heavenly sympathy. Cosmic forces are often seen working in Crane's writings, though there has been much spurious speculation and too little reliance upon the author's words: in section seven of "The Open Boat," Crane writes that Nature "did not seem cruel . . . nor beneficent, nor treacherous, nor wise. But she was indifferent, flatly indifferent" (p. 443). Throughout *The Red Badge*, notwithstanding the well-known claim of "psychic affinity,"[26] Nature is shown to be indifferent, at times to the surprise of the immature and romantic Henry (in contrast to the more mature and realistic Henry at the novel's end). Note particularly the last paragraph of chapter five:

> As he gazed around him the youth felt a flash of astonishment at the blue, pure sky and the sun gleaming on the trees and fields. It was surprising that Nature had gone tranquilly on with her golden process in the midst of so much devilment. (p. 265)

In spite of such evidence, one still encounters untrue and unsupportable statements like "[Henry's] simple, secure world of romantic pretentions is sundered by the sublime confusion of the universe."[27] It is not the universe that is confused, and Crane says so in unmistakable terms; neither is it actively hostile, although it has been posited that one of Crane's recurring themes is "that man is an alien in an alien universe."[28] What Crane says is that Nature is unaware and unconcerned, not alien; the universe is clearly indifferent, not antagonistic. Henry learns this lesson and at the novel's end he can smile though slogging "in a trough of liquid brown mud under a low, wretched sky" (p. 370). The language describing Henry's surroundings is realistic—as is his recognition of the world with which he is now compatible. Seeing "a golden ray of sun . . . through the hosts of leaden rain clouds" is not the same kind of perception that construed Nature as sympathetic or saw the sky as "fairy blue" (p. 241). As I pointed out earlier, only a mistaken perception finds the end of *The Red Badge* to be inconsistent: "It has been Crane's view all along that nature is alien to man. Having read the novel up to the last page, no sensitive reader is going to accept signs from nature as meaningful."[29]

There are no advertent signs, just observable processes, and none but the romantic and immature will see in that activity a personal gesture. Therefore, the "signs" are not supposed to be meaningful—but Henry's response is: the book has established the fact that man's response is the only thing that is meaningful. In Crane's work, natural forces over which man has no control appear often—the sea in "The Open Boat," the storm in "The Blue Hotel," the fire in "The Veteran"—as well as man-made social forces such as those Dr. Trescott faces in "The Monster," or changing life in "The Bride Comes to Yellow Sky," or war, which is certainly man-made; but Crane's characters do have some control over their response to all these forces.

Henry responds—there can be no doubt of that. Yet one critic regards the novel as defective because, as he sees it, Henry's becoming a man "is largely a matter of accident, [and] lacks the authority of a consciously willed readiness to work out the hard way of salvation. Crane, I think, had his own doubts about the validity of Henry's transformation."[30] To make such an extrapolation is to ignore certain facts of the novel. For instance, it is no accident that Henry and Wilson, after overhearing the commanding general of their division predict that not many of the "mule drivers" will survive the next battle—which is imminent—both keep the secret and make the charge. Crane leaves no doubt that the decision is both heroic and moral, i.e., a consciously willed one: at the end of chapter eighteen, Henry and Wilson, "the only ones who possessed an inner knowledge," regard each other knowingly: "It was an ironical secret. Still, they saw no hesitation in each other's faces, and they nodded a mute and unprotesting assent when a shaggy man near them said in a meek voice: 'We'll git swallowed'" (p. 337). In case any doubt lingers, the reader is directed to the flag-carrying scene at the beginning of chapter twenty which makes clear each man's "willingness to further risk himself" (p. 343).

There should be no question of his transformation if we follow Henry carefully through the novel. When he first meets combat, in chapter five, he feels the potency of "the subtle battle brotherhood"—a phrase that is echoed in "The Open Boat" as "the subtle brotherhood of man" (p. 426)—and he temporarily loses "concern for himself" because he is part of "a common personality" (p. 261). Hence he does not run, but slips into a kind of "battle sleep" which sees him through this encounter. Transcending of self in community is a human ideal, and for the moment he achieves it, or so he believes. But he has not yet become a man. Later, when he deserts, it is because he yields to selfish motivations (animal instinct) and disregards his human responsibility to his fellow soldiers.

Note also the language: before Henry flees, the characters in his regiment are described impersonally, "the tall soldier," "the loud soldier," "corporal," "private;" however, when he returns, he becomes one of them and they are consistently referred to in terms of "friend" and "comrade." (From chapter thirteen to the end, Wilson is referred to as "companion" twice, "comrade" 9 times, and the word "friend" appears a total of 68 times; "fellowship" is mentioned and demonstrated: the other members of the regiment are referred to 6 times as "companions," 9 times as "comrades," once as "friends," and 6 times as "his fellows.") The change is meaningful: friendship and loyalty are human values that are presented as important—the correspondent in "The Open Boat" acknowledges that, despite their awful circumstances, the comradeship in the boat is "the best experience of his life" (p. 427).

His friends reveal to Henry "that he had been a barbarian, a beast. He had fought like a pagan who defends his religion. Regarding it, he saw that it was fine, wild, and, in some ways, easy. He had been a tremendous figure, no doubt" (p. 331). Observe that the "barbaric" terms elicit no revulsion and that they are presented in admiration: Henry is not repelled by them as he was formerly by "chicken" and "worm" and other lowly terms. Indeed, the words *fine, wild*, and *tremendous* seem to be equated in Henry's mind, and all the language seems antithetical to a religious interpretation. A barbarian is a person not living in a Christian country, but in a savage, primitive state, a state which Henry thought secular and religious education had effaced; a pagan is not a Christian—the word derives from *pāgānus*, worshipper of false gods, and not a soldier of Christ. Nevertheless, none of these words is used disparagingly in the passage quoted above, and it appears that Crane recognizes and accepts the animal nature man has inherited, but sees that man has a responsibility to reconcile, to syncretize, and to utilize that animality for the sake of brotherhood. (It is a paradox of life, and not a Crane paradox, that man can join in brotherhood to destroy his fellow man.) Henry, in harmony with his nature and his comrades, knows that being forgetful of self in the face of duty is human and good. The pejorative animal imagery disappears and the words *barbaric* and *wild*—or some form thereof—appear frequently throughout the rest of the novel. At the end, when Crane says, "He was a man" (p. 369), there is no ironic undercutting and this judgment seems to echo the close of chapter twenty: "And they were men" (p. 348), a phrase devoid of irony. But Cazemajou's antipodal opinion has it that "only an oversimplified interpretation could see in Henry's final charge the proof that he has become, as he himself thinks, 'a man.'"[31] Not recognizing the inadequacy of his own interpretation, this reader imposes the pattern of "a spiritual journey" upon the novel, then levels an indictment against Crane's artistry for failing to accommodate itself to a foreign design.

Henry's growth is certainly as real as the parallel transformation of Wilson, who is introduced as a craven loudmouth and emerges a stalwart, reliable soldier. Both have learned the meaning of humanity—the essence of which is man's duty to man—and that life, like war, is not a romantic and beautiful dream brimmed with glory, but is hard and filled with pain. Life is not dream but responsibility; still, there is a joy to be found in community, in real human values, as Henry recognizes when he returns to "the creed of soldiers"—the creed of responsibility and fellowship. Although the world of battle is grotesque and lethal, Nature offers only indifference, loneliness, and the arena for a truly animal existence, which Henry rejects.

In the course of one day, a torturous, frightful, but enlightening day, Henry has achieved a profound understanding. The "soft and eternal peace" at the end of the novel is the peace Henry has made with himself through a process of self-actualization. No longer at war with the animal within or the world without, he is comfortable with himself and his commitments. The red badge of courage is his courage to accept the reality of existence and to act in accordance with his choice. And it seems to me that acceptance means affirmation: to accept the universe is to affirm it, and to accept life is to affirm life.

Notes

1. John Fraser, "Crime and Forgiveness: *The Red Badge* in Time of War," *Criticism*, 9 (Summer, 1967), 243-56.

2. In the Introduction to the Oxford edition, V. S. Pritchett is on record as saying, "It is a poetic fable about the attempt of a young man to discover a real identity in battle" (*The Red Badge of Courage and Other Stories* [London: Oxford University Press, 1960], p. viii)—but any critic who describes "The Blue Hotel" as a "half-comic" story (p. ix) and declares *The Red Badge of Courage* to be a sustained bugle call without plot (as he did in *The Living Novel*) can be sure of provoking skepticism, if not disregard. Assuming that not all readers are mistaken, how can the divergent understandings be explained? Some scholars believe the polarity of interpretations results from disunity in the novel itself—an easy explanation, but unsatisfactory because art and disunity are seldom compatible. (Organic integrity is now often questioned: disregarding Aristotelian principles, John Bayley in *The Uses of Division* [New York: The Viking Press, 1976] argues that contradictions and divisiveness add strength to masterpieces, and that critics are apt to *impose* unity on a work of art for the sake of a preconceived order and tidiness.) In *The Red Badge*, however, there is no inherent contradiction or disorder, but there has been much imposition as a result of pure misinterpretation.

3. Jean Cazemajou, *Stephen Crane* (Minneapolis: University of Minnesota Press, 1969), p. 21.

4. James Trammell Cox, "The Imagery of *The Red Badge of Courage*," *Modern Fiction Studies*, 5 (Autumn, 1959), 209-19.

5. Mordecai and Erin Marcus, "Animal Imagery in *The Red Badge of Courage*," *Modern Language Notes*, 75 (February, 1959), 108-11.

6. Eric Solomon, "The Structure of *The Red Badge of Courage*," *Modern Fiction Studies*, 5 (Autumn, 1959), 220-34.

7. Mordecai and Erin Marcus, p. 110. We are informed by another critic that "Crane's tremendous power of imagery creates an atmosphere of un-reason in which the boy's naturalistic code can thrive" (Winfred Lynskey, "Crane's *The Red Badge of Courage*," *Explicator*, 8 [December, 1949], Item 18). And Alfred Kazin, not content with merely calling Crane a naturalist, but straining to relate the author's personality to

the philosophy, proclaims that "the ferocious pessimism of naturalism suited his temperament exactly" (*On Native Grounds* [New York: Harcourt, 1942], p. 87).

8. Naturalism is defined as "a manner and method of composition by which the author portrays life *as it is in accordance with the philosophic theory of determinism*. (exemplified in Zola's *L'Assommoir*). In contrast to a realist, a naturalist believes that man is fundamentally an animal without free will" (Lars Åhnebrink, *The Beginnings of Naturalism in American Fiction* [Uppsala and Cambridge: Uppsala University Press, 1950], pp. vi-vii). The following is from a definition in *The Reader's Encyclopedia of American Literature* by Max J. Herzberg, *et al.* (New York: Thomas Y. Crowell Company, 1962), p. 783: "Human life is pessimistically viewed as being at the mercy of uncontrollable exterior forces—the environment—or of interior drives—fear, hunger, sex." According to most definitions, deterministic philosophy is the major ingredient of naturalism; for a discussion of the general tenets, see Malcolm Cowley's "'Not Men': A Natural History of American Naturalism," *Kenyon Review*, 9 (Spring, 1947), 414-35.

9. *The Red Badge of Courage*, from *Stephen Crane: An Omnibus*, R. W. Stallman, ed. (New York: Alfred A. Knopf, 1952), p. 229. This work is used for all references to the novel as well as to any other Crane material mentioned in the text, and all inserted page numbers refer to this *Omnibus* edition,

10. Donald B. Gibson, *The Fiction of Stephen Crane* (Carbondale, Illinois: Southern Illinois University Press, 1968), p. 76.

11. Ibid., p. 77.

12. Ibid., p. 78.

13. Eric Solomon, *Stephen Crane: From Parody to Realism* (Cambridge: Harvard University Press, 1966), p. 78.

14. Robert F. Gleckner, "Stephen Crane and the Wonder of Man's Conceit," *Modern Fiction Studies*, 5 (Autumn, 1959), 270.

15. Solomon, p. 80.

16. Mordecai Marcus, "The Unity of *The Red Badge of Courage*," in *Stephen Crane's The Red Badge of Courage: Text and Criticism*, ed. Richard Lettis *et al.* (New York: Harcourt, Brace & World, Inc., 1960), p. 191.

17. Gibson, p. 79. Cf. Lynskey (note 7): her contention is that Henry's reward is "undeserved."

18. Marston LaFrance, "Stephen Crane's *Private Fleming: His Various Battles*," in *Patterns of Commitment in American Literature*, ed. Marston LaFrance (Toronto: University of Toronto Press, 1967), p. 121. That free will is an intrinsic quality of man is inherent in this argument and seems to be evident in Henry Fleming's actions; yet Åhnebrink (*op. cit.*, note 8) flatly states that Henry has "no free will" (p. 193) and that "Crane seems to have held, throughout his life, that man's will was enslaved" (p. 189).

19. The author sees religion as one means of coping with the problem of animality, not as an aid to its acceptance. Christianity, in addition to teaching self-denial, the subordination of the body to the spirit, and the subduing of many animal desires, also emphasizes the belief that earth is not man's home. In this regard, it is important to note that Henry, at the very end of the novel, "saw that the world was a world for him" (p. 370). Also, according to John Fraser, *op. cit.*, "Henry is no longer bothered by the pre-

sumed hostility of the 'big gods and little gods' because he has ceased to bother about them [and] he has ceased, too, to bother about retribution or to introduce supernatural values into the activities of battle. Hence the act of fighting is no longer some kind of ultimate moral testing of the self . . . and even death becomes simply death and not a stage en route to further judgment."

20. See "Notes Toward an Analysis of *The Red Badge of Courage*," from the Introduction to the Modern Library Edition of *The Red Badge of Courage* (New York: Random House, 1951), pp. xxii-xxxvii; and also *Omnibus*, pp. 191-201; a tempered, less insistent interpretation is in *Stephen Crane: A Biography* (New York: George Braziller, 1968), pp. 168-88.

21. James B. Colvert, "Structure and Theme in Stephen Crane's Fiction," *Modern Fiction Studies*, 5 (Autumn, 1959), 199-208.

22. Cox, p. 217.

23. Bernard Weisberger, "*The Red Badge of Courage*," in *Twelve Original Essays*, ed. Charles Shapiro (Detroit: Wayne State University Press, 1958), pp. 96-123.

24. In "The Imagery of *The Red Badge of Courage*," *Modern Fiction Studies*, 8 (Winter, 1962), 410-15, James W. Tuttleton sees "constructs of impressionistic (not symbolic) religious imagery" and divides the religious "impressions" into two patterns, one of Christian and another of pagan images, for an examination of the irony they provoke in juxtaposition.

25. Scott C. Osborn, "Stephen Crane's Imagery: Pasted Like a Wafer," *American Literature*, 23 (November, 1951), 362. This brief article compares Crane's wafer image to a similar one in Kipling's *The Light That Failed* and argues that "in both the sun seems compared to a red wafer of wax used to seal an envelope." In a footnote, Professor Osborn states his belief that the wafer or seal is an indication of "the ironically enigmatic indifference of heaven to the youth's blasphemy against war." Without offering any explanation or support, Maxwell Geismar makes an assertion to the contrary by assuring us that the image "actually referred of course to the flesh and the blood of the martyred God, or the bleeding Son" (*Rebels and Ancestors: The American Novel, 1890-1915* [Boston: Houghton Mifflin, 1953], p. 85).

26. Stallman, all 3 sources.

27. Jay Martin, *Harvests of Change* (Englewood Cliffs, New Jersey: Prentice-Hall, 1967), p. 53. For some reason, critics simply refuse to listen to Crane and go on imposing their ideas upon him. Oscar Cargill, for example, declares that in writing *The Red Badge* Crane was "doubtless inspired by Zola's *La Débâcle*, which he denied reading" (*Intellectual America* [New York: The Macmillan Company, 1941], p. 86). Here Cargill ungenerously calls Crane a liar rather than give up the predetermined "source."

28. Gibson, p. 64.

29. Ibid., p. 65.

30. John W. Shroeder, "Stephen Crane Embattled," *The University of Kansas City Review*, 17 (Winter, 1950), 119-29. Shroeder also thinks the novel is confused, primarily because he cannot determine whether Henry's salvation is based on Naturalism or a recognition of humanistic values. (I must point out that Crane differentiates between the display of physical courage and true heroism which is associated with the ideal of

brotherhood, and the best way to perceive this difference is by comparing "The Open Boat" with "A Mystery of Heroism.")

31. Cazemajou, p. 19. Stallman, despite his claim of "regeneration" (*Omnibus*, p. 199), also sees Henry back where he started, a view shared by many. C. C. Walcutt is adamant in his declaration that all of Henry's judgments are "delusions," and are not meaningful: "If there is any one point that has been made it is that Henry has never been able to evaluate his conduct. . . . He has been through some moments of hell, during which he has for moments risen above his limitations, but Crane seems plainly to be showing that he has not achieved a lasting wisdom or self-knowledge" (*American Literary Naturalism, a Divided Stream* [Minneapolis: University of Minnesota Press, 1956], pp. 81-82). Joseph X. Brennan echoes Walcutt's judgment in saying Henry "clearly has learned little or nothing of any permanent value about himself" ("Stephen Crane and the Limits of Irony," *Criticism*, 11 [Spring, 1969], 190).

The Red Badge of Courage:
Text, Theme, and Form

Donald Pizer

During the last several years, Hershel Parker and his former student Henry Binder have argued vigorously that *The Red Badge of Courage* which we have been reading since 1895 is a defective text.[1] Crane, they believe, was forced by his editor Ripley Hitchcock to eliminate from the version accepted by D. Appleton & Co. an entire chapter as well as a number of important passages—particularly from the close of the novel—in which he underlined with biting irony the fatuousness and wrong-headedness of Henry Fleming. It is therefore the original and uncut version rather than the censored version of *The Red Badge*, Parker and Binder maintain, which we should be reading. In response to this contention Parker arranged for the uncut version of *The Red Badge* to be included in the prestigious, widely used, and in general textually responsible *Norton Anthology of American Literature* and Binder has published the version in a separate volume.[2]

This effort to rescue Crane's uncut draft of *The Red Badge* from exclusively scholarly use (the omitted portions of the novel have been known and available since the early 1950s) would have little significance except for the coincidence of Parker's editorial involvement in the Norton anthology and thus its presence in that widely circulated form. For there is no direct external evidence that Crane cut *The Red Badge* under pressure from Hitchcock. There are only inferences and assumptions derived from long-known collateral external evidence and from the critical belief that the uncut novel is the superior work of art—the novel which presents Crane in the form of his initially more honest and powerful intentions rather than in the emasculated and muddled form of these intentions in the first edition. The Appleton text, Parker, Binder, and yet another Parker student Steven Mailloux argue, is hopelessly flawed because of the unintentional ambivalences created in its themes and form by Crane's destruction, through his omissions, of his previously consistent and clearly evident contemptuous attitude toward Henry.[3] Thus, if we wish to read "the *Red Badge* that Crane wrote"[4] rather than the one forced upon him by Hitchcock's desire for a less negative portrait of a Civil War recruit, we must read it in the form available to us in the *Norton Anthology* and Binder's edition.

I have already discussed elsewhere the weaknesses in the argument from external evidence that Crane was forced by Hitchcock to cut *The Red Badge*.[5] I would now like to tackle the more problematical but equally vital issue of the argument from internal evidence that the ambivalences and ambiguities in the 1895 Appleton text constitute proof that Crane was forced to warp the themes of the novel through his revision and that the more immediately clear and consistent uncut draft is thereby the superior text. I have found it best in undertaking this task to concentrate initially and for a good deal of my paper on a portion of the novel which Crane wrote early in his composition of the work and which he left uncut and unrevised in its printed version—the first two paragraphs of *The Red Badge*. By demonstrating the purposeful and thematically functional ambivalences in this passage and then in the revised novel as a whole I wish of course to demonstrate that Crane's intent from the first was toward the expression of the ambivalent nature of Henry's maturation under fire and that his revision and cutting were toward the refinement of this intent. And I would also like to push on to a demonstration of the thesis that the presence of major thematic ambivalences in *The Red Badge* can be explained to a large degree by their apt relationship to major changes occurring at that time both in Crane's ideas and in the history of American thought.

Here are the first two paragraphs of *The Red Badge of Courage*:

The cold passed reluctantly from the earth, and the retiring fogs revealed an army stretched out on the hills, resting. As the landscape changed from brown to green, the army awakened, and began to tremble with eagerness at the noise of rumors. It cast its eyes upon the roads, which were growing from long troughs of liquid mud to proper thoroughfares. A river, amber-tinted in the shadow of its banks, purled at the army's feet; and at night, when the stream had become of a sorrowful blackness, one could see across it the red, eyelike gleam of hostile campfires set in the low brows of distant hills.

Once a certain tall soldier developed virtues and went resolutely to wash a shirt. He came flying back from a brook waving his garment bannerlike. He was swelled with a tale he had heard from a reliable friend, who had heard it from a truthful cavalryman, who had heard it from his trustworthy brother, one of the orderlies at division headquarters. He adopted the important air of a herald in red and gold.[6]

The opening paragraph of the novel describes the coming of spring to an army which has been in camp for the winter.[7] One major stream of imagery in the paragraph is that of awakening—awakening both after the cold of night and the fogs of dawn and after the brown of winter. The army awakens eagerly and expectantly—life is more than the cold and darkness of sleep, and in daylight and warmth passage can be made (the roads now "proper" rather than liquid mud) in the direction of one's destiny. The setting and its images are those of the beginning of a journey in which the emotional cast or coloration of the moment is largely positive; something is going to happen, and this something is better than the death in life of coldness, darkness, and immobility. The opening of the novel thus suggests that we are to be engaged by an initiation story, since both the initial situation and its images are in the archetypal form of an awakening to experience. Out of the blankness and emptiness of innocence, youth advances through experience to maturity and manhood.

Of course, the journey will have its difficulties. Indeed, without these it would not be an initiation journey. One is of those others in life who have aims different from ours and who therefore appear before us as the contradictory, belligerent principle in experience. So there is in the first paragraph the image of a mysterious and potentially dangerous enemy whom one sees in the night. But perhaps the greater difficulty will be in knowing in truth both the nature of the journey as it occurs and its full meaning at its conclusion. This difficulty is anticipated in the first paragraph by three references to the difficulty of knowing which are expressed through images of seeing and hearing. Fogs often obscure the landscape, the army hears only rumors, and the river is in shadow. The only unequivocally clear image of knowing is that the immediate avenue of movement—the roads—are now passable. Moreover, both the awakening and opposing forces are given an animal cast (the army "stretched out on the hills"; the "low brows" of the distant hills where lies the enemy), which suggests the limited rational equipment of those seeking to know.

The first paragraph of *The Red Badge of Courage* reveals Crane in a typically complex interweaving of images. Although the images in the paragraph imply that Henry's adventures may shape themselves into an initiation story, they also suggest that Henry himself will be an inept and inadequate interpreter of what has happened to him, that he will be unable to see and know with clarity and insight. And since the narrator will choose to tell the story through Henry's sense of its nature and importance rather than with a clear authorial underlining of meaning, we as readers will be left in a permanent state of ambivalence or ambiguity. Are we to respond to Henry's experiences principally in their symbolic character as milestones in the archetype of initiation, or are we to respond to them, because of Henry's limited understanding, as fogridden, shadowy, and misunderstood markers on a dimly perceived road?

The second paragraph reinforces and extends the notion that we are to have difficulty fully comprehending Henry's experiences. The first paragraph rendered the distinction between a possible progressive movement through time and the difficulty of knowing what occurs in time by means of symbolic and potentially allegorical images. The second paragraph increases our sense that the conventional means of evaluating experience are not to be trusted but does so now by means of the narrator's ironic voice in his reporting of such efforts. A tall soldier goes to wash a shirt with a belief that this enterprise requires virtue and courage. (As always in Crane's narrative style, the terms describing an action—here "developed virtues" and "went resolutely"—though superficially authorial in origin are in fact projections into the third person narrative voice of the doer's own estimation of his action. It is the soldier who believes he is behaving virtuously and resolutely, not Crane.) The statement, beginning as it does with major values and ending with the minor task to which these have been applied, is couched in the classic form of ironic anticlimax. One may think that it takes virtue and courage to wash a shirt, but there is a sharp and large distinction to be made between the actual character of the act and one's estimation of it. The implication which this distinction has for the general nature of self-knowledge, for the estimation of the worth of our acts, is that we will generally both aggrandize the significance of the event and overvalue our own attributes in relation to it.

The remainder of the paragraph contains two further implications for the problem of knowledge, both of which are also expressed in habitual forms of Crane's irony. The "tale" which the tall soldier has heard is rendered suspect despite the soldier's belief in its truth by Crane's account of its distant source and by his ironic repetition of the reliability, truthfulness, and trustworthiness of each of the tellers in the tangled history of its transmission. Much of what we learn about experience from our fellows is tainted by the difficulty of communicating accurately both what has occurred and what lies in store for us. Group knowledge, in short, is as suspect as personal self-evaluation.

As a further indication of the complications inherent in the acquisition and transmission of knowledge, the tall soldier—in his belief that he has something important to tell—begins to play a traditional role. He carries a banner and adopts the air of a herald. Man, when he has something to communicate, will adopt various roles to dramatize the worth both of his information and of himself. But the role will often obscure the emptiness and valuelessness of that which is being communicated. In short, Crane appears to be saying in this paragraph, the process of gaining and transmitting knowledge is warped by powerful weaknesses within both human nature and social intercourse. And the knowledge communicated by this process—that which we believe is true about ourselves and our fellows—is thus suspect.

The two opening paragraphs of *The Red Badge of Courage* constitute a paradigm for the themes and techniques of the novel as a whole. In its events and in much of its symbolism, the novel is a story of the coming of age of a young man through the initiatory experience of battle. But our principal confirmation of Henry's experiences as initiation myth is Henry himself, and Crane casts doubt—through his ironic narrative voice—on the truth and value of Henry's estimation of his adventures and himself. And so a vital ambiguity ensues.

* * *

The initiation structure of *The Red Badge* is evident both in the external action of the novel and in a good deal of the symbolism arising from event. A young untried soldier, wracked by doubts about his ability to perform well under fire, in fact does flee ignominiously during his first engagement. After a series of misadventures behind his own lines, including receiving a head wound accidentally from one of his own fellows, he returns to his unit, behaves estimably in combat, and receives the plaudits of his comrades and officers. On the level of external action, *The Red Badge* is thus a nineteenth-century development novel in compressed form. In such works, a young man (or woman) tries his mettle in a difficult world, at first believes himself weak and unworthy in the face of the enormous obstacles he encounters, but finally gains the experience necessary to cope with life and thus achieves as well a store of inner strength and conviction. Much of the symbolism in *The Red Badge* supports a reading of the work as developmental fiction, for one major pattern of symbolism in the novel rehearses the structure of the initiation myth. Henry is at first isolated by his childlike innocence. But after acquiring a symbol of group experience and acceptance (the red badge), he is guided by a supernatural mentor (the cheery soldier) through a night journey to reunion with his fellows; and in the next day's engagement he helps gain a symbolic token of passage into manhood (the enemy's flag).

But much in the novel also casts doubt on the validity of reading the work as an initiation allegory. Chief among these sources of doubt is Crane's ironic undermining at every turn of the quality of Henry's mental equipment and therefore of the possibility that he can indeed mature. Whenever Henry believes he has gained a significant height in his accomplishments and understanding, Crane reveals—by situational and verbal irony—how shallow a momentary resting place he has indeed reached. A typical example occurs after the enemy's first charge during the initial day of battle, when Henry grandiosely overestimates the character of a minor skirmish. ("So it was over at last! The supreme trial had been passed. The red, formidable difficulties of war had been vanquished" [p. 34].) This ironic deflation of Henry's self-evaluation continues unrelieved throughout the novel and includes as well Henry's final summing up, when, after in effect merely having survived the opening battle in the spring of a long campaign (with Gettysburg to follow!), he concludes that "the world was a world for him, though many discovered it to be made of oaths and walking sticks" (p. 109).

In addition, Crane casts doubt on the depth of Henry's maturity at the close of the novel by revealing Henry's exercise in sliding-door conscience. Henry, at the end of the second day's fighting, is still troubled by two of his less estimable acts—his desertion first of his unit and later of the tattered soldier. But what troubles him most is less the intrinsic nature of these acts than that they might be discovered, and when he realizes that this is not likely, he "mustered force to put the sin[s] at a distance" (p. 109) and revels instead in his public accomplishments. It was this aspect of Henry's intellect—his conscience-troubled rationalizations of his behavior and his closely related fury at fate for having placed him in conscience-troubling situations—which Crane, after concluding the first draft of the novel, realized he had overdone and thus cut heavily in the interval between the draft and publication.

Crane also undermines the initiation structure of *The Red Badge* by including in the novel two major counterstructures. Initiation is essentially a mythic statement of a faith in the potential for individual growth—that the forward movement of time is meaningful and productive because through experience we acquire both the capacity to cope with experience and a useful knowledge of ourselves and the world. But *The Red Badge* also contains two major structures which imply that time is essentially meaningless, that all in life is circular repetition, that only the superficial forms of the repetition vary and thus are capable of being misunderstood as significant change and progress. One such symbolic structure is that of the rhythmic movement of troops. The novel begins with the advance to battle by Henry and his regiment, it ends with their departure from battle, and the body of the work contains a series of charges and countercharges, advances and retreats. Since these movements occur in an obscure landscape in connection with an unnamed battle, and since little meaning attends the various movements aside from their impact on Henry and his regiment, significance is attached to the fact of movement itself rather than to movement in relation to a goal or direction. One of the symbolic structures of *The Red Badge* is therefore of a flow and counterflow of men, a largely meaningless and directionless repetition despite Henry's attribution of deep personal meaning to one of its minor phases, a moment of flow which he mistakes for a moment of significant climax.

Another such circular symbolic structure is even more consciously ironic in character. Henry runs on the first day of battle because of two psychic compulsions—an animal instinct of self-preservation and a social instinct to act as he believes his comrades are acting. On the next day—in a far more fully described series of combat experiences—

Henry responds to battle precisely as he had on the first day, except that he now behaves "heroically" rather than "cowardly." Again an animal compulsion (that of the cornered animal made vicious and powerful by anger and fear at being trapped) is joined with a social one (irritation at unjust blame attached to the regiment) to produce a similar "battle sleep" of unconsciousness in action. These underlying similarities in Henry's battle performances reveal not only Crane's attack on the conventional notions of courage and cowardice but—in their role as "equal" halves in a balanced symbolic structure—his belief that life is essentially a series of similar responses to similar conditions in which only the unobservant mistake the superficially different in these conditions and responses for a forward movement through time.

These two powerful drives in *The Red Badge*—the initiation plot, structure, and symbolic imagery, and the undercutting of a development myth by a variety of ironic devices which imply that the belief that man can adequately interpret the degree of his maturity is a delusion—these two drives come to a head in the final chapter of the novel. The second day's battle is over, and Henry has behaved well in his own eyes and in those of his fellows. Yet he continues as well to overvalue his accomplishments and deny his failings. The imagery of the conclusion reflects this ambivalence. Henry, now that the battle is over, thinks of "prospects of clover tranquility" (p. 109). But in fact it is raining, and "the procession of weary soldiers became a bedraggled train, despondent and muttering, marching with churning effort in a trough of liquid mud under a low, wretched sky. Yet the youth smiled, for he saw that the world was a world for him. . ." (p. 109). In this passage, the fatuousness of Henry's conception of what awaits him and therefore of what he has achieved is inherent in the sharp distinction between Henry's belief and the permanent condition of the group to which he belongs, of all mankind, in effect, despite his conviction that he lies outside this condition.

It might thus be argued that Crane wishes us, at this final moment, to reject completely the validity of an initiation experience for Henry.

Yet, in the final sentence of the novel, added after the completion of the full first draft, Crane wrote: "Over the river a golden ray of sun came through the hosts of leaden rain clouds" (p. 109). This flat, bald imagistic statement reaffirms the essential ambiguity of the work as a whole, despite the possibility of reading the final chapter as a confirmation of one position or the other. For the image is not attributed to Henry; it occupies a paragraph of its own, and is the narrative voice's authoritative description of a pictorial moment rather than of Henry's suspect response to the moment. And the narrative voice wishes us to be left, as a final word, with the sense that life is truly ambivalent—that there are rain clouds and that there is the sun. The darkness and cold (and lack of vision) of the opening images of the novel are part of the human condition, but the promise of daylight and spring warmth and of vision which are also present in the opening images have in part been fulfilled by the ray of sunlight.

* * *

I would now like to explore the implications of Crane's ambiguity in *The Red Badge of Courage* for his career and for his place in American literary and intellectual history. Crane's career can be divided into the usual three major phases, of which *Maggie* (1893) is the principal work in the first phase, *The Red Badge* in the middle period, and the novellas of 1897 and 1898 (of which I shall discuss "The Open Boat") the most important work of the last phase.

Maggie has always been rightfully considered the most naturalistic of Crane's works. Each of its characters is locked in a prison of self-delusion from which he never escapes. Maggie believes that Pete is a chivalrous knight who will rescue her from poverty and the oppression of her home; Pete believes that he is a formidable lover and that he has behaved well toward Maggie; Jimmie believes that his family honor requires defense; and Mary Johnson believes that she has been a Christian parent to Maggie. These delusions are made so grossly evident by the distinction between a character's self-conception and the circumstances of his life—between Mrs. Johnson's notion of the home she has created and the actual nature of that home—that we are left with little doubt that one of Crane's principal intents in the novel is to depict the overpowering role of emotional self-interest in the handicapping of the capacity to see life and oneself fully and clearly. No one knows anything of truth in *Maggie*—neither what they are nor what he or she wants to believe about himself and the world at large. Some are destroyed by this limitation (Maggie goes to her death); some are in decline (Pete and Mrs. Johnson); and some continue on their way (Jimmie). But all are locked into a world of blindness which effectively thwarts any possibility of growth based on understanding. Although the physical setting of *Maggie* is a slum, its symbolic setting is a surrealistic hall of mirrors, where the characters see only grotesque versions of themselves, versions, however, which they accept as real. And since there are no exceptions to this principle in *Maggie*, it must be assumed that Crane, at this stage of his career, believed self-delusion to be the universal human condition, with only its degree and level of sophistication a matter of variation.

"The Open Boat," written some five years later, is at the other end of Crane's depiction of the human condition. The allegorical context of the story, however, does not differ radically from the slum of *Maggie*; here, too, life is principally a matter of coping with the destructiveness present in all existence. The four men in the open boat find the sea (the immediate setting of their lives) dangerous; the sky (God) empty; and the shore (society) unknowing. But unlike the characters of *Maggie* in their absolute social and emotional isolation, the four men in "The Open Boat" come to rely on each other—to lean heavily on each other in order both to bear their condition and to survive it. Much in the story details a growth in their mutual interdependence, from a sharing of duties in the boat to a sense of comradeship which all feel. In the end, after the adventure is over, Crane tells us that the men, hearing the sound of the sea at night, "felt that they could then be interpreters."

Text, Theme, and Form

Few readers have viewed this closing line as ironic. Our sense of a successful resolution of the adventure for its survivors, of something gained through the experience, is too great to cast doubt on the "reliability" of this final statement. Thus, the principal question to be asked of the statement is what indeed can the men now properly interpret? Crane replies to this question within the story as a whole, and his answer also replies, in a sense, to the issues raised by *Maggie*. There is no God, he appears to be saying, and isolation is therefore the quintessential human condition. But within this unchanging situation men can both establish temporary communities based on mutual need and entertain compassion for those ranges of human experience which also reveal man's essential loneliness. To be more precise, the correspondent learns, within the story, that there are no temples to cast stones at in blame for their fate, but that the men can establish a "subtle brotherhood" in their mutual understanding and aid on the boat, and that his realization of these truths of experience can at last bring him to a recognition of the universal pathos surrounding the soldier of the legion, alone and dying far from home.

"The Open Boat" thus suggests that Crane has come some distance from *Maggie*. We are still battered by life, and some, like the oiler, are mercilessly destroyed. But we can now understand this condition and, to some extent, through our understanding, lessen its effect on us, both physically and emotionally. We need not all be victimized by the human capacity for self-delusion; some of us have the capacity to mature, under pressure, to understanding. Which returns us to *The Red Badge of Courage*. In relation to Crane's career, the novel, in an image appropriate to its setting, is a kind of battleground in which the two views of human nature and experience which I have identified as flourishing in *Maggie* and "The Open Boat" struggle for dominance, without either succeeding in gaining the day. The plot and a good deal of the symbolic structure of the novel imply growth on Henry's part in coping with the eternal "war" which is human experience. But Crane's ironic voice and other symbolic structures imply that Henry is as self-deluded at the close of the novel as he is uncertain about himself at the opening. The theme of the value of social union in *The Red Badge* has something of the same ambivalence. Henry does gain a sense of a "subtle battle brotherhood" (p. 31) at various times during combat, and his return to his regiment is depicted as a productive reunion. But at other times, when he opposes the blind obedience which "union" requires of him, he is described as locked into a "moving box" (p. 21) of social and psychic compulsion as viciously destructive as is the Johnson household in imposing its values and demands on its weakest members.

The Red Badge of Courage is thus a work whose ambivalences and ambiguities are an appropriate and probably inevitable reflection of those of its author at that particular moment in his career. Crane in the novel was "working out" his then divided and uncertain notion of the balance of emphasis to give to the human capacities both for self-delusion and for insight and understanding.

The Red Badge of Courage also reflects in its ambivalences a major moment of transition in the history of American belief—that of a period in American thought when, broadly speaking, there was a movement from nineteenth-century certainties to modern doubts, from a willingness to affirm large-scale notions about the human enterprise to an unwillingness to do more than represent the immediacies of experience itself.

The origins of this state of mind in the 1890s lie less in the events of the decade itself than in the realization by a generation coming of age during the decade of changes which had been occurring in the American scene and American belief since the Civil War. In brief, and with some of the melodramatic overemphasis and overgeneralization inherent in the art of intellectual history, young writers of the 1890s were now no longer sure of two transcendent faiths which had buttressed American belief for over a hundred years. The first was a faith in human nature in general—or more specifically in the Christian notion of man as God's special creature as that notion was refined and extended by late eighteenth-century Enlightenment idealism and early nineteenth-century romantic transcendentalism. The second was a more special-ized faith in America as a world in which the Edenic possibilities of man could indeed flourish—that in this new-found-land man's capac-ity for productive self- and national development could best be real-ized.

Challenging these two faiths in the 1890s were the growing aware-ness of the impact of a Darwinian explanation of man's origin on the belief that man was principally a reflection of God's own capacity for wisdom and goodness, and the growing awareness that American soci-ety in its present state of development was indeed an apt symbolic re-flection of man as a jungle, rather than an Edenic, creature. The animal degradation of life in the slums and factories and the cut-throat charac-ter of economic life everywhere made such an endorsement of the met-aphor of America as jungle so obvious than even the popular mind could grasp the analogy.

Yet always—along with these realizations—there remained a pow-erful vestige of a continuing faith, one that took many forms but which had in all its shapes an emotional center of belief that America was in-deed a new birth for the best that was in man—that the experiment could yet succeed. It is out of this tension between old belief and new doubts that a work such as *The Red Badge of Courage* emerges in the mid-1890s. And as so often occurred in the Americanization of the nineteenth-century great debate between faith and doubt, the specific poles of tension among writers of the 1890s were less within religious or even social categories of belief than within epistemological ones: can man know and translate into experience the great transcendent truths of life? If one can posit the two extremes in the American ver-sion of the debate, they might thus be Emerson's celebration of man's capacity to grasp intuitively the large truths analogically present in ex-perience (that is, in nature) and the early Hemingway's lack of confi-dence in all but the concrete immediacies of experience itself, of his immense distrust of all large abstractions which men seek to impose on life.

Henry's experiences in *The Red Badge of Courage* appear to confirm, in their symbolic analogue to an awakening at dawn and a concluding ray of sunshine after battle, the great nineteenth-century faith in the human capacity for growth and development through a self-absorbed projection into life. But the novel also contains an equally powerful edge of "modern" doubts about the capacity of man to achieve wisdom, doubts expressed in the "modern" form of an ironic undercutting through voice and structure of the protagonist's belief that the traditional abstraction of courage is real and can be gained. It is thus an irony of a different kind that in seeking to universalize his story, to have it be not a depiction of a specific battle but an expression of a permanent human condition, Crane in fact also brought his account of Henry Fleming closer to the specific state of mind of his own historical moment—to the uncertainties about the possibility for growth and self-knowledge which had begun to gnaw at the American consciousness in his own time.

The Red Badge of Courage therefore plays seemingly contradictory roles in relation to the career of its author on the one hand and its historical moment on the other. In relation to Crane's career, the novel lies between Crane's deeply pessimistic view of man's blindness in *Maggie* and his far more affirmative sense in his later novellas of man's capacity to grow in insight and moral courage through experience. In relation to American thought, however, the novel affirms an earlier nineteenth-century faith in man's ability to mature while offering as well a modernistic critique of man's fatuous belief in his own ability to evaluate correctly both himself and experience. But this paradox, this cross-stitching, so to speak, of past and present in the work, in which it looks both backwards and forwards depending on whether one adopts a biographical or historical perspective, is one of the major sources of the novel's richness and permanence. *The Red Badge of Courage* is not a work flawed in its ambivalences. Rather, as its first two paragraphs suggest, it holds them in meaningful suspension to reflect what in the end is perhaps the modern temper in its essence—not so much a reaffirmation of faith or an announcement of the triumph of doubt as a desire to explore the interaction between these two permanent conditions of man.

Notes

1. See Binder's "*The Red Badge of Courage* Nobody Knows," *Studies in the Novel* 10 (Spring, 1978): 9-47 and Parker's comments on *The Red Badge* in his "Aesthetic Implications of Authorial Excisions," in *Editing Nineteenth-Century Fiction*, ed. Jane Millgate (New York, 1978), pp. 99-119 and "The New Scholarship," *Studies in American Fiction* 9 (Autumn, 1981): 181-97.

2. Ronald Gottesman et al., ed., *The Norton Anthology of American Literature*, Vol. 2 (New York, 1979) and Henry Binder, ed., *The Red Badge of Courage* (New York, 1982). Parker is one of the editors of the Norton Anthology.

3. See Mailloux's *Interpretive Conventions: The Reader in the Study of American Fiction* (Ithaca, N.Y.: Cornell University Press, 1982), pp. 160-65, 178-91.

4. Binder, "*The Red Badge of Courage* Nobody Knows," p. 10.

5. "'*The Red Badge of Courage* Nobody Knows': A Brief Rejoinder," *Studies in the Novel* 11 (Spring 1979): 77-81.

6. *The Red Badge of Courage*, A Norton Critical Edition, ed. Donald Pizer (New York, 1976), p. 5. Citations from this edition will hereafter appear in the text. The text of *The Red Badge* in the Norton Critical Edition is that of the 1895 Appleton edition conservatively emended, principally to correct typographical errors.

7. The reading of *The Red Badge of Courage* which follows has been evolving in my own thinking about the novel and about Crane's career and his times for some years. See, for example, my "Stephen Crane's *Maggie* and American Naturalism" and "Late Nineteenth-Century American Naturalism" in my *Realism and Naturalism in Nineteenth-Century American Literature* (Carbondale, Ill., 1966); "A Primer of Fictional Aesthetics," *College English* 30 (April 1969): 572-80; "Nineteenth-Century American Naturalism: An Approach Through Form," *Forum* (Houston) 13 (Winter, 1976): 43-46; and my edition of *American Thought and Writing: The 1890s* (Boston, 1972). I have also drawn upon my awareness of the vigorous debate in Crane studies on the nature, role, and worth of the ambiguities in *The Red Badge*. For a survey of the debate, see my "Stephen Crane," in *15 American Authors Before 1900: Bibliographical Essays on Research and Criticism*, ed. Earl N. Harbert and Robert A. Rees (Madison, Wisc., 1984), pp. 128-84.

Humor and Insight Through Fallacy in Stephen Crane's *The Red Badge of Courage*_____

Jacqueline Tavernier-Courbin

Stephen Crane's multifaceted approach to reality departs from the naturalistic credo of straightforward objectivity. His premises are essentially the same as most realists' and naturalists', but his technique is distinctive, indirect, and humorous, requiring more perceptiveness on the reader's part to understand the complexities and implications of the novel. While his brilliant use of fallacious reasoning, one of the most complex forms of humor in the novel, is superficially unnaturalistic, it nevertheless makes a strong social comment by implication, which falls well within the mandate of the naturalistic novel. Indeed, it exposes not only human nature through Henry's self-serving hypocrisy in rationalizing his own behavior but also the fallacy of received ideas concerning war, education, religion, and civilization, as well as the shallowness of socially accepted abstractions, such as courage, cowardice, and man's place in nature. Henry's fallacious reasoning evidences both modern society's pious illusions about itself and the confusion its denial of basic human instincts creates for the individual who is attempting to understand his own conflicting desires and perceptions.

About to face his first battle, Henry rebels against the whole world, regrets his having enlisted, and switches the blame over to the government to exonerate himself from personal responsibility: "He had not enlisted of his free will. He had been dragged by the merciless government. And now they were taking him out to be slaughtered."[1] On the superficial level, this is blatantly untrue since he very much wanted to enlist, even doing so against the expressed wishes of his mother. Nevertheless, he unknowingly voices a naturalistic truth: the fact that both body and mind are largely controlled by heredity and the milieu. Henry has indeed been dragged, psychologically rather than physically, into the war, not so much by the merciless government but by a society which glorified war and courage for centuries, and made them a test of manhood, and of both social and self-acceptance—that is, society manipulated Henry into wanting to go to war to prove his manhood. However, the fault is not society's alone, for the various human communities the world has known since the stone age would not have been so successful in ensuring their own survival through the idealization of war and courage if fighting was not an atavistic need in man, and if the protection of self, family, and territory was not a deeply rooted instinct, inevitably linking man to the rest of the animal world. Indeed, it is not only the government, society, and his collective unconscious, but also his own human nature which has dragged Henry into the war. Thus, as we peel off the layers of fallacy in Henry's reasoning, we are brought back to Henry himself and his instinctive desire to fight and prove his worth as a man.

In *The Red Badge of Courage*, Crane focuses on the contrast between modern Western society, which, in peacetime, frustrates the aggressiveness of young males by castigating the trait as primitive and immoral, and earlier societies which rewarded male aggressiveness and exalted it continually through literary works. In that respect, *Red Badge* is remarkably contemporary since our late twentieth-century society has gone much further than Crane's in denying or repressing the fighting instinct. Henry's ambivalent perception of the war at the beginning of the novel evidences clearly his confusion:

> He had, of course, dreamed of battles all his life—of vague and bloody conflicts that had thrilled him with their sweep and fire. In visions he had seen himself in many struggles. He had imagined people secure in the shadow of his eagle-eyed prowess. But awake he had regarded battles as crimson blotches on the pages of the past. He had put them as things of the bygone with his thought-images of heavy crowns and high castles. . . .
>
> . . . He had long despaired of witnessing a Greeklike struggle. Such would be no more, he had said. Men were better or more timid. Secular and religious education had effaced the throat-grappling instinct, or else firm finance held in check the passions. (83)

Many conflicts are dramatized in this passage, the most important one summarized by the sentence: "Men were better or more timid." "Men are better," if one is to believe that fighting and the enjoyment of it was barbarous and that the fighting instinct has been erased by civilization. But "better" is equated with "more timid," suggesting the instinctive contempt which Henry feels towards those who will not fight.

That Henry should be confused regarding this basic issue is hardly surprising since he has received two conflicting messages from society. Every instinct makes him equate morality with timidity and regret a past, more simple in psychological terms, when the aggressiveness of youth was glorified and channelled through "those great affairs of the earth." Having read some of the epics of literature and history has reinforced and sublimated those instincts, leading him, naturally, to visualize himself in heroic terms. However, his education has taught him that civilization has erased "the throat-grappling instinct"—a fallacy if there is one, but one which Henry does not know as such. He believes in the concept, but it does not correspond to an inner reality, either physical or psychological. It is an intellectual conviction which has no echo in the self. As he will discover through combat, the throat-grappling instinct is alive and well, and living in every individual with the will to live and a reluctance to being "badgered of his life, like a kitten chased by boys." Henry's mixed feelings toward war clearly reflect the duality of human nature.

Moreover, the archetypal myth of the hero is far too deeply ingrained in our unconscious to disappear so easily. Courage on the battlefield has been glorified for thousands of years, reaching its perfect justification in the concept of knighthood, which Crane refers to sarcastically as the people whom Henry imagines "secure in the shadow of his 'eagle-eyed prowess.'" While Crane is gently mocking the young country boy's dream of embodying the concept of knighthood, his implied criticism of a society which teaches its youth to regard knighthood as "crimson blotches on the pages of the past" is perhaps sharper, since knighthood allowed for the sublimation of physical force into an instrument of protection of the weak and the helpless. However, Henry is not only attracted by the nobility of the chivalric ideal but also by its pageantry and its gentlemanly concept of fair play. When the second enemy charge follows hard on the heels of the first, Henry "waited as if he expected the enemy to suddenly stop, apologize, and retire, bowing," as though it were still the eighteenth century, when warring generals bowed to each other before attacking, giving the adversary the opportunity to fire first—as Count d'Auteroche did, for instance, at the battle of Fontenoy in 1745 where the Maréchal de Saxe defeated both the British and the Dutch. Auteroche was commanding the French Guards, and his phrase, "*Messieurs les Anglais, tirez les premiers*" became famous.

On the other hand, Henry has also been taught to believe that education, religion, and finance improved human nature and erased wars. The irony here is bitter, and made even more so because of Henry's complete lack of awareness that religion and finance have in fact been the two basic motivations for wars. The name of God has been used since the beginnings of religion to justify, and even sanctify, man's selfish greed, lust for power over others, and aggressiveness. The very war in which Henry enlists is itself an instance of economic and political motivation camouflaged as ideology. Historically, passions have been stirred rather than held in check by religion and finance, and Henry's naivete is a device used by Crane to hold society up to the reader's scrutiny, in a way which recalls *Huckleberry Finn*. Indeed, it exposes the social manipulation of human psychology; and Henry's acceptance merely mirrors the uncritical conformism of the majority.

Henry's bidding farewell to his mother is also revealing:

Still, she had disappointed him by saying nothing whatever about returning with his shield or on it. He had privately primed himself for a beautiful scene. He had prepared certain sentences which he thought could be used with touching effect. But her words destroyed his plans. . . ."If so be a time comes when yeh have to be kilt or do a mean thing, why, Henry, don't think of anything 'cept what's right, because there's many a woman has to bear up 'ginst sech things these times, and the Lord'll take keer of us all." (85)

Here, Crane is making fun of Henry's self-image as a Greek warrior. However, there is more. Appearances are what attracts Henry throughout—heroic poses and the coveted red badge of courage—and his fascination for appearance prevents him from seeing reality. His mother, in fact, does tell him to come back with his shield or on it; but she does so in her own way devoid of grandiose images, and he does not hear her. Throughout the novella, Crane mocks Henry's penchant for the theatrical, always reminding us that our self-image is formed through the models which have been flaunted before our eyes and imagination by society.

Henry's mother's belief that concern for her might cause Henry to be cowardly ironically foreshadows Henry's running like a rabbit. However, concern for her will be the last thing on Henry's mind at that time, self-concern and self-preservation being his only thoughts. While a cause may be the initial reason for fighting, the actual combat is intensely personal, tapping into primitive emotions and instincts which belong to our shadow and collective unconscious, and has little to do with causes or loved ones, unless their physical presence becomes a factor in the confrontation.

Courage and cowardice, the two notions which obsess Henry and his concept of self, are reduced by Crane to the two basic emotions of anger and terror. This deflation of two major concepts is furthered by his allowing the same individual to be both cowardly and courageous in situations which are almost identical.

Just as the youth has barely finished congratulating himself on his courage during his first battle, convinced that he is now the man he always hoped to be—"So it was all over at last! The supreme trial had been passed. The red, formidable difficulties of war had been vanquished. . . . He perceived that the man who has fought thus was magnificent" (117)—the enemy attacks anew, and he runs. However, it is less the new attack which makes Henry run than the turn he allows his thoughts to take, exaggerating

> the endurance, the skill, and the valor of those who were coming. . . . They must be machines of steel. It was very gloomy struggling against such affairs, wound up perhaps to fight until sundown. . . .
>
> To the youth it was the onslaught of redoubtable dragons. He became like the man who lost his legs at the approach of the red and green monster. . . . He seemed to shut his eyes and wait to be gobbled. (119)

Indeed, the workings of his imagination terrify him far more, in that he allows it to transform the enemy into something they are not, perhaps unconsciously justifying his wish to run. His later rationalization of his behavior by comparing himself to a squirrel follows the same pattern, but is deliberately sophistic:

> The squirrel, immediately upon recognizing danger, had taken to his legs without ado. He did not stand solidly baring his furry belly to the missile, and die with an upward glance at the sympathetic heavens. (126)

Clearly Henry is not a squirrel, as Marston LaFrance points out,[2] nor are soldiers expected to stand stolidly, passively awaiting oncoming missiles. More importantly, though, the comparison of the two situations is entirely sophistic, for the squirrel is not confronting another aggressive squirrel, but an actual formidable dragon (given his and Henry's respective sizes), while Henry is merely fighting other men with equal weapons. Because it serves his self-justification, he now tramples the theatrical and romantic poses he has admired so far and coveted for himself. His comparison of a fighting and dying soldier with a squirrel baring his furry belly and dying with an upward glance at the sympathetic heaven is funny and cute, but bitter when one parallels it with the death of the tall soldier. It is also an amusing parody of Henry himself, who keeps expecting nature to sympathize with him and is amazed that it should go "tranquilly on with its golden process" despite the horror of the battlefield.

The situation is sensibly the same at the beginning of the next battle, once Henry has rejoined his regiment after his desertion. Again Henry feels that he has earned the opportunity for contemplation and repose, and again he exaggerates the power of the enemy and his own helplessness, feeling chased around like a rat, and vulnerable like a kitten in a bag. This time, however, his mental processes turn to anger rather than terror:

> He had a wild hate for the relentless foe. . . . He was not going to be badgered of his life, like a kitten chased by boys, he said. It was not well to drive men into final comers; at those moments they could all develop teeth and claws. . . . The tormentors were flies sucking insolently at his blood, and he thought that he would have given his life for a revenge of seeing their faces in pitiful plights. (172)

Thus, two similar situations may bring about dramatically different results in the same individual, depending on his initial psychological reaction to the stimuli. In both cases, Henry has a strong feeling of impotence brought about by a momentary belief that his rifle is useless—not loaded (111) or an impotent stick (173). However, in one case, the feeling of helplessness leads to fear and desertion, while, in the other, it leads to rage and aggression. Indeed, it is not so much what the situation is as the emotional reaction to it which controls the outcome.

Crane is making the point that courage and cowardice are abstract and moral concepts which have no objective reality. The same individual may be both courageous and cowardly, depending on the direction in which his imagination directs his surge of adrenaline under stress. Henry, of course, does not understand this, and keeps dreaming of himself in heroic terms: "he had been a barbarian, a beast. He had fought like a pagan who defends his religion. . . . And he had not been aware of the process. He had slept and, awakening, found himself a knight" (175). He is unaware that, in closely linking the animal and human worlds, he removes the concept of courage from its moral pedestal and brings it down to the physical level. The equation between barbarian, beast, pagan, and knight reveals that they are effectively based on the same premise. Indeed, the paradox is that, in order to be a knight and protect others as well as oneself, one must allow the beast in oneself to surface and take over.

Crane is also indicating that both running and fighting, being prey and predator, are part of the animal world, and that man is basically an animal despite his inflated opinion of himself. It is not accidental that animal imagery is consistently used to describe Henry's behavior and emotions: he is a "pestered animal, a well-meaning cow worried by dogs" (113) at the beginning of the first battle; he runs like a rabbit and is like the proverbial chicken during the second battle; during the third, he is a wild cat. The running soldiers are like terrified buffaloes, while the fighting soldiers have teeth and claws, and are like "animals tossed for a death struggle into a dark pit" (173). Both prey and predator, dominant and subservient members within each breed, belong to nature and within society. Man belongs to the animal world, and it is somehow his choice to be either prey or predator.

While the reasoning mind has very little to do with actual combat, it plays a major role before and after the action. Before the first engagement, Henry realizes that he is "an unknown quantity" and would again have "to experiment as he had in early youth":

> For days he made ceaseless calculations, but they were all wondrously unsatisfactory He found that he could establish nothing. He finally concluded that the only way to prove himself was to go into the blaze, and then figuratively to watch his legs to discover their merits and faults. He reluctantly admitted that he could not sit still and with a mental slate and pencil derive an answer. To gain it, he must have blaze, blood, and danger, even as a chemist requires this, that and the other. (91)

Henry discovers the obvious here: that it is only through actualization that one can verify one's self-image; and that it is only through battle that he will find what manner of a soldier he is. However, the fallacy of the argument is rather humorous, for Crane attributes a naturalistic viewpoint to Henry, which is entirely negated by the personal stake he has in the experiment—i.e., the chemist cannot be both the dispassionate observer carrying out the experiment and the experiment itself. In dissociating his legs from his mind, Henry appears to be objective—the mind analyzing the body—but instead foreshadows ironically the fact that his mind will not only have little control over what his body does but will be unable to assess the situation with any objectivity because of its emotional involvement in it. Indeed, Henry's body will act and his mind will be reduced to watching the action and attempt a pathetic rationalization of the fait accompli afterwards.

Henry's courage in the first and third battles is largely the result of two things: his surge of adrenaline directed toward aggressiveness rather than blind terror, and his loss of personal identity. When the fighting begins, he takes leave of his reasoning mind and stops thinking altogether. In "his battle sleep" he does not know the direction of the ground, nor that he is standing up or has fallen, nor even that a lull has taken place. He loses "sense of everything but his hate, his desire to smash into pulp the glittering smile of victory which he could feel upon the faces of his enemies" (173). Crane's description of courage as a reflex action, which is not controlled by the will, calls into question the concept of courage as a moral virtue but not its effectiveness.

This animal instinct is also dramatized by Crane as a "temporary but sublime absence of selfishness" (183): "He suddenly lost concern for himself, and forgot to look at a menacing fate. He became not a man but a member" (26). The loss of identity is therefore double: man becomes both a raging animal and a selfless component whose identity is submerged into "a common personality which [is] dominated by a single desire" (112). While the two concepts are in ironic contrast, their result is the same: the individual mind gives control over to something powerful which takes over, the immediate reward being a strong feeling of brotherhood which is more potent than either cause or self.

The reasoning mind, however, need not be entirely absent. It can indirectly control the body, once it has recognized that the body will not consult it in life-threatening emergencies. That is, one may manipulate one's own mind into forcing the chosen animal instinct to surface and block out the unwanted one. It seems that, by the end, Henry intuitively learns that focusing on a physical thing, such as the adversary's flag, or taking his foe's resistance as a personal insult will allow him to summon a desperate purpose, and, therefore, eradicate fear. Then, bullets and shells are no longer instruments of death "with rows of cruel teeth that grinned at him" (120), but merely things that can prevent him from reaching his goal:

> The youth had centered the gaze of his soul upon that other flag. Its possession would be high pride. It would express bloody minglings, near blows. He had a gigantic hatred for those who made great difficulties and complications. They caused it to be a craved treasure of mythology, hung amid tasks and contrivances of danger. (206)

Amusingly, though, Henry's single-minded determination remains wrapped up with mythological and archetypal tests of manhood, suggesting that he has not really learned much about his own human nature from the experience.

Henry can never relinquish his heroic self-image, and, once combat is over and his rational mind is in control again, he is even able to rationalize cowardice:

> He had done a good part in saving himself, who was a little piece of the army. He had considered the time, he said, to be one in which it was the duty of every little piece to rescue itself if possible. Later the officers could fit the little pieces together again, and make a battle front. If none of the lit-

tle pieces were wise enough to save themselves from the flurry of death at such a time, why, then, where would be the army. His actions . . . were the work of a master's legs. (124)

The sophism of this reasoning is extremely funny, for Henry has considered nothing before running, merely reacting in blind terror. There has been no sagacity or strategy in the work of his legs, as he would have himself believe. Indeed, he keeps jumping back and forth on both sides of his own argument to convince himself that his actions were not really what they were. Since he has set himself up to be judged by the work of his legs, his legs, then, cannot possibly have done anything wrong. Moreover, his rationale for an efficient army is in fact a rationale for a parody of an army—one which breaks up and runs any time there is combat. It might make for great comedy, but not for winning battles.

Actually, Henry's desperate desire to justify himself entails horror as much as comedy.

> He had been overturned and crushed by their lack of sense in holding the position, when intelligent deliberation would have convinced them that it was impossible. . . . He felt a great anger against his comrades. He knew it could be proved that they had been fools. (124)

Again, while the reasoning appears logical, it is faulty because based on false premises. The proof being in the result, the impossibility of a task can only be determined by trying it with all possible effort, not by deliberating about it. Ironically, in his desperate attempt to make theory the proof of fact, Henry reverses his earlier realization that his behavior would establish his identity. Here, the facts must be wrong since they do not fit his theory. Much of Henry's rationalizing follows the same pattern, and the "hateful" facts always prove him wrong, making him project his self-hatred onto the world and others. This is where the seed of the horror resides. In order to be vindicated, Henry wishes his own side defeated—that is, by implication, his comrades and many others dead. While this is only a temporary emotion for Henry, it nevertheless illustrates the motivating pattern for fanaticism, which involves the need of proving oneself right by forcing others to do or believe as one does. The overwhelming need to be right entails that those who do not believe or act as one does are wrong and must be persuaded to change. If they are changed, they verify one's own beliefs and justify one's right to convert them, even by force if necessary. If they resist, then they deserve to die because they are wrong.

Clearly, Henry is no dictator, murdering maniac, or religious fanatic, but he is representative of humanity at large. Not only a young man undergoing his first tests of manhood, he is also representative of what may happen to the mind as a result of self-hatred and the resulting psychological isolation. Crane makes it clear throughout the novel that Henry's self-loathing breeds a hatred of his own comrades because he believes that they can perceive his guilt—in Jean Paul Sartre's words: "*l'enfer, c'est les autres.*" He, therefore, wishes them dead. However, when his hatred is directed at the enemy, it brings about acts of valor, self-love, and love for his comrades. Paradoxically, Henry's hatred is not so much directed at other men in a different uniform as against those who interfere with his wishes and well-being—that enemy's flag bearer, for instance, who will not relinquish the flag Henry desires as a symbol of his own pride and greatness, or his own officers who called him and his comrades "mule drivers" and "mud diggers."

Ironically, despite his experiences, Henry does not seem to learn much about himself or to become conscious of those assumptions which prevail in his society and which he takes for granted—those very assumptions which Crane's humorous viewpoint challenges indirectly. To the end, Henry remains a conformist, one who has a limited knowledge of himself but who is still self-deluded in his belief that he knows all. He has proven objectively that he is both a coward and a courageous man, but he has not figured out how he can be both at the same time, and what mental processes brought about dramatically different outcomes to identical situations. Crane's original ending to the story—"He had been to touch the great death, and found that, after all, [it] was for others"—makes it clear that Henry remains a rather silly young man who has merely derived a feeling of invulnerability from his accidental survival. Appleton's ending—"He had been to touch the great death, and found that, after all, it was but the great death" (212), on the other hand, brings a further dimension to Henry's psychology, but one which is not really warranted by what we see of his mental processes. Appleton's ending essentially suggests that Henry has learned what Francis Macomber realizes in Ernest Hemingway's short story "The Short Happy Life of Francis Macomber": that "a man can die but once; we owe God a death . . . and he that dies this year is quit for the next."[3] Nothing in *Red Badge* suggests that Henry has reflected about his own mortality and has understood that it is how we live that counts, and not how long.

The Red Badge of Courage is a complex work in its revelation of human nature and of the illusions and delusions bred by society. In associating closely the positive concept of courage with the negative emotion of hatred, the idealized concepts of heroism and knighthood with the killer instinct, Crane dramatizes the relativity of social beliefs, and the fact that, when one is actually fighting for one's life, morals and ideals yield the stage to the unconscious, going back into the primitive—what Jack London calls "the womb of Time." The will to live takes second place to the will to kill—the latter being, paradoxically, far more effective in the protection of life than the former. Through his ironical use of fallacious reasoning, Crane also calls into question both society's glorification of heroism and courage and its denial of man's primitive nature. Ironically, glorification makes for sublimation and control of a primitive instinct, while denial leads to denigration, confusion, and even chaos.

From *Stephen Crane in War and Peace*, edited by James H. Meredith, special edition of *War, Literature & the Arts* (1999): 147-159. Originally published by the U.S. Air Force Academy Department of English.

Notes

1. Stephen Crane, *The Red Badge of Courage*, in *Stephen Crane: Prose and Poetry* (New York: The Library of America, 1984), p. 101. Subsequent references to this text are parenthetical.

2. Marston LaFrance, *A Reading of Stephen Crane* (New York: Oxford University Press, 1971), p. 112.

3. Ernest Hemingway, "The Short Happy Life of Francis Macomber," *The Short Stories of Ernest Hemingway* (New York: Charles Scribner's Sons, 1966), 32.

The Imagery of *The Red Badge of Courage*_____

James W. Tuttleton

The Red Badge of Courage continues to provoke the liveliest kind of criticism. One of the most significant and provoking studies is Robert W. Stallman's criticism scattered throughout his essays in *Stephen Crane: An Omnibus*,[1] *Critiques and Essays on Modern Fiction*,[2] and in his Introduction to the Modern Library edition of the novel.[3] Briefly, Stallman sees in the novel a structure of Christian symbols—actions and images—which play a vital role in the salvation of the major character, Henry Fleming, and which relate his particular experience to the universal significance of the Christian myth. Stallman's interpretation of the action and imagery of the novel has provoked expostulation and reply. John Hart[4] and James T. Cox[5] have complemented Stallman's approach to the "symbolism" of Crane's fiction, but others—particularly Scott C. Osborn,[6] Stanley B. Greenfield,[7] and Philip Rahv[8]—have seriously criticized the Stallman approach as well as some of the conclusions he had reached. Their criticisms include not only flat denials of the imagery as Christian imagery but also flat denials of the validity of a symbolic or mythic interpretation of the novel.

According to Stallman, one of the effects of Jim Conklin's life and death is to bring about the spiritual regeneration of Henry Fleming. Such an idea is based upon the symbolic function of Jim Conklin: "He goes under various names. He is sometimes called the spectral soldier (his face is a pasty gray) and sometimes the tall soldier (he is taller than all other men), but there are unmistakable hints—in such descriptive details about him as his wound in the side, his torn body and his gory hand, and even in the initials of his name, Jim Conklin—that he is intended to represent Jesus Christ."[9] The efficacy of Conklin's death, Stallman contends, takes on significant meaning for Henry Fleming after he has run from the battle. This controversial reading of the novel is so well known that perhaps one need not go further into the other details that Stallman adduces to support his contention. That Stallman's interpretation of the novel has proved unacceptable to so many serious critics of the novel, however, suggests that the imagery he has isolated (and it is there) is either meaningless or coincidental, or that it has some other function in the novel. Granting that Stallman's imagery is indeed there, though not granting that it means what he says it means, this paper proposes that the Christian imagery is really only one of two constructs of impressionistic (not symbolic) religious imagery which, when juxtaposed, evoke an irony of opposites hitherto unmentioned in the criticism of the book.

I

Given the Christian imagery as the first cluster of religious impressions, the second cluster of images—pagan religious images—has at its center the pagan god War. There are several references to him. The first is this: "They were going to look at war, the red animal—war, the blood-swollen god" (p. 46). Consistently throughout the novel, war is defined as a pagan god. Again, "The army, helpless in the matted thickets and blinded by the overhanging night, was going to be swallowed. War, the red animal, war, the blood-swollen god, would have bloated fill" (p. 137). Moreover, the pagan god War is consistently presented in the image of a huge serpent or dragons. For instance, "Staring once at the red eyes across the river [Henry] conceived them to be growing larger, as the orbs of a row of dragons advancing" (p. 25). The regiment was "like one of those moving monsters wending with many feet" and there was "an occasional flash and glimmer of steel from the backs of all these huge crawling reptiles" (pp. 26-27). Both the enemy army and Henry's regiment are identified with this god War.

As the regiment marches, it is described as "two serpents crawling from the cavern of night" (p. 27), and as the boy is thrown into battle, it seemed to him "an onslaught of redoubtable dragons. He became like the man who lost his legs at the approach of the red and green monster" (p. 78). As he ran from battle, Henry felt that "death must make a first choice of the men who were nearest; the initial morsels for the dragons would be then those who were following him" (p. 81), but he could nevertheless imagine their "rows of cruel teeth" (p. 81). The columns of wagons and men moved from the front lines with "the sinuous movement of a serpent" (p. 125). Again, "the dragons were coming with invincible strides" (p. 137). The line of troops under fire "curled and writhed like a snake stepped on" (p. 191). Finally, after his desertion, Henry congratulates himself on escaping after having "been out among the dragons" (p. 173).

This god War has his worship. His temple is the forest, which is bathed in a "cathedral light" (p. 47). "Through the *aisles* of the wood could be seen the floating smoke from . . . rifles" (p. 47; italics mine). The soldiers in battle are likened to "slaves toiling in the temple of this god" (p. 76), to "pursued imps" (p. 78), and to "ugly fiends" (p. 244; misprinted as "friends" here and in the 1895 edition). In addition, the temple has its priests: the smoke clouds of battle drift "slowly and insolently across the fields like observant phantoms" (p. 52); they are called "the swirling battle phantoms which were choking him, stuffing their smoke robes down his parched throat" (p. 66).

There is of course a congregation of worshipers who participate in all of the traditional elements of worship. The "congregation" (p. 63), likened in one place to pupils in a schoolroom—perhaps catechists in a Sunday school room—is called "the subtle battle brotherhood," a "mysterious fraternity born of the smoke and danger of death" (p. 65). Henry had fought like "a barbarian, a beast. He had fought like a pagan who defends his religion" (pp. 194-95). He feels "a desire to chant a paean" (p. 86), "to sing a battle hymn" (p. 137). The preaching is performed by the guns: "Batteries were speaking with thunderous oratorical effort" (p. 72). "They belched and howled like brass devils guarding a gate" (p. 141). The chorus is a chorus of shell and shot: "The din in front swelled to a tremendous chorus" (p. 56); "The chorus pealed over the still earth" (p. 96); "there was a mighty song of clashes and crashes . . ." (p. 186) that created "a most awe-inspiring racket in the wood" (p.

240). Like Greeks the men read the flight of rumors as if birds of omen (p. 179). In the heat of battle worship, "Many of the men were making low-toned noises with their mouths, and these subdued cheers, snarls, imprecations, prayers, made a wild, barbaric song that went as an undercurrent of sound, strange and chantlike with the resounding chords of the war march" (pp. 66-67). It seems hardly necessary to indicate that the foregoing quotation adds prayer to the list of offices in this satanic ritual. One is reminded by it of Wilfred Owen's "Anthem for Doomed Youth."

Surely blood sacrifice is a signal element of pagan worship, of this mad religion of war. Just before Henry falls back, he realizes that "they were all going to be sacrificed" (p. 45). Later on he felt "the daring spirit of a savage religion-mad. He was capable of profound sacrifices, a tremendous death" (p. 251). One of the frightened boys who was fleeing from battle was apprehended by the lieutenant: "The man was blubbering and staring with sheeplike eyes at the lieutenant, who had seized him by the collar and was pommeling him. He drove him back into the ranks with many blows. The soldier went mechanically, dully, with his animal-like eyes upon the officer. Perhaps there was to him a divinity expressed in the voice of the other—stern, hard, with no reflection of fear in it" (pp. 68-69). In another place the officers are likened to "critical shepherds struggling with sheep" (p. 204). Certainly these officers were representatives of the mad divinity of the god War, who must have his sacrifices. As we have noted before, Henry during his flight saw himself and his comrades as "taken out to be slaughtered" (p. 41), as "morsels for the dragons" (p. 81)—an inverse Eucharist in which the God devours the body and blood of the worshiper. "The brigade was hurrying briskly to be gulped into the infernal mouths of the war god" (p. 83). Even the teamsters and their wagons fled "like fat sheep," like "soft, ungainly animals" (p. 124). Crane has not described these men simply and tritely as cannon fodder; they are sheep for the slaughter in sacrifice to the War God.

The pattern of these pagan religious images is perhaps less striking than the pattern of Christian images, for the pagan imagery is scattered throughout the novel, whereas the Christian imagery is primarily concentrated in the first half of the book. Nevertheless, a pattern of images is there, and it emerges upon careful reading. We see a demoniacal, mad, satanic religion of the god War, imaged as a dragon. He has his temple, his slaves, his priests, his congregation, and his Black Mass in preaching, song, prayer, and blood sacrifice. Into the horrible service of War the boy Henry Fleming is plunged. He emerges from it, Crane says, as a man.

II

"The youth had been taught that a man became another thing in battle. He saw his salvation in such a change" (p. 48). Henry Fleming experiences battle and achieves a kind of heroism by his fearlessness in the face of fire. Yet for Henry Fleming, war was not altogether what he thought it would be, and the salvation which he achieved, the growth of his soul, was achieved not through war, for he almost became its slave as a "war devil" (p. 194) but through the later contemplation of his experience. What Henry had been taught about war—from the pagan War of Troy in Homer's *Iliad*—was false, a false concept of the glory of militarism which Crane objectified in the image of the religion of war. What Henry eventually learned was that "the world was a world for him, though many discovered it to be made of oaths and walking sticks. He had rid himself of the red sickness of battle" (p. 266). He enlisted for reasons of personal glory and ambition only to discover that war is a sickness, a social disease perhaps rooted in the imperfections of the universe itself.

Crane expresses this indictment of war by juxtaposing these images of pagan religion, liturgy, and ritual, against images of the Christian religion. The result is a masterful piece of irony. The nature of this juxtaposition suggests not only the eternal antagonism between war and the Christian ethic, but also the tension within the boy himself. Both war

---

and ethical sacrifice are real and actual facts of experience, the materials of the novel. Crane has illuminated them both by two clusters of impressionistic imagery, which when juxtaposed become the form of the reality he is presenting.[10]

The resolution of these opposites, or the third thing created from them, is implicit in the significance of the chapel of the woods into which Henry stumbles as he retreats from the battle. Standing between the Christian imagery and the pagan is the imagery of the religion of Nature in Chapter VII. Nature seems to give Fleming its sign of approval for having run; and the religion of nature seems to Henry one of peace. But the dead man within the chapel of boughs negates Henry's hope and suggests that nature is neither malign nor benevolent, but simply indifferent or uncognizant of man as an independent part of its process. The "religious half-light" (p. 92) of the chapel ironically indicates its lack of full illumination. Yet it stands midway between the darkness of the religion of War and the light of the religion of peace suggested by the sacrificial ethic of Christianity. Crane's goal in juxtaposing these polar religious images was in part certainly to show Henry Fleming's salvation, enlightenment, growth, maturation, initiation, or whatever we choose to call it. War was to be for Fleming "a deity laying about him with the bludgeon of correction."[11] But Crane never really succeeded in demonstrating that the youth was appreciably corrected. Crane merely says that he changed. Toward the end of the novel, Henry ruminates: "He had been to touch the great death, and found that, after all, it was but the great death. He was a man" (p. 266). This conclusion, however, sounds suspiciously like the "brass and bombast of his earlier gospels" (p. 265), his belief that "a man with a full stomach and the respect of his fellows had no business to scold about anything that he might think to be wrong in the ways of the universe, or even with the ways of society" (p. 172). The manuscript copy of the novel, in fact, supports this contention, for there Henry says, "He had been to touch the great death, and had found that, after all, it was but the great death [and was for others]."[12] Such a conclusion is not the wisdom of a man who has, after such battle experience, grown, matured, been initiated, enlightened, or saved. Crane's irony gets in the way of the conclusion he is driving toward. If Henry's soul does change, it is only much, much later than the conclusion of the novel that it does so. Crane only states that Henry Fleming has changed; he does not demonstrate from the boy's actions that an actual change has occurred. In this respect, the novel fails of its intention.

From *Modern Fiction Studies* 8, no. 4 (1962): 410-415. Copyright © 1962 by Purdue Research Foundation. Reprinted with permission of the Johns Hopkins University Press.

Notes

1. (New York, 1958).

2. "Stephen Crane: A Revaluation," *Critiques and Essays on Modern Fiction, 1920-1951*, ed. John W. Aldridge (New York, 1952), pp. 249-269.

3. (New York, 1951).

4. "*The Red Badge of Courage* as Myth and Symbol," *University of Kansas City Review*, XIX (1953), 249-256.

5. "Stephen Crane as Symbolic Naturalist: An Analysis of 'The Blue Hotel,'" *Modern Fiction Studies*, III (Summer, 1957), 147-158.

6. "Stephen Crane's Imagery: 'Pasted like a Wafer,'" *American Literature*, XXIII (1951), 362.

7. "The Unmistakable Stephen Crane," *PMLA*, LXXIII (1958), 562-572.

8. "Fiction and the Criticism of Fiction," *The Kenyon Review*, XVIII (Spring, 1956), 276-299.

9. "Introduction," *The Red Badge of Courage* (New York: Modern Library, 1951), pp. xxxiii-xxxiv. All quotations from the novel are taken from this edition, unless otherwise stated.

10. It is perhaps worth pointing out that this juxtaposition of images implies an indictment of a society in which war is glorified, romanticized, indeed almost worshiped, and that in the 1890's militarism provided an instrument of policy justified by "science" for achieving imperialistic aims. See Richard Hofstadter, *Social Darwinism in American Thought* (Boston, 1959), 190 ff.

11. *Stephen Crane: An Omnibus*, p. 369. In the final holograph version this statement was not canceled but unaccountably was not printed in the 1895 book edition.

12. *Stephen Crane: An Omnibus*, p. 369.

The Imagery of *The Red Badge of Courage*_____

James Trammell Cox

"The red sun . . . pasted in the sky like a wafer" of Stephen Crane's *The Red Badge of Courage* continues to generate more critical heat than light. Since the publication in 1951 of R. W. Stallman's much-debated introduction to the Modern Library edition of the novel and his later expansions of this reading, contemporary criticism has been sharply divided on at least three issues: the significance of the religious imagery, the closely related problem of Henry Fleming's development or lack of it, and the question of Crane's fictional method, naturalist or symbolist. Seldom however are these fundamental points of disagreement recognized as such; all too frequently they are obscured or simply avoided in a dispute over critical method. If the imagery gets re-examined, the examination is likely to limit itself to this single image in isolation. Only a single article is devoted primarily to a study of the imagery as a whole.[1] Another look is urgently needed.

Of what has been done, the best on the significance of the religious imagery is Bernard Weisbarger's recent suggestion that "There is going to be rebirth, indeed, but not a supernatural one. Here is a negation of the Christian conversion."[2] This obvious obverse significance of the Christian symbolism, noted but misinterpreted by Stallman and quite consistent with Henry Fleming's naturalistic re-education, seems to have occurred to no one but Mr. Weisbarger. On the problem of Henry Fleming's development, more specifically on its significance in the naturalistic universe depicted in the novel, Stanley B. Greenfield's summation is thoughtful and valuable, especially to the extent that it reconciles what seems a discrepancy between Crane's determinism and the manifest value he attaches to individual insight and moral behavior:

> Crane's magnum opus shows up the nature and value of courage. The heroic ideal is not what it has been claimed to be: so largely is it the product of

instinctive responses to biological and traditional forces. But man does have will, and he has the ability to reflect, and though these do not guarantee that he can effect his own destiny they do enable him to become responsible to some degree for the honesty of his personal vision.[3]

Closer textual analysis—a method Mr. Greenfield inconsistently ridicules and utilizes at will—reveals a need for considerable qualification of the cheerful indifference of Nature and of the "decided growth in moral behavior"[4] he finds in Henry Fleming's development. For the imagery suggests that this cheerful appearance of Nature is a part of its treacherous hostility. As Crane expresses the idea in an expunged passage from an earlier manuscript version, "It [Nature] could deck a hideous creature in enticing apparel."[5] The imagery also insists upon the irony of Henry's discovery of unselfishness and courage through the wounded vanity of egocentrism, so that the decided growth toward moral manhood posited by Greenfield ignores this basic irony, as well as its chief philosophical implication: that man's relationship to his universe is paradoxical. He becomes least an animal when most an animal. On the question of Crane's fictional method, Stallman is still significantly right in his recognition of the extent to which "Crane puts language to poetic uses, which is to use it reflexively and symbolically."[6] And it is past time that this fundamental question be considered apart from any given interpretation, for a full understanding and appreciation of the better works of Stephen Crane are absolutely dependent upon an awareness of this method.

What makes this awareness so very important, in particular, to a reading of *The Red Badge of Courage* is that the novel is an initiation story, the account of a young man's discovery of the nature of reality, and the definition of this reality, symbolically presented to the reader through the imagery, provides Henry Fleming's slow discovery with a pervasive dramatic irony as essential to a full appreciation of the work as, for example, a foreknowledge of Oedipus' origin is in *Oedipus Rex*.

Briefly paraphrased, the definition Crane provides us with is largely the same naturalism to be found in "The Blue Hotel." The earth and all life on it originated from the fierce fire of the sun, which continues ultimately to determine both life and death on the earth in the dependence of all life here upon its warmth and light for existence. It is this condition of things, further, which requires that all life—specifically man, animal, and plant, as enumerated by Crane—must alike struggle to survive. Whatever the decking or coloration for the plant or animal, whatever the disguises for man—which would include all the myths of man's mind that obscure this conception of himself and his universe, notably his pretense to honor and glory, his romantic concept of nature, and his belief in eternal life—all are engaged in an endless struggle to survive that necessitates a conflict relation to environment. For this reason the inner nature of all life is hostile. Its battles are for existence, and the essence, in fact, of existence is a battle. This being true, all attempts either to escape or to deny this conflict are doomed to meaninglessness. For meaning, man's only recourse in such a universe is to heed the general's exhortation, "t' go in—everlastingly—like blazes—anything"; that is, to embrace life as conflict. In so doing, man achieves a paradoxical harmony with his hostile universe that allows him, like the regiment, to proceed "superior to circumstances until its blazing vitality fades." It also allows him to know, for a moment, "a temporary but sublime absence of selfishness" and the undeceived brotherhood which his nature, his condition, and his disguises otherwise preclude. And with full knowledge comes, finally, a certain dignity, nothing more.

What is of further interest in the imagery as a whole is that Crane employs here the same images for the same symbolic purposes he later uses in "The Blue Hotel." To symbolize life as an eternal conflict, he uses a battle in the novel as a "way that seemed eternal" and two fights in the short story, one of which is also described as "eternal to his [the Easterner's] sense." To suggest the deterministic inevitability of this conflict and its destructive power, he uses machine images in both, while its ferocity and its limited grandeur are compared to a firework display. To equate man with other forms of life in the identity of their struggle for survival, he relies heavily upon comparisons to animals. To call attention to the timelessness and also the brutality of this struggle, comparisons to primitive warriors are abundant. To make a mockery of man's chief delusion, which is Christianity with its promise of eternal life, Stephen Crane—no matter whose son he is—compares the victims of both conflicts to Jesus Christ. Inferno images abound for roughly the same purpose. To define the essence of reality as treacherous in that its facade conceals the inner hostility which emerges only when existence is threatened, Crane employs a blue exterior with a fire or simply red within in both works. To suggest that death is an inevitable consequence of this fire within, actually differing from life only as colors on the spectrum differ—in degree, not in kind—yellow is used to symbolize death in both. To represent miseducation, particularly in regard to Nature, green and brown have identical functions in both. To symbolize fear, white is used in both, though white in the novel is also linked with stoic calm or love—all three of which associations possess commonality in being opposites to the red of hostility and anger. Only black shows change: in the novel it is the equivalent of red, while in the story it is the oblivion of death, grey in the novel assuming approximately this significance. The two works, in fact, are companion pieces: studies of fear and courage and awareness in a naturalistic universe.

Consistently overlooked, even by Edward Stone,[7] in the long wrangle over the wafer image is the central role of the sun, metaphorically and philosophically, in the novel as a whole. It is set up in the beginning of the novel in the account of Henry's misconceptions as a youth: "There was a portion of the world's history which he had regarded as the time of wars, but it, he *thought*, had been *long gone over the horizon* and had disappeared forever" (6).[8] To this Crane adds, "He had long despaired of witnessing a Greek-like struggle. Such would be no more. Men were better, or more timid. Secular and religious education had effaced the throat-grappling instinct, or else firm finance held in check the passions." Furthermore, this whole idea, with the last two sentences verbatim, is repeated on page 13. Consequently, it cannot be without significance and irony that the general who is in charge of the fighting that Henry has deserted on the first day of battle is described first as "much harassed" with the appearance "of a business man whose market is swinging up and down" (84), secondly, as having in his eyes "a desire to chant a paean" (86), and thirdly as one who "beamed upon the earth like a sun" (86).

Here is ample evidence, indeed, manifest in the action and explained in the imagery, that the time of wars is anything but "long gone over the horizon." As a Greek, an ironically unfirm representative of firm finance, and a sun, this general as the immediate cause of the conflict that ensues is still very much on Henry Fleming's horizon. The explanation provided by the imagery is first of all that finance is neither firm nor capable of holding in check men's passions. Further, in their common identity through metaphor, the imagery also calls attention to the common relation both the general and the sun have to the conflict which follows: it is causal, the general immediate and the sun ultimate. This is again the chief significance and the chief irony in the timely reappearance of the "red sun . . . pasted in the sky like a wafer" (115) when Henry has just observed in Jim Conklin's fall that his "side looked as if it had been chewed by wolves." The time of wars has still to go over the horizon because religious education has also failed to efface "the throat grappling instinct."

The lieutenant is thus ironically profounder than he knows when he observes, "'I was willin' t' bet they'd attack as soon as th' sun got fairly up'" (184). This role of ultimate responsibility would also seem to be the implication of the abrupt appearance of the sun in this picture of the dead soldiers: "A dead soldier was stretched with his face hidden in his arm. Farther off there was a group of four or five corpses keeping mournful company. A hot sun had blazed upon the spot" (98). Other corpses are described as "dumped out upon the ground from the sky" (71) or as "stricken by bolts from the sky" (245). The din of this battle is indeed, as Crane tells us, "fitted to the universe" (242), and the sun, though capable of appearing "bright and gay in the blue, enameled sky," is ultimately red and responsible, as the "cloud of dark smoke, as from smoldering ruins" (196), which goes up toward it, reveals like an accusing finger.

The red badge that Henry Fleming wears is seed and sign of this same sun. For in the necessity imposed by the sun on all life to struggle for survival, man retains within a fiery hostility as revealed in the description of his hut, where it is not surprising that we find a fire in a "flimsy chimney of clay and sticks [that] made endless threats to set ablaze the whole establishment" (5). Philosophically, it is the same fire. It is the same fire that disturbed Henry when he "burned to enlist" (6). In the heat of battle, with existence threatened, it is this fire that has now emerged upon Henry's "red and inflamed features" (207) and upon the general's face, "aflame with excitement" (85). The regiment itself is a "firework that, once ignited proceeds superior to circumstances until its blazing vitality fades" (65).

Of course fiery hostility is not the only reaction Henry and the regiment show to this conflict threatening existence. Fear is common and is invariably denoted with expressions suggesting the emergence of white upon the features instead of fire or red, as when Henry "blanched" before turning to run. For fear, like hostility, is a constituent part of the make-up of the inner man as again he is defined in his quarters, with the suggestion that it is from his environment or the outside that his fear derives: "A small window shot an oblique square of whiter light upon the cluttered floor" (5).

Confirming the determining role of the sun as overhanging or providing the conditions under which man, so defined, exists, the sun appears here too: "The sunlight, without, beating upon it [the folded tent which serves as a roof] made it glow a light yellow shade" (5). Thus besides giving the fire necessary to existence, it demands finally as a consequence of this fire death. For yellow is consistently associated with death. The first corpse Henry sees is dressed in a suit of "yellowish brown" (43), and the mouth of the corpse in the chapel of the trees has changed from red "to an appalling yellow" (92). And overhanging the battle area Henry flees from exactly as it overhangs his quarters is "a yellow fog [that] lay wallowing on the treetops" (87). Though the exterior of this hut is brown, careful readers of "The Blue Hotel" cannot fail to note the astonishing similarity between these quarters and the "proper temple" of the short story.

A further aspect of man's nature is symbolically revealed in this interior: his tendency, deriving from his hostility, to screen from himself his inner nature, wreathing it in constructs of belief and value which only obscure the truth, as the smoke from the fire here "at times neglected the clay chimney and wreathed into the room" (5), obscuring this fire as the smoke of battle so often obscures the flames of the enemy guns, making it "difficult for the regiment to proceed with intelligence" (212). A part of this tendency is laziness and ignorance, qualities frequently associated with smoke: "some lazy and ignorant smoke curled slowly. The men, hiding from the bullets, waited anxiously for it to lift and disclose the plight of the regiment" (224). Primarily however it is the fear of death which leads man to construct his own smoke-screens, as suggested in the frequent linkage of smoke with the color gray. For the face or prospect of death is gray in each of the deaths that Henry has occasion to observe closely: in the "ashen face" (44) of the first, in "the gray skin of the face" (92) of the corpse in the chapel of the trees, and in "the gray appalling face" (106) of Jim Conklin. Also revealing is its identification with phantom: "Smoke clouds went slowly and insolently across the fields like observant phantoms" (52). For both Jim Conklin and the guilt Henry feels over his desertion of Jim are repeatedly referred to as a "specter" or "somber phantom." The implication of the linkage would seem to be that the guilt Henry feels is a part of the "clogged clouds," from which Henry's brain must emerge before his eyes are opened to new ways and the old sympathies are defeated. It derives from those systems of false belief and value which only obscure from man the fiery essence of the naturalistically conceived universe finally recognized and accepted by Henry Fleming. As such, this "sin" may be put "at a distance" by Henry with somewhat less callousness.

Aside from the false concept of heroism and the emptiness of its values, honor and glory, which it is the obvious purpose of the story to expose as so much smoke obscuring the true nature of man and his conflicts, a romantic concept of Nature, as a part of Henry's secular education, must also be included in this smoke. This romanticism is especially apparent in the sentimental pantheism which leads him to see in the landscape he comes to in his flight "a religion of peace" (90), where the arching boughs in a grove of trees "made a chapel" (92), with the sunlight in them providing "a religious half light" (92) and the wind "a hymn of twilight" (95). The low branches are "green doors" (92) to this chapel and the pine needles "a gentle brown carpet" (92). But exactly as the sentimentality of his earlier reaction to "the gentle fabric of softened greens and browns" which "looked to be a wrong place for a battlefield" (43) is revealed when it becomes the scene of the holocaust he flees, so here are his illusions shattered: within these green doors, resting on this gentle brown carpet is a rotting corpse, its uniform, once blue, now faded to a "melancholy shade of green" (92). However gentle green and brown may seem to the miseducated Henry Fleming, Crane makes it shockingly clear to the reader here and elsewhere that green and brown are the colors of the earth which requires death and decay for its fertility.

In the further relation of image to incident, Crane tells us a great deal more about Nature in this particular passage. The eyes have the "dull hue to be seen on the side of a dead fish" (92), linking the corpse to the frequently noted fish devoured previously by the small animal. The corpse, in other words, is like the fish in its failure to survive. What is not so frequently noted is that on five other occasions we are reminded of this resemblance. Henry, for example is a "'Fresh fish!'" (15) and the courageous Lieutenant Hasbrouck "a whale" (265). Also war is twice a "red animal" (46 and 137) and more than twenty times either war or the enemy is a monster about to devour the men, whose frequent fear is "'We'll git swallowed'" (205). Thus through its connection with this meal of the small animal and the corpse, the conflict that takes place on the battlefield becomes itself a symbol of the struggle for survival. And the connection is repeated, emphasizing that all life is involved in this struggle, in the detail of the ant on the lip "trundling some sort of bundle" (92), for again through simile and metaphor Crane elsewhere identifies this bundle as the soldiers being devoured by the red animal, war: they are "Grunting bundles of blue" (247) that drop here and there "like bundles" (69). Henry himself is "a parcel" (154).

Also significant in this passage is the threat of the branches "to throw him over upon it [the corpse]" (93), symbolizing Henry's involvement in the natural order which demands ultimately a return to the earth like that of the corpse. Furthermore this involvement is carefully elaborated through the tree symbolism. Not only are Henry and the men frequently entangled in Nature's trees or her "brambles [which] formed chains and tried to hold him back" (97), but they are repeatedly likened to a tree to reveal the identity of their mutual struggle, as in the song of the soldiers:

> A dog, a woman, an' a walnut tree,
> Th' more yeh beat 'em th' better they be
> (96)

If they survive, that is. The tattered soldier, whose wounded arm dangles "like a broken bough" (102), and Jim, whose body swings forward as he goes down "in the manner of a falling tree" (114), can hardly be described as "better." To indicate that this bit of homely naturalism is to be taken seriously, incidentally, Crane frequently repeats the beating or thrashing imagery like this picture of Henry, who sprawls in battle "like a man who had been thrashed" (193), and compares the soldiers also to women and dogs.

The idea of entanglement is also carried over into the machine imagery, which is used more than fifteen times to describe the battle, suggesting both the deterministic inevitability of this struggle and its destructive power. For instance, as Henry joins the column of the wounded: "The torn bodies expressed the awful machinery in which the men had been entangled" (101). And this machinery is not only the battle but the fixed processes of the natural order demanding conflict and death: "The battle was like the grinding of an immense and terrible machine to him. Its complexities and powers, its grim processes, fascinated him. He must go close and see it produce corpses" (98). A flood is also used on several occasions for the same symbolic purpose. The meaninglessness of this conflict, morally speaking, is apparent in Crane's mention only once of the causes over which the Civil War was fought and then as less important than "the subtle battle brotherhood" of the men, and it is symbolically stated in comparisons of the battle to a circus or carnival and to sporting events. Jim Conklin, for example, gestures toward the battle and says, "'An', Lord, what a circus!'" (108). Over seventy comparisons of the men to animals contribute to this significance of the battle, and in this line, its immediate source is defined as the animal-like hostility of the inner man: "A dull animal-like rebellion against his fellows, war in the abstract, and fate grew within him" (89). To suggest that man is as helpless as a babe in the grinding machinery of the natural order and his fury against it as foolish as that of a child, there are over twenty-five comparisons like these of the men to infants and children: An officer displays "infantile features black with rage" (211) and another "the furious anger of a spoiled child" (59), while Henry before his first battle feels "in the face of his great trial like a babe" (41). This is Nature as it really is—hardly the "woman with a deep aversion to tragedy" (91) Henry Fleming conceived it to be.

Nature's processes are not simply grim however. It is a part of its essence to conceal its inner violence behind a bright facade of blue or blue and gold, so that Nature on occasion parades a gleaming sun in a "blue, pure sky" (73) even as the recruits strut in the "blue and brass" of

---

their new uniforms. Previous to contact with that which threatens existence, man knows only this facade, and Henry on the march to the front
sees the sky as a "fairy blue" (28) and does not see "The rushing yellow
of the developing day [that] went on behind their backs" (27). Before
the march the men themselves are still but a part of this facade, being
referred to four times as only a "blue demonstration." And because isolation from the known breeds fear, the same linkage of blue and white
is used here that appears in the short story: Wilson tells Henry,
"'You're getting blue, my boy. You're looking thundering peaked'"
(32). But note what happens to both this fairly blue sky and this blue
uniform when Jim Conklin falls: "As the flap of the blue jacket fell
away from the body" it exposes Conklin's side, which "looked as if it
had been chewed by wolves" (115)—in other words a red and bloody
side. And then as a repetition on the cosmic level temporally of the
same exposure we have just observed spatially, Crane reveals a "red
sun" in what was a bright, blue sky. All nature is alike. This is its double essence—the red of violence within the blue of innocence. Innocence in the sense both of inexperience and of beguiling beauty. This
spatial relation of blue and red is even preserved in the movement of
the troops from their "eternal camp," where they are only a "blue demonstration." For as they prepare to move off toward the front "their uniforms glowed a deep purple" (25), and when they arrive in the battle
area "these battalions with their commotions were woven red and startling into the gentle fabric of softened greens and browns" (43).

As a further aspect of the miseducation which obscures from Henry
Fleming the fiery essence of his naturalistic universe, his religious education is also responsible. It too is a part of the "clogged clouds" and
the old sympathies, as revealed not only in the imagery depicting Jim
Conklin's death but also in the inferno imagery and in the imagery of
the primitive warrior-worshiper. In the ironic resemblances of Conklin
to Christ, Crane is perhaps naively, but clearly and powerfully, saying
that in this red world Jesus Christ is a grim joke. It is to this climactic
conclusion that Crane builds in this crucial chapter exactly as he built

up to the shattering revelation of the corpse in the trees. Only here it is the reader who gets the shock instead of Henry, for to have had Henry consciously perceive the resemblance would have been both too obvious and too implausible.

The resemblances are manifestly here however. Since Stallman has noted many of them, I would call attention only to the principal resemblance he's missed: when Jim Conklin falls, his "body seemed to bounce a little way from the earth" (114-15). Here, the point of this carefully and subtly prepared resemblance to Christ, with eight preceding hints, becomes clear. We know why, as Henry rushes to the fallen body, he discovers that "the teeth showed in a laugh" (115). It is because this death, which is all too real, makes of the other a palpable absurdity with its Ascension to the right hand of God. The only ascension here is a grotesque bounce "a little way from the earth." And when then the ultimate source and seal of this grimly naturalistic death appears in the sky in the shape—of all things—of a wafer, the irony is devastating and the significance no less: this *red* wafer symbolizes that there will be *no* miraculous transubstantiation from this mangled and meaningless corpse. Rather, it is a reminder of what we have seen of another corpse: the "red animal, war" and the ants will be the unholy communicants that devour this quite untransubstantiated and unrisen body which is left "laughing there in the grass" (118)—laughing at the appalling joke Henry Fleming's religious education has perpetrated upon him in its promise of eternal life.

What has confused some readers in this resemblance is that Crane does the same thing with his religious imagery here that he does in the short story, where Scully is at one moment God and Satan the next. Jim Conklin is *also* compared to the imps of hell in his "hideous hornpipe," his arms flailing about "in expression of implike enthusiasm" (114), and the "'God!'" that the tattered soldier exclaims upon the fall is starkly changed to "'Hell—'" (115). The significance of this apparent inconsistency is simply that all of heaven and hell man will ever know is here on earth, the product of his own efforts to obscure from himself the truth of his hostile nature in a hostile universe. And inferno imagery, like this line linking Jim to these imps, abounds throughout the text: "The black forms of men, passing to and fro before the crimson rays made weird and satanic effects" (31). They dodge "implike around the fires" (32). War, like life, is hell.

It is in the interesting sense in which Crane uses "enthusiasm" that the religious imagery becomes most revealing, for this enthusiasm is "the daring spirit of a savage religion mad" (251). Again it may be traced from the very beginning of the novel in the "enthusiast" (8) who rings the church bell with news of battle. In Henry too we see it on the march where for a moment "The thrill of his enthusiasm made him . . . fiery in his belief in success" (33-34). Finally, it is this religious enthusiasm of the pagan worshiper and warrior that defines the state of mind necessary for the performance of unselfish or heroic deeds:

> The men, pitching forward insanely, had burst into cheerings, moblike and barbaric. . . . It made a mad enthusiasm. . . . There was the delirium that encounters despair and death, and is heedless and blind to the odds. It is a temporary but sublime absence of selfishness. (209)

In a sense Crane seems to be saying that the Dionysiac fury of the pagan worshiper, who at least recognized his universe as hostile, was closer to a valid view of man and his universe than the Christian is with his humanistic veneer and false promise of eternal life. If the general, who gives us the central thematic statement of the novel—"t' go in—everlastingly—like blazes"—were to chant his paean, it would with more validity be addressed to the red sun than to the Heavenly Father.

This pattern is further revealing if we examine the source of this enthusiasm more closely. For it is in the flames of man's inner egotism, stirred up through wounded vanity to a pitch of hatred that is repeatedly described as "a dream" (191), a "delirium" (209), and a "state of frenzy" (251), precluding the consciousness necessary to will. As Crane tells us on the occasion of Henry's first experience of it, from which he awakes a knight or hero, "he lost sense of everything but his hate, his desire to smash into pulp the glittering smile of victory which he could feel upon the faces of his enemies" (191). And it is not only his enemies: "his greater hatred was riveted upon the man, who, not knowing him, had called him a mule driver" (220). The friendly jeers of the veterans produce the same reaction, the praise of the lieutenant an infantile swelling of the same vanity. Before the final charge of the enemy it is again the recollection of being called mud diggers that determines the men to hold and again "some arrows of scorn" (246) that generate "the strange and unspeakable hatred" in Henry, who desires nothing so much as "retaliation upon the officer who had said 'mule drivers' and later 'mud diggers'" (246). To see in this childish hatred with its subsequent "enthusiasm of unselfishness" (250) a "decided growth in moral behavior" is a misreading quite as mistaken as a Christian redemption. Both interpretations miss the point of the paradox Crane *labors* throughout the latter half of the book: that the selfless behavior of heroism paradoxically emerges only from the grossest, most infantile, animalistic, fiery hatred born of the vanity of egocentrism. Though in his non-conscious "enthusiasm" he may be temporarily a man (see 227), it is only after Henry Fleming's "eyes seemed to open to some new ways" (265) that he feels "a quiet manhood" (266). Awareness—the ability to perceive truthfully the nature of this symbolically revealed, hostile universe—alone confers this new quiet, this new dignity.

From *Modern Fiction Studies* 5, no. 3 (1959): 209-219. Copyright © 1959 by Purdue Research Foundation. Reprinted with permission of the Johns Hopkins University Press.

Notes

1. John E. Hart, "*The Red Badge of Courage* as Myth and Symbol," *University of Kansas City Review*, XIX (Summer 1953), 249-257. The value of Mr. Hart's analysis is limited by his purpose, which is to compare Henry Fleming to the mythic hero, thus reflecting more the anthropological interests of 20th century criticism than the naturalism of late 19th century fiction.

2. Bernard Weisbarger, "*The Red Badge of Courage*," *Twelve Original Essays on Great American Novels*, ed. by Charles Shapiro (Detroit, 1958), pp. 104-105.

3. Stanley B. Greenfield, "The Unmistakable Stephen Crane," *PMLA*, LXXIII (December 1958), 572.

4. *Ibid.*, 569.

5. R. W. Stallman, *Stephen Crane: An Omnibus* (New York, 1952), p. 292.

6. *Ibid.*, xlv.

7. Edward Stone, "The Many Suns of *The Red Badge* of *Courage*," *American Literature*, XXIX (November 1957), 322-326.

8. Italics mine. All text references are to the Modern Library edition.

Insensibility in *The Red Badge of Courage*_____
William B. Dillingham

When Henry Fleming, the youth of Stephen Crane's *The Red Badge of Courage*, charges ahead of his comrades and fearlessly carries his flag into the very jaws of death, he seems to be a romantic hero rather than the protagonist of a naturalistic novel. But for Crane appearance was seldom reality. Bearing the symbol of his country's cause, Henry is unquestionably courageous, but the underlying causes of his deeds are neither noble nor humane. Throughout his life Crane deeply respected heroic action. His attitude was, as Daniel G. Hoffman has said, that it was "among the very few means man has of achieving magnificence";[1] nevertheless, he considered courage the product of a complex of non-rational drives. The difference between the external act of courage and the internal process that leads up to that act created for Crane one of the supreme ironies of life.

The Red Badge has frequently been read as the story of how a young soldier achieves some sort of spiritual salvation. One critic sees Henry Fleming's "growth toward moral maturity";[2] another, his "redemption" through "humility and loving-kindness."[3] His initiation has been called the successful search for "spiritual and psychological order," the discovery of a "vision of pattern."[4] Some readings emphasize Henry's new sense of brotherhood and call the book the story of a young man's developing awareness of social responsibility.[5] Such views as these offer more insight than may be indicated by a brief quotation and comment, but they also tend to obscure the central irony of the novel, that of the nature of courage, by making Henry Fleming as distinctive and as individually interesting a character as, say, Raskolnikov, Huckleberry Finn, or Isabel Archer. The young soldier whom Crane seldom calls by name is, as Alfred Kazin has suggested, Everyman—or at least every man who has the potentiality for courage.[6] The chief purpose of the novel is to objectify the nature of heroism through Henry Fleming. Through witnessing his actions and changing sensations we discover the emerging paradox of courage: human courage is by its nature sub-human; in order to be courageous, a man in time of physical strife must abandon the highest of his human facilities, reason and imagination, and act instinctively, even animalistically.[7]

In developing and illustrating this paradoxical definition of courage, Crane used a simple structural arrangement. The novel is divided into two parts of twelve chapters each. The first twelve chapters tell of Henry Fleming's early insecurities about himself; his first battle, where he fights and then runs; his various adventures during his retreat; and finally his encounter with the fleeing soldier and then his wound. Chapter 13 begins with Henry's coming back to his own camp to begin anew, and the remainder of the book takes the reader through the battles of the next day, in which Henry fights with great courage.

The first part of the book deals with the anatomy of cowardice, which is in Henry the result of an active imagination and a disposition to think too much. Until he receives the head wound in Chapter 12, he is characterized by a romantic and thoughtful self-consciousness. In his anxiety about how he will conduct himself in combat, he speculates constantly about himself and the nature of battle: "He tried to mathematically prove to himself that he would not run from a battle" (p. 30).[8] Trying to comfort himself through reason, he makes "ceaseless calculations" for days. Finally he has to admit that "he could not sit still and with a mental slate and pencil derive an answer" (p. 35). Henry's "own eternal debate" is frequently interrupted by the terrifying images of his imagination. In the darkness he sees "visions of a thousand-tongued fear that would babble at his back and cause him to flee" (p. 44). This constant activity of Henry's reason and imagination compels him to feel isolated until he experiences a vague sense of unity with his fellows during the first battle. Here he becomes suddenly caught up in the fight almost by accident. In contrast to his insensibility in later battles, "he strenuously tried to think," but he is luckily carried along by the momentary excitement of his comrades. The first encounter with the enemy is very brief, and his courage is not seriously tested. In the second engagement, his imagination is rampant: "He began to exaggerate the endurance, the skill, and the valour of those who were coming" (p. 73). He imagines the enemy as dragons and sees himself as being "gobbled." No longer feeling enclosed in the "moving box" of his first encounter and now stimulated by wild imaginings, Henry runs in terror from the battle.

In "The Veteran," a short story written as a sequel to *The Red Badge*, Henry, now an old man, reminisces about his war experience and tells how his imagination and his reliance on reason compelled him to run: "The trouble was . . . I thought they were all shooting at me. Yes, sir, I thought every man in the other army was aiming at me in particular, and only me. And it seemed so darned unreasonable, you know. I wanted to explain to 'em what an almighty good fellow I was, because I thought then they might quit all trying to hit me."[9]

After his retreat, he wanders behind the lines, still relying upon his reason and imagination, attempting to convince himself that he is the reasonable man, "the enlightened man," who "had fled because of his superior perceptions and knowledge" (p. 81). When he comes upon the group of wounded men, he is still debating his case. He then witnesses the death of his friend Jim Conklin. But even at this point he shows no significant change.[10] Shortly thereafter, his imagination still controls him as he magnifies "the dangers and horrors of the engagement" from which he fled (p. 104). Until he is wounded in Chapter 12, he is still rationalizing, still trying mathematically to prove to himself that his cowardice was "in truth a symmetrical act" (p. 104).

The episode in which Henry is struck by a retreating Union soldier occurs at the center of the novel both physically and thematically. The incident has frequently been called the ironic peak of the story. A Union soldier, not the enemy, gives Henry his wound, and unlike his comrades he is wounded with the butt of a gun, not with a bullet. Upon this highly ironic "red badge" Henry builds his courage. In addition to its function as irony, the wound serves as the chief symbol of the book. Significantly, the wound is inflicted on the *head*. Almost from the moment he is struck, Henry starts to set aside his fearful and potent imagination and his reason. Symbolically, the head wound is the damage the experience of war gives to these highest human faculties. The chaos of war teaches the necessity of insensibility. After the symbolic wound, Henry finds his way back to his regiment, and the last half of the book portrays a youth initiated into the ways of courage. From here on, Henry runs from himself; he escapes his essential humanity in order to avoid running in battle.

Henry's inner voices and visions, then, are obliterated by the head wound. Through one half of the story, his mind has been tried and found wanting. Henry's wound forces his attention to his physical being. The only voices now heard are those of the body. After he returns to camp, "he made vague plans to go off into the deeper darkness and hide, but they were all destroyed by the voices of exhaustion and pain from his body" (p. 120). When he awakes, "it seemed to him that he had been asleep for a thousand years, and he felt sure that he opened his eyes upon an unexpected world" (p. 127). The Henry Fleming who before looked into the future, saw imagined horrors, and speculated constantly about himself, now thinks little of the future: "He did not give a good deal of thought to these battles that lay directly before him. It was not essential that he should plan his ways in regard to them" (p. 136). He has become instinctively aware of a truth taught by intense experience, that man can and must cultivate a dullness which will serve as armor against the stings of fear and panic. The totality of Henry's war experience thus far has helped to show him that "retribution was a laggard and blind."

In contrast to the thoughtful and romantic boy of the first part of the book, the young warrior of the last twelve chapters is capable of unreason, even self-abandon. At the first sight of the enemy, he "forgot many personal matters and became greatly enraged" (p. 141). He becomes a prideful animal, seeking the throat of the enemy with self-forgetfulness. The feelings of the imaginative young soldier, who once thought of war as a glorious Greek-like struggle, now are constantly described in terms of bestiality, unreason, and even insanity. He "lost sense of everything but his hate" (p. 148). Suspending all thought, he fights as a "barbarian, a beast . . . a pagan" (p. 150). His actions are frequently described as "wild." He is "unconsciously" out in front of the other troops, looking "to be an insane soldier." "There was the delirium that encounters despair and death, and is heedless and blind to the odds. It is a temporary but sublime absence of selfishness" (p. 160). The selflessness implied here is not self-sacrifice but insensibility, which enables Henry to escape thoughts and suspend imagination, to get outside of himself while the emotions of rage and hatred control his actions. As he cultivates personal insensibility his mental position as an observer becomes more and more pronounced: "He was deeply absorbed as a spectator; . . . he did not know that he breathed" (pp. 184-5). Henry's self-abandon spreads to the others, who were "again grown suddenly wild with an enthusiasm of unselfishness" (p. 189). Henry is no longer aware of the personal element in the danger that he faces. Now he does not think of the enemy as attempting to kill him personally. He looks upon their bullets vaguely as "things that could prevent him from reaching the place of his endeavour" (p. 189). So separated from meditation and imagination is Henry that he finds it difficult after the battle to become himself again: "It took moments for it [his mind] to cast off its battleful ways and resume its accustomed course of thought. Gradually his brain emerged from the clogged clouds, and at last he was enabled to more closely comprehend himself and circumstances" (pp. 196-7).

Henry's change is thus the result of intensely dangerous experience which reveals to him intuitively the impersonal nature of the forces that defeat men. After glimpsing the powers of "strange, squalling upheavals" he is able to control his fear. This ability comes to men not through intellectual or spiritual processes but through habit in being exposed to violence. As Henry becomes more accustomed to battle and the sight of death, he no longer thinks about the implication of these overwhelming experiences. He sinks into a subhuman dullness and is thereby able to act courageously. He does not learn to know himself, as one critic asserts,[11] but to escape himself—to make his mind blank, to become a "spectator."

Otherwise, Henry remains essentially unchanged during the course of the novel. It is a mistake to think of him as having become rejuvenated through humility or in any way changed into a better person morally. He has simply adapted himself through experience to a new and dangerous environment.[12] When the last battle is over, he is the same prideful youth, bragging on himself as he reviews his deeds of valor. The Christian references, which have so frequently been a subject of controversy, do not point to "rebirth" or "salvation" for Henry. The pattern of religious imagery built up through the use of such words as "sacrifice," "hymn," and "cathedral" is part of the pervasive irony of the book.[13] Just as Henry is not "selfless" in the usual sense of the word, neither is he "saved" in the Christian sense. It is his body that is saved, not his soul. He is trained by war to realize, in contradiction of Christian ideals, that he must desert the mind and spirit and allow his physical being—even his animal self—to dominate. Through Henry, Crane is saying with St. Matthew that whosoever will lose his life will find it. But the Christian paradox is in direct opposition to Crane's. Henry finds and retains his physical life by losing that sensibility characteristic of the highest forms of life.

The evidence for a "naturalistic" interpretation of *The Red Badge is* overwhelming.[14] Creating, chiefly through irony, a considerable degree of aesthetic distance, Crane studies the change in the behavior of a soldier. Through half the book this character is a sensitive youth. But sensitivity is incompatible with physical courage and the ability to kill. In the center of the story occurs the symbolic head wound, which damages the youth's sensibility and causes him to rely more on the physical and instinctive, less on the mental. For the rest of the book, Henry is brave in battle, having arrived at that state of self-discipline which makes one in danger resemble more an animal than a man. An iconoclast, Crane enjoyed laughing as he destroyed the illusions of a former tradition. He does not rejoice that Henry has found courage; he does not change him into a better person. Nor does he mourn as did Wilfred Owen for the tenderness and the innocence that war destroys in those who must kill.[15] With a keen sense of the incongruity of things, he simply shows that courage has been misunderstood. In order to be a Greek (in a Greek-like struggle), one must be a barbarian.

From *College English* 25, no. 3 (1963): 194-198. Originally published by the National Council of Teachers of English.

Notes

1. Daniel G. Hoffman, *The Poetry of Stephen Crane* (New York, 1957), p. 150.

2. James B. Colvert, "Structure and Theme in Stephen Crane's Fiction," *Modern Fiction Studies*, 5 (Autumn 1959), 204.

3. Robert Wooster Stallman, introduction to *The Red Badge of Courage*, Modern Library (New York, 1951), p. xxxii.

4. Earle Labor, "Crane and Hemingway: Anatomy of Trauma," *Renascence*, 11 (Summer 1959), 195.

5. John E. Hart, "*The Red Badge of Courage* as Myth and Symbol," *University of Kansas City Review*, 19 (Summer 1953), 249-56. See also M. Solomon, "Stephen Crane: A Critical Study," *Mainstream*, 9 (January 1956), 25-42.

6. Alfred Kazin, *On Native Grounds* (New York, 1956), p. 50.

7. Although the focus of his article is somewhat different from the present discussion, James Trammell Cox also states this central paradox of *The Red Badge*: ". . . the selfless behavior of heroism paradoxically emerges only from the grossest, most infantile, animalistic, fiery hatred born of the vanity of egocentrism." "The Imagery of *The Red Badge of Courage*," *Modern Fiction Studies*, 5 (Autumn 1959), 219. Hoffman suggests the paradox in his treatment of Crane's indebtedness to Tolstoi: introduction to *The Red Badge of Courage and Other Stories* (New York, 1957), p. xii.

8. Page references are to *The Work of Stephen Crane*, ed. Wilson Follett (New York, 1925), I.

9. *Work*, I, 204.

10. For an opposite opinion, see Stallman, p. xxxiii.

11. Norman Friedman, "Criticism and the Novel," *Antioch Review*, 18 (Fall 1958), 356-61.

12. Crane never ceased to be interested in the molding influence of environment. His favorite situation shows man pitted against a new and quite different environment. In some cases, as in "The Blue Hotel" and "The Bride Comes to Yellow Sky," characters find it impossible to undergo the necessary change to survive and are either de-

stroyed or disillusioned. In *The Red Badge* as in "The Open Boat," however, the chief characters manage to adapt to the dangerous new environment and thus to survive.

13. Two critics have made similar statements about the Christian imagery of the book: Bernard Weisbarger, *"The Red Badge of Courage,"* in *Twelve Original Essays on Great American Novels*, ed. Charles Shapiro (Detroit, 1958), pp. 104-105; and Cox, pp. 217-18.

14. Several naturalistic interpretations are available. See, for example, Winifred Lynskey, "Crane's *The Red Badge of Courage," Explicator*, 8 (Dec. 1949), 3; Richard Chase, introduction to Riverside Edition *of The Red Badge* (Boston, 1960); and Charles Child Walcutt, *American Literary Naturalism, A Divided Stream* (Minneapolis, 1956).

15. Owen's poem "Insensibility" is, however, a remarkably similar statement of the definition of courage:

> Dullness best solves
> The tease and doubt of shelling,
> And Chance's strange arithmetic
> Comes simpler than the reckoning of their shilling.
> . . . .
> Happy are these who lose imagination:
> They have enough to carry with ammunition.
> . . . .
> Having seen all things red,
> Their eyes are rid
> Of the hurt of the colour of blood for ever.

Depersonalization and the Dream in *The Red Badge of Courage*_____

Robert M. Rechnitz

I

Studies of *The Red Badge of Courage* continue to question whether the intention of the novel's final paragraphs is literal or ironic. Most of the recent critics lean toward a literal interpretation and assert that Henry Fleming gains a measured and realistic understanding of himself and his world.[1] James B. Colvert's conclusion is representative: ". . . when he [Henry] sees them in spectator fashion . . . events in reality seem to fit into a comprehensible order."[2]

I believe that the possibility of Henry's gaining any such spectator-like objectivity is highly unlikely. In believing so, I am partially reverting to Charles C. Walcutt's judgment that the final four paragraphs of the novel

> are a climax of self-delusion. If there is any one point that has been made it is that Henry has never been able to evaluate his conduct. He may have been fearless for moments, but his motives were vain, selfish, ignorant, and childish. . . . He has . . . for moments risen above his limitations, but Crane seems plainly to be showing that he has not achieved a lasting wisdom or self-knowledge.[3]

Walcutt suggests that Henry's ultimate understanding is clouded because it is distorted by the subjective delusions which have infused his perceptions throughout the novel. I depart from Walcutt, and take the position that Henry, in the course of his experience, exchanges his subjective delusions for a socially derived and sanctioned vision, an alleged objectivity, which is as far removed from reality as was his abandoned private vision. In exchanging private delusion for public, Henry finds a home in the army, just as Jim Conklin had before him, but the price is exorbitant. Becoming the good soldier, he becomes less the individual being; and he emerges in the concluding paragraphs in serene possession of an unauthentic soldier-self, ominously ready to follow his leader.

The little autonomy he possesses at the beginning is immediately threatened. He had entered the army intent upon realizing youthful dreams of glory. These private delusions are soon replaced by the incommunicable anguish and fears which are a natural part of the lull before the battle. Alone in the "light yellow shade" of his hut, he wonders whether he will have guts enough to stand and fight when his time comes.[4] His imagination, which is nourishing this private fear, gains its matter not from Henry's own limited experience but from that of his society. The veterans have told him of the enemy, "gray, bewhiskered hordes . . . tremendous bodies of fierce soldiery who were sweeping along like the Huns." Though Henry does not "put a whole faith in veterans' tales," he does tend to give greater credence to their reports than to the witness of his own senses. The tales of the veterans follow and displace his own observation of the rebel picket who had called him a "'right dum good feller'" (p. 9).

This contest between individual and group perceptions, or, more precisely, between individual and social evaluation of personal perceptions, continues throughout the novel. Much of the action depicts Henry's attempts to honor his personal interpretations, but the final outcome is foreshadowed in this present episode. The authority of personal interpretation crumbles under the massive testimony of the group. Eventually, Henry cannot believe his eyes.

He is by no means mere victim in this process. Henry is tempted to surrender his interpretive faculties to the group upon discovering that his fears are abated when leagued with those of his comrades. After hearing Jim Conklin say that he might run if the others did, Henry "felt gratitude for these words of his comrade. He had feared that all of the untried men possessed a great and correct confidence. He now was in a measure reassured" (p. 12). Henry can thus choose to sink his individuality in group anonymity and diminish his fear by partaking of the group's strength.

Since such a maneuver, demanding a surrender of autonomy, simultaneously appeals to and repels him, Henry compromises; he maintains an ambivalence toward his group allegiance, wryly dubbing his outfit "the blue demonstration" (p. 8). This ambivalence, this desire to assert his individuality and the equally pressing need to abandon it, runs through not merely the opening chapters but the entire book. Yet in the world of *Red Badge*, there can be no doubt whatsoever about the outcome. Henry must surrender his individuality for the sake of simple survival.

He does so, however, begrudgingly, his ambivalence always in evidence. For example, Henry relies upon and damns his officers with monotonous regularity. One morning, in the ranks of his regiment ready at last to march into the unknown under the red eyes of the enemy troops across the river, Henry gazes into the east, and in his need for leadership he sees against the sun "black and patternlike . . . the gigantic figure of the colonel on a gigantic horse" (p. 14). *Patternlike* is the key word here, the presence of the officer obliterating Henry's fear and confusion. But *black* is equally important, carrying as it does the threat of annihilation of self. This probability is forgotten though, as "the rolling crashes of an engagement come to his ears," and the officer, displaying beneficent self-control, "lift[s] his gigantic arm and calmly stroke[s] his mustache" (p. 14).

The threat of lost individuality is also forgotten when the men finally move into combat and Henry yields himself totally to the saving embrace of the group:

> He became not a man but a member. He felt that something of which he was a part . . . was in a crisis. He was welded into a common personality which was dominated by a single desire. . . . [The noise of the regiment] gave him assurance. . . . It wheezed and banged with a mighty power. . . . There was a consciousness always of the presence of his comrades about him. He felt the subtle battle brotherhood more potent even than the cause for which they were fighting. It was a mysterious fraternity born of the smoke and danger of death. (p. 31)

Crane's description of the fearlessness his soldiers enjoy during this part of the battle is similar to an account of the loss of fear on the part of concentration-camp inmates given in Bruno Bettelheim's *Informed Heart*. Forced to stand in the cold without adequate clothing and any chance to help their dying friends, the prisoners confronted a "situation which obviously the prisoner as an individual could not meet successfully."

> Therefore, the individual as such had to disappear in the mass. Threats by the guards become ineffective because the mental attitude of most prisoners was now changed. Whereas before they had feared for themselves and tried to protect themselves as well as possible, they now became depersonalized. It was as if giving up individual existence and becoming part of a mass seemed in some way to offer better chances for survival, if not for the person, at least for the group.[5]

But just is the prisoners are unable to sustain their fearlessness and sense of power, so Henry soon feels his courage drain from him, and in the following exchange of fire he runs away. Henry's flight has been foreshadowed by more than his fearful anticipations before the battle. His perception of the officers as benign authorities who promise an end to chaos and the comfort he has derived from the ambience of the "blue demonstration" has been qualified by his growing suspicion that.the officers are idiots who send the men "marching into a regular pen" (p. 23). The "blue demonstration" threatens to rob him of his will; marching into battle he sees "that it would be impossible for him to escape from the regiment. It inclosed him. And there were iron laws of tradition and law on four sides. He was in a moving box" (p. 21).

Consequently, though motivated by fear, Henry's flight has implications of which Henry remains unaware but which suggest themselves to the reader because of the traditional nature of the flight itself. Like a great number of American literary figures—Huck, Rip, Goodman Brown, the *persona* of "Song of Myself," an endless list of others—

Henry abandons his society and lights out for the territories. One more romantic egoist, Henry resigns his membership in the society which would demand from him the relinquishment of his perfect freedom. Though he is most assuredly no student, he would seem to have imbibed his share of Transcendentalism from the very air of nineteenth-century America and would claim for himself Emerson's "infinitude of the private man."

But in the following moment, the reader is reminded that this is *Red Badge* and not Emerson's *Nature*. Henry enters the forest chapel and learns, most hideously, that the woods will no longer serve as nursery to the burgeoning soul:

> Near the threshold he stopped, horror-stricken at the sight of a thing.
>
> He was being looked at by a dead man who was seated with his back against a column-like tree. The corpse was dressed in a uniform that once had been blue, but was now faded into a melancholy shade of green. The eyes, staring at the youth, had changed to the dull hue to be seen on the side of a dead fish. The mouth was open. Its red had changed to an appalling yellow. (pp. 43-44)

This scene marks the impasse at which, one after the other, the romantic heroes of the last half of the nineteenth century find themselves. Buck discovers that the Mississippi flows inexorably into the heartland of slavery, and James's Isabel Archer, to name only one other, discovers that the highroad of unlimited choice terminates within the walls of the Palazzo Roccanera. Henry Fleming learns to his horror that nature culminates in the forest chapel.

Nature and morality, once fused by the transcendentalists, are now divided, and the division has wide-ranging consequences. First, nature itself becomes foreign and treacherous. The branches in the forest chapel threaten to push Henry onto the corpse. Second, the individualism that Henry is capable of imagining as a substitute for his life in the army is no longer Emersonian, no longer expansive and life-enhancing, but isolating, atomistic. Self-reliance, drained of moral content by the time Crane is writing, has degenerated to mere selfishness. Whitman's "man in the open air" has become only a corpse propped against a tree. The third consequence is societal and needs a further paragraph of amplification.

Made aware of his experience with the corpse of the inadequacy of his individualism, Henry tries to rejoin the army. Marching up the road in a crowd of soldiers, Henry "regarded the wounded soldiers in an envious way. He conceived persons with torn bodies to be peculiarly happy. He wished that he, too, had a wound, a red badge of courage" (p. 49). This image appears in the first paragraph of chapter 9 and is paired at the end of the chapter with a highly similar image, the notorious: "The red sun was pasted in the sky like a wafer" (p. 53). The referent of "wafer" must remain a puzzle, but perhaps it is of little importance. The crucial fact about the sentence is its reductive effect. The setting sun is reduced to a trivial, two-dimensional dot merely pasted in the sky. This reduction may be considered as a further consequence of the lost transcendental fusion of nature and morality. Associating the paired images suggests, and added consideration confirms, that the image at the first part of the chapter is also perhaps reductive. To think of a wound as a badge is, indeed, to trivialize human suffering. Furthermore, we may say that if the nature-morality split diminishes nature, the same split brutalizes society. Henry knows that it is in society's eyes that a wound is a badge of courage. Society, stripped of morality, then, is not community, but is brutal collectivity. Consequently, Henry's hungering for a wound signifies a desire to surrender personal morality to the demands of collectivization, a sacrifice which perhaps Crane sensed might be increasingly demanded of men in the twentieth century.

Henry, on the other hand, has no comprehension of the moral implications of the wound, but he is a witness to its physical import when he sees Jim Conklin die. Conklin has served from the novel's opening as a warning, apparent only in retrospect, against wholehearted identification with the group. Prior to their first battle, Conklin exhibits a blissful unconcern. This compliance with the dictates of the war machine marks him for destruction; and in the moments of his death, he remains in some hideous, indefinable way, a willing collaborator in the perverted mystic ceremony of war: "There was something ritelike in these movements of the doomed soldier. And there was a resemblance in him to a devotee of a mad religion, blood-sucking, muscle-wrenching, bone crushing" (p. 52). Like a "devotee of a mad religion," Conklin enacts the roles of both priest and sacrifice. The passive surrender of personal initiative in his early behavior culminates in a sort of self-destruction.

Having witnessed Conklin's death, Henry can no longer yearn for a red badge, that emblem of membership in the group, for he sees that the badge is deadly. He is forced in chapter 10 to take up the other alternative, which if not he then at least the reader already realizes is equally hopeless, his earlier atomistic individualism. In fact, so empty are the alternatives, that it is not until he is goaded into choosing by the mindless yammering of the zombie-like tattered soldier that Henry decides to run. But as the forest chapel scene demonstrated, individualism offers no adequate sanctuary, and in a short time Henry is led back to his regiment.

II

With Henry's return at the beginning of the second half of the novel, the dominant motif, that archetypal American movement of alternating escape and return, is several times repeated, even though there is no possibility of any genuine escape. The attempted escapes, however, are no longer physical; rather, they become a matter of allegiances and commitments. When Henry's individuality dominates, he curses the army. As the novel moves closer to its conclusion, he identifies increasingly with the army.

Quite understandably, Henry's initial loyalty upon returning is to the regiment. Wounded and exhausted, he sees in the figures of the sleeping men an image of content, and after having his wound dressed he sleeps among his comrades. But in chapter 14 he awakes: "He believed for an instant that he was in the house of the dead, and he did not dare to move lest these corpses start up, squalling and squawking" (p. 73). Only a moment passes before he realizes that "this somber picture was not a fact of the present, but a mere prophecy." The prophecy is accurate on two levels: first, of course, many of the men will be killed in the forthcoming skirmishes. But, second, the men are all doomed to die in a spiritual sense as they surrender themselves more and more to the demands of the army.

With same sort of recognition of this second meaning, Henry is unwilling to accept the officers' leadership. At the beginning of the new day's combat, furious at the evidence of the Union defeat, Henry cries out, "'B'jiminey, we're generaled by a lot 'a lunkheads.'" Wilson, however in terms reminiscent of Jim Conklin's, defends the commanding general: "'Mebbe, it wa'n't all his fault—not all together. He did th' best he knowed. It's out luck t' git licked often,' said his friend in a weary tone. He was trudging along with stooped shoulders and shifting eyes like a man who has been caned and kicked" (p. 81). Wilson may have the better of the argument, but he is a beaten man. The great cost of what we may call his collective vision is but partially revealed in this passage.

It is more fully revealed as further instances of the collective vision are disclosed. In the following action, "deeply absorbed as a spectator" (p. 109), Henry observed the battle:

The regiment bled extravagantly. Grunting bundles of blue began to drop. The orderly sergeant of the youth's company was shot through the cheeks. Its supports being injured, his jaw hung afar down, disclosing in the wide cavern of his mouth a pulsing mass of blood and teeth. And with it all he made attempts to cry out. In his endeavor there was a dreadful earnestness, as if he conceived that one great shriek would make him well. (p. 110)

Though the events being described here are horrible, the style drains them of emotional content. This is precisely the cost of the collective vision—affectlessness. Throughout the novel, Crane's famous irony insists upon the unspeakable lesson: as he continues to surrender his autonomy to the overwhelming pressure of collectivization, modern man will most likely lose even the capacity to feel.

Another characteristic of the collective view might be noted here. Possibly, it is not so "enlarging and ruthlessly revealing" as critic James Colvert says.[6] On their way to fill the canteens, Henry and Wilson have a chance for a collective view of the battle:

> From their position . . . they could of course comprehend a greater amount of the battle than when their visions had been blurred by the hurling smoke of the line. They could see dark stretches winding along the land, and on one cleared space there was a row of guns making gray clouds, which were filled with large flashes of orange-colored flame. Over some foliage they could see the roof of a house. One window, glowing a deep murder red, shone squarely through the leaves. From the edifice a tall leaning tower of smoke went far into the sky. (p. 89)

It is true that this view is enlarging, but only in spatial terms, and with such a view one is bound to feel insignificant. But it should be noted that it is in such passages that Crane's style is at its most impressionistic. Though the view is broad, it consists of no more than a bundle of discrete images, for neither Henry nor the narrator supplies the conceptual strands which would weave the images into a fabric of meaning. The passage even suggests that meaning might be impossible to achieve on any plane more profound than the purely aesthetic one, impressionism having, as Richard Chase points out, "implications that are pessimistic, irrationalist, and amoral since its technique is to break down into a shimmering flow of experience the three dimensions that symbolized rationality and religious and social order in traditional art."[7]

Finally, on the psychological level, it must be noted that these paragraphs of the collective mass view follow immediately upon a passage that demands distancing and impressionism if one is to retain his sanity. Jimmie Rogers has been wounded: "He was thrashing about in the grass, twisting his shuddering body into many strange postures. He was screaming loudly. This instant's hesitation seemed to fill him with a tremendous, fantastic contempt, and he damned them in shrieked sentences" (p. 89). And off Henry and Wilson go with the canteens. The collective view here, then, seems motivated not by any desire to see reality, but rather to escape it. Motivation need not wholly determine perception, but it certainly qualifies it as we know. At any rate, all the considerations I am discussing here combine to suggest that the collective view may serve not only to humble a man but to delude and diminish him.

More references to man's diminished stature follow. The officers are referred to as "critical shepherds struggling with sheep." The regiment itself is lost in the noise of battle, the battle, in turn, lost in a world "fully interested in other matters" (p. 92). These images serve as background for Henry's and Wilson's crucial withholding from the men their knowledge of the great dangers involved in the impending charge. As a consequence, the virtues implicit in that decision are undermined. Without doubt, their choice to remain silent has elements of selflessness, loyalty, and certainly valor. But the context of the decision suggests that they remain mute also because they are feeling the pressures of the collective vision and its attendant, self-diminishing impressionism.

In the climactic battle of the book, Henry yields to those pressures. Charging across the field "like a madman," Henry undergoes the change he had yearned for before the battle. Unprotected and essentially alone, thirsting for help and protection, he finds it in the flag, "a creation of beauty and invulnerability . . . a goddess, radiant . . . that called him with the voice of his hopes. Because no harm could come to it he endowed it with power" (pp. 96-97). Unable to protect himself, Henry again chooses to submerge himself in the group; but this time he does so wholeheartedly, abandoning that remnant of individuality that had insisted earlier upon a wry aloofness from the group, derisively dubbing it the "blue demonstration." With the identification he makes now, Henry finds the strength to conduct himself nobly in battle, but there can be no mistake about the price he has unwittingly paid. The flag he carries, the emblem of group allegiance, does not belong to living men. The corpse from whom they wrest it tries to warn Henry and Wilson that to serve the flag is to die, but the warning is of no avail. "One arm [of the corpse] swung high, and the curved hand fell with heavy protest on the friend's unheeding shoulder" (p. 97).

In the final chapters, the ultimate consequences of Henry's unqualified identification with the group unfold. This is accomplished primarily by a continued alternation of two points of view, the private and the collective, until Henry wholly surrenders his belief in the validity of his own perceptions and memories.

Having driven off the light contingent of rebels, the regiment, at the end of chapter 20, regains the "impetus of enthusiasm" (p. 102). But when they return to their line and the mockery of the veterans, they quickly lose it. Henry looks back at the ground they have just covered:

> He discovered that the distances, as compared with the brilliant measurings of his mind, were trivial and ridiculous. The stolid trees, where much had taken place, seemed incredibly near. The time, too, now that he reflected, he saw to have been short. . . . Elfin thoughts must have exaggerated and enlarged everything, he said.
>
> It seemed, then, that there was bitter justice in the speeches of the gaunt and bronzed veterans. (p. 103)

Now the point is not that here, regarding his actions in spectator fashion, he is right and earlier wrong, for actually both impressions are correct. At the time of the battle, Henry's perception was accurate, the way was long and hard; in denying this, in accepting the point of view of the veterans, Henry betrays himself and his fellows. The glance of disdain he gives them is, however, not simply unjust. It is a tacit denial of the testimony of his own senses. Having made this, Henry is all the more vulnerable to the opinion of the general that the men are nothing but "a lot of mud diggers" (p. 104). Of course the men all rage at this unjust treatment. Their personal perceptions are still weighty enough to prevent their utter abasement by the opinion of the officer. But Crane is extremely shrewd at this point. If the men are able to maintain their personal points of view in the face of the officers' condemnations, they are not able to hold out against their praise. Told that the colonel said they deserve to be "major generals," Henry and Wilson are elated, "and their hearts swelled with grateful affection for the colonel and the youthful lieutenant" (p. 107). Given what Crane has told us about the psychology of the battlefield, we question whether the officers' praise has any meaning. But the real importance of the chapter lies in its revelation of the degree to which Henry's opinion of himself is becoming increasingly determined by the official version of his behavior.

Therefore, after the following victory and subsequent retreat (the logic of the battlefield remaining absurd to the end) when Henry remembers his behavior, his reflections are not easily acceptable as reliable judgment of his past:

> he began to study his deeds, his failures, and his achievements. Thus, fresh from scenes where many of his usual machines of reflection had been idle, from where he had proceeded sheeplike, he struggled to marshal all his acts.
>
> At last they marched before him clearly. From this present viewpoint he was enabled to look upon them in spectator fashion and to criticize them with some correctness, for his new condition had already defeated certain sympathies. (p. 117)

By now there can be little doubt in our minds that viewing events in "spectator fashion" offers no assurance of discovering the truth. The spectator's way is the collective way, the way of the officers, remote, impressionistic, inhumanly dispassionate. Contrary to his opinion, Henry has not been "good," a moral term which has questionable validity as applied to men in the chaos of combat. And in a moment, his self-congratulations congeal as, in a "wretched chill of sweat," he recalls his desertion of the tattered soldier. "A specter of reproach came to him. There loomed the dogging memory of the tattered soldier—he who, gored by bullets and faint for blood, had fretted concerning an imagined wound in another; he who had loaned his last of strength and intellect for the tall soldier; he who, blind with weariness and pain, had been deserted in the field" (p. 117).

But this recollection, too, is inaccurate. It is true that Henry deserted him, and it is perhaps true that this was indeed profoundly criminal; but in being inaccurate, in constructing as he does here a sentimentalized version of the tattered soldier, a version replete with the sentimental cadences of the fundamentalist pulpit, he is being criminal again. He left the tattered soldier because of a complex of reasons and circumstances, which we can sum up by saying that he was being forced to take up the red badge of the mass man but chose at that desperate moment the alternative of atomistic individualism.

Perhaps the choice was wrong. It certainly served as no viable alternative. But in not adequately comprehending in this last chapter the stakes and circumstances that were then involved, and in "maturely" forgiving himself a little for that "sin"—without fully understanding its real nature—Henry runs a great risk of slipping ever more deeply into the role of mindless foot soldier. And we must consequently shudder when Henry, marching along with his fellows, knows "that he would no more quail before his guides wherever they should point" (p. 118). For we end almost where we began: to escape his fear of isolation, Henry will lose himself, not in the wryly dubbed "blue demonstration," but in something far more insidious, the "procession of weary soldiers" of the novel's final page.

III

Given the reading I have offered, it is impossible to take the final four paragraphs as either intentionally straightforward or ironic in tone. My insistence upon the wholly unambiguous implications of Henry's final commitment to his regiment nullifies the possibility of a straightforward reading and renders the irony so painfully obvious as to make of Crane a hopelessly inept artist. That being emphatically not the case, I conclude with Richard Chase that these paragraphs reflect Crane's embarrassment "about the necessity of pointing a moral."[8]

Yet, I would go further and suggest the possibility that Crane was a victim of more than just the demands of the reading public of his time. In including these final paragraphs, Crane is being strongly prompted to refuse to acknowledge the logic of his own art by a cultural force. In spite of the corpse in the forest chapel, the death of Emersonian self-reliance it symbolizes, Crane is compelled to insist upon his anti-institutional legacy, the anarchic dream of Emerson and Thoreau. Henry again escapes, if only in thought, to roam fields of clover and fresh meadows.

Crane insists in these last paragraphs upon Emersonian individualism, upon the impossible American dream of escape from history. Though it tear art works apart, as it does the last of this one, as it does the final fifth of *Huckleberry Finn*, and though it sink the nation, as it does the *Pequod*, the dream persists, measuring our institutions and, no less important, our lives. Having dramatized the forces in modern America which were increasingly demanding the subservience of human needs to those of the machine, Crane insists at the final moment—unconvincingly—that man might escape his self-imposed servitude. By doing so, Crane in effect redefines the dream, showing in the vastly limited possibility of its realization how precious is its vision of Emersonian individualism.

Red Badge, then, takes its place with those other works in our literature that constitute an evolving definition of that complex, protean American Dream of anarchic freedom. Wildly extravagant, certainly no proper goal if we are to survive as a free society, that dream must yet be cherished, indeed now more than in the past, as the profoundly valuable counterweight to the increasingly urgent search for community that is properly bound to occupy Americans in the decades to come.

Notes

1. See, for example, any of the following: Stanley B. Greenfield, "The Unmistakable Stephen Crane," *PMLA*, 73 (Dec. 1958), 562-72; John E. Hart, "*The Red Badge of Courage* as Myth and Symbol," *University of Kansas City Review*, 19 (Summer 1953), 249-56; Maynard Solomon, "Stephen Crane: A Critical Study," *Masses and Mainstream*, 9 (Jan. 1955), 32-41; and, of course, R. W. Stallman, Introduction to the Modern Library edition of *The Red Badge of Courage*. Other straightforward readings are to be found in the excellent Norton critical edition of *Red Badge*, eds., Sculley Bradley, R. C. Beatty, and E. H. Long, for example, the essays by Eric Solomon and Edward Stone. For two more recent straightforward readings see John Fraser, "Crime and Forgiveness: The Red Badge in Time of War," *Criticism*, 9 (Summer 1967), 243-56; and John J. McDermott, "Symbolism and Psychological Realism in *The Red Badge of Courage*," *Nineteenth-Century Fiction*, 23 (Dec. 1968), 324-31.

2. James B. Colvert, "Structure and Theme in Stephen Crane's Fiction," *Modern Fiction Studies*, 5 (Autumn 1959), 207.

3. Charles Child Walcutt, *American Literary Naturalism, A Divided Stream* (Minneapolis: Univ. of Minnesota Press, 1956), pp. 81-82.

4. Stephen Crane, *The Red Badge of Courage*, ed. Richard Chase (Boston: Houghton Mifflin, 1960, Riverside Editions), p. 4. Subsequent references to this edition will appear in my text.

5. Bruno Bettelheim, *The Informed Heart* (Glencoe: The Free Press, 1960), p. 137.

6. Colvert, p. 200.

7. Richard Chase, Introduction to *The Red Badge of Courage* (Boston: Houghton Mifflin, 1960), p. xii.

8. Ibid., p. xiii.

Violence as Ritual and Apocalypse_____

Harold Kaplan

The naturalist obsession with violence can, when conditioned by an imaginative sensibility and raised to the level of revelation—emerge in the form of ritual observations and ceremonial drama. Stephen Crane had that kind of sensibility, tightening what is loose allegory in Norris, and in *The Red Badge of Courage* he developed a poetry of violence that singles that book out in the mainstream of naturalist fiction.

Crane did not need to know the Civil War personally because he knew it so well imaginatively; all that he needed were the naturalist myths that fed his imagination. His book is powerful, standing out above the works of Norris, London, and even Dreiser, not because it documents the life of camp and battle but because it is highly focused on primitive mysteries in battle and death. Crane is clearly attempting to give a religious coloring to these revelations. Nature contains a god, and his service is sacrifice and death. War is nature's stormy Mount Sinai, "war, the red animal—war, the blood-swollen god" (RB 23).[1] All that nature contains of great force, pain, death, extreme physical effort, and ultimate physical collapse are given their high ground of revelation in war. It is there that these naturalist truths meet and converge on a metaphysical level. And when Henry Fleming is most absorbed by the battle, he knows war in this way: "He himself felt the daring spirit of a savage, religion—mad. He was capable of profound sacrifices, a tremendous death" (RB 103).

But since Henry is entirely oblivious of the political or moral justifications of this war, his battle crisis reveals only the cosmic processes of survival and death. Here can be found naturalism's nearest approach to religious transcendence, and it occurs at the boundaries of biological fate. And this is the essence of naturalist heroism: to approach the mystery of nature depends on the will to confront its most savage truth, sacrificing a mundane safety. Crane mentions "profound sacrifices," but it is clear that these sacrifices have no specific moral purpose. The value is metaphysical and personal, and the antagonist is not a human being but natural violence and death.

Violence possesses awesome meaning here because it opens toward death. The major confrontation with naturalist mystery is not in battle itself, for it comes to Henry Fleming when he is running away from battle. The scene is described in explicitly religious terms:

> he reached a place where the high, arching boughs made a chapel. He softly pushed the green doors aside and entered. Pine needles were a gentle brown carpet. There was a religious half light.
>
> Near the threshold he stopped, horror-stricken at the sight of a thing. [RB 41]

The "thing" is a dead man, seated with his back against a tree, and the chapel containing that thing expresses the lucid power of Crane's imagination. Crane of course complicates the religious references with the irony that is characteristic of all his writing, but here the irony is complex, not obviously reductive. Nothing of the shock of physical death is withheld; the eyes of the dead man have "the dull hue to be seen on the side of a dead fish," and

> Over the gray skin of the face ran little ants. One was trundling some sort of bundle along the upper lip. [RB 41]

In the midst of all this horror, "The dead man and the living man exchanged a long look." Then the scene draws softly to a close, as if it had brought spiritual comfort:

> The trees about the portals of the chapel moved soughingly in a soft wind. A sad silence was upon the little guarding edifice. [RB 42]

A fuller initiation into the mystery of death takes place later, in the prolonged agony of Henry's friend, Jim Conklin. As he walks beside

Henry in the parade of the wounded, Jim is dying on his feet, staring into the unknown: "he seemed always looking for a place, like one who goes to choose a grave" (RB 47), and, already spectral in his look, he says, "don't tech me—leave me be" (RB 49). The dying man is preparing himself: "there was something ritelike in these movements of the doomed soldier" (RB 49). When the place and the moment are finally reached, there is an effect of ennoblement and transfiguration: "He was at the rendezvous . . . there was a curious and profound dignity in the firm lines of his awful face" (RB 49, 50).

The dignity might reflect natural process: Conklin's last moment is like the falling of a tree, "a slight rending sound." But, with his mouth open, "the teeth showed in a laugh" (RB 50). The laugh dismisses a sentimental primitivism, and Conklin, when he falls, reveals the side of his body, which looks "as if it had been chewed by wolves." Fleming at this moment shakes his fist at the battlefield, getting out only one word, "Hell——." Following this is a line that has stirred debate among various critics as to its serious or ironic implication: "The red sun was pasted in the sky like a wafer."[2] Given the context, it would seem absurd to miss the irony of this reference to Christlike dying and to the Communion. Still, if Crane is here employing his characteristic irony, he is at the same time confirming the universal ritual modes for confronting the experience of death.

The allusion to Christ emphasizes the vulnerability of the religious imagination, a pathos that is frequent in naturalist writing. Here irony and pathos come together in the seeming laugh of the dying man, enforcing his stoic dignity. He dies as a tree falls, and he has chosen his place to die after walking for a long time with a horrible wound in his side. There is not only a natural mystery here but a moral lesson. Conklin himself has no doubt transcended the motivation of pride in his personal bearing, but Fleming seems to have learned something from it, and this is related to the ostensible theme of Crane's book, the "red badge" of an initiation into courage. Just as the mystery religions of nature reached their deepest revelations in death, so here a specifically naturalist ethic is death-oriented. Almost immediately after Conklin's death, which might have confirmed him more than ever in his desire to run away, Henry begins to envision, instead, a return to his comrades, among whom, restored to self-respect by leading a charge in battle, he sees himself "getting calmly killed before the eyes of all. . . . He thought of the magnificent pathos of his dead body" (RB 55).

The awe and fierce dignity of Conklin's death confirmed that "magnificent pathos." It is a death-pathos now linked to the spirit of "a savage religion" requiring "profound sacrifices." The forest chapel of death, where ants trailed over the dead soldier's lips, affirmed the harsh terms of a soldier's religion, and further, and conclusive, emphasis is placed on Henry's redemptive initiation in battle: "He had been to touch the great death, and found that, after all, it was but the great death. He was a man" (RB 109). The values of this manhood are vitalist, and Crane views their implications with detachment: "He had been where there was red of blood, and black of passion, and he was escaped. . . . He saw that he was good" (RB 107). Did the "good" reside in Henry's escape or in his authentication by blood and passion? At that margin of experience it is not possible to distinguish between survival and authenticity, or self-realization.

Critics have argued about this conclusion of Crane's story. Some have accepted Fleming's apotheosis in courage, while others continue to challenge the notion that Crane was seriously attempting to define a code of virile honor. I doubt, myself, that Crane was capable of writing a line describing subjective human commitments without leaving the door open for implicit irony. He was that kind of naturalist—indeed, in his uncorrupted detachment he resembles Flaubert or Joyce—and it is from that perspective, with a lucidity that is almost inevitably ironic, that he viewed the male-oriented vitalism of hunting, fighting, and survival. In this he presents a precise contrast with Adams's cult of the Virgin. Yet it might seem that, moved by the same intellectual needs as Adams, Crane was led to a parallel sexual vitalism but one almost inevitably "machoist" in tendency (later to be elaborated in the works of Hemingway and Norman Mailer).

The naturalist ethic in which the red of blood and the black of passion are the banner of manhood and lead the way to the "good" finds easy reinforcement in the group. The battle ordeal and the natural laws of pain and death set the conditions for the "subtle battle brotherhood" of the men who fight together. In the end, after both loss and victory, the regiment has become "a mysterious fraternity born of the smoke and danger of death" (RB 31). The brotherhood of soldiers expresses the force of the vitalist cult as it might be applied to nations, races, and classes. These are collectivities committed to historic conflict and survival. Promoting the ethic of conflict, they learn to translate danger into fraternity; perhaps they even invite violence in order to learn fraternity.[3]

In Crane's completely clear view of this theme, the only suffering that exceeds physical suffering, and could make the latter welcome, is that of the moral outcast. Similarly, the only emotion that can compete with fear is shame. After Henry Fleming has run from battle, his fear lessens and he is gradually possessed by the self-ostracism of the moral refugee. As he walks among the wounded, he encounters the "tattered man," and the latter's desire to compare wounds probes into his cowardice. "The simple questions of the tattered man had been knife thrusts to him. They asserted a society" (RB 53). What Henry needs now is a wound of his own, and he longs for it, his "red badge of courage." The blow he receives from another fleeing soldier gives him what he wants, and he is able to return to his regiment. The wound is unworthy, but the link between its sign and his self-respect has been emphasized. Now he has the chance to redeem himself in another battle, and he does.

The power of emulation thus matches the power of pain and death. It is perhaps this equation in naturalist thought that is the key to some of its deepest political implications. Nature's force and process are absorbed and dominated by the social process, but this in turn is ruled by natural law. In an army the reasons for valuing courage and the ability to endure pain and face death are obvious. Nevertheless, Crane's descriptions of the army as a social unit and a moral force establish it as something much greater than an instrument for winning wars. His imagery is, as usual, concise and telling: "It [the regiment] inclosed him. And there were iron laws of tradition and law on four sides. He was in a moving box" (RB 21). The army as a thing, a box, alternates with images of the army as a serpent, a dragon, a monster. The interesting question is how this imagery supports rather than undercuts the army's function as a disciplined moral instrument, capable of collective judgment: "The regiment was like a firework" (RB 31), Crane writes, a thing ready to explode with its force. The point is actually to eliminate a traditional concept of judgment. This collectivity, enforcing behavior, is viewed as power in itself in its ability to evoke emulation, fear, shame, and pride.

The "naturalness" of this power is emphasized by the clarity with which Crane saw that to bring up the cause for fighting would have no relevance. There is no war here in the ordinary political and geographic sense. There are two armies, but they are distinguished only by the color of their uniforms. And the generals, who think they have control over the battle, actually do not. They send only inconsistent and incomprehensible orders, and they preside over actual confusion; for, whether running away or running forward, "the running men . . . were all deaf and blind" (RB 28).

Accordingly, when the group power of the army is not a prisonlike enclosure of tradition and law, it becomes simply a "floodlike force." Either way, the species dominates, absorbs, and transcends individual instincts and all personal interests, including survival itself. The group is not led but driven, both from within and from without; it either compulsively obeys tradition or anarchically surrenders to chaos. The army as a mob is as definite a force as the army under discipline. Nothing really distinguishes this society from simple organic or mechanical force except the spirit of emulation. If the approach of battle reveals to Henry that "he knew nothing of himself" and that "he was an unknown quantity" (RB 11), it also reveals that there is not much to know beyond the realities of fear and courage, strength and weakness. For the rest, "he continually tried to measure himself by his comrades" (RB 14); it was their good opinion he wanted. Henry's mind is at times filled with conventional battle romanticism, with notions of breathless deeds observed by "heavy crowns and high castles," but this traditional idealization of war is treated as a thin layer of childlike fantasy superimposed on more basic forces: the "moving box" of the army and the "throat-grappling" instinct for battle.

Still, as I have noted, these more basic forces are themselves the source of idealizations, of purely naturalist values. One is the vitalist virtue of proven manhood, of macho courage. Another is Henry's feeling of sublimity in the presence of "tremendous death" or in "the magnificent pathos of his [own] dead body" (RB 55). This might be called the moral code of Thanatos, calling for "an enthusiasm of unselfishness," "a sublime recklessness . . . shattered against the iron gates of the impossible" (RB 103). The highest virtue learned in naturalist conflict thus seems to be self-immolation. Behind war, "the blood-swollen god," stands death, a greater god, and the question that needs review is the extent to which the naturalist myth finds itself in service to the gods of *greatest* strength. The death pathos has no rival in its power to stir human emotions; recognizing this, Crane went further than most naturalist writers in appreciating the primitive compulsions of attraction and dread that death exerts.

Let us then trace the clear outline of Crane's naturalist values. Primordial violence, "the red animal," releases the most elemental and unsocialized passions and instincts. But since in Crane's work this occurs in the context of opposed armies, it results in elemental socialization. Henry Fleming's only defense against the fear of death, and perhaps against the attractions of death, is the approval of his comrades. He knew his greatest despair when he was alone, isolated from the rest of the army. Confronting death, he comes back to the army and experiences great relief, as if here was the only alternative to metaphysical panic. Social membership is almost as absolute as death, and it receives from death a kind of existential sanction, giving to Henry all the confidence of being that he can have. In all of this the crisis of violence is indispensable, for it proves the need for high group discipline and, in a naturalist paradox, juxtaposes primitive savagery with highly organized behavior. The battle scene brings together the reality of power and conflict and a primitive social ethic at its point of inception. In fact, if one wonders why the ethos of naturalist political movements, whether fascist or communist, is imbued with authoritarian discipline, the most direct answer would be that, in assuming the universality of group conflict as the premise for their existence, they needed to organize and motivate themselves like armies.

Redemptive Violence

In *The Red Badge of Courage*, a novel of war, where the opportunity to expose social illusions and oppressions was most available, Crane chose to concentrate on primitive collective psychology and instinctual experience. He pointedly avoids the social and historical issues of the Civil War. The deepest reading of Crane, I myself believe, emphasizes a tragic naturalism or a pessimism directed at both natural violence and social rule. But it is arguable, to a degree limited somewhat by his ironic sensibility, that Crane, in both *Maggie* and *The Red Badge of Courage*, is a vitalist in whom high respect for truth fuses with stoic faith in nature. Certainly he traces the growth of a neoprimitive, stoic religion of nature in his characters, as in Henry Fleming's inchoate respect for the gods of death and war. Essential to it is the ordeal, the arena in which the hero finds value in pain, violence, and even death—accepts them as productive of good. The ethos that naturalism develops is thus based on the struggle for survival, and it features that combination of sacrificial and stoic virtues described by Lovejoy as "hard primitivism."[4] Nietzsche was the modern teacher of these stoic values when he said, in making his own great claim to naturalist revelations, that he would rather perish than renounce the truth that "life sacrifices itself—for the sake of power!"[5] The various forms of redemptive or cathartic violence expressed in the works of Crane and Hemingway and by many later disciples, in both fiction and film, are specifically Nietzschean motifs in the modern myth of power.[6]

Notes

1. Quotations from *The Red Badge of Courage* are from *The Red Badge of Courage*, ed. Sculley Bradley et al., rev. ed. (New York: Norton, 1976).

2. For this debate, see R. W. Stallman, ed., *Stephen Crane: An Omnibus* (New York: Knopf, 1952), pp. 223-24.

3. Authority for this statement can be found in the works of one of the best students of modern responses to violence. Hannah Arendt writes as follows:

> As far as human experience is concerned, death indicates an extreme of loneliness and impotence. But faced collectively and in action, death changes its countenance; now nothing seems more likely to intensify our vitality than its proximity. Something we are usually hardly aware of, namely, that our own death is accompanied by the potential immortality of the group we belong to and, in the final analysis, of the species, moves into the center of our experience. It is as though life itself, the immortal life of the species, nourished, as it were, by the sempiternal dying of its individual members, is "surging upward," is actualized in the practice of violence. [*On Violence* (New York: Harcourt, Brace & World, 1970), p. 68]

4. Arthur O. Lovejoy, in Arthur O. Lovejoy and George Boas, eds., *A Documentary History of Primitivism and Related Ideas* (Baltimore, 1935), pp. 9-11.

5. *Thus Spake Zarathustra*, trans. R. S. Hollingdale (Baltimore: Penguin Books, 1962), p. 136.

6. There are strong political analogies here; the therapeutic justifications of political terrorism in the writings of Frantz Fanon come first to mind. The fact that during the civil rights movement his ideas were frequently echoed in statements of the blacks' need to assert self-respecting manhood is general testimony to the popular influence of his thinking. A more complex implication is found in the mood and actions of Israelis since the Holocaust and in the very bitter criticism often directed at the passivity of the Jews before the Nazis, suggesting that there were more virile and noble ways to be slaughtered.

Reading "Race" and "Gender" in Crane's *The Red Badge of Courage*_____

Verner D. Mitchell

Taking my cue primarily from Nobel Laureate Toni Morrison's "Unspeakable Things Unspoken: The Afro-American Presence in American Literature" (1989) and *Playing in the Dark: Whiteness and the Literary Imagination* (1993), I want to offer, in this brief paper, what I trust will be a relatively new look at Stephen Crane's classic civil war novel, *The Red Badge of Courage*. In a 1992 review of Melville scholarship, critic Andrew Delbanco writes that Morrison's "Unspeakable Things Unspoken"[1] "opens new entrances into Melville in ways that earlier estimable works . . . had not quite managed to do. It will be a long time, he adds, "before these entrances are closed."[2] Morrison's critical work offers, I would contend, an equally fortuitous opening into Crane. For with the exception of criticism on *George's Mother* and *Maggie*, and on "The Monster," signs of "gender" and "race" in Crane's fiction have gone largely uninterrogated—or, in Morrison's language, they have been unspeakable and unspoken. The foregrounding of constructions of "gender" and "race" therefore promises to offer new openings into *The Red Badge* and, perhaps more importantly, suggests that in his most successful work Crane challenges, and in some instances subverts categories which controlled much of nineteenth-century Euro-American thought.

Ralph Ellison in his 1986 work *Going to the Territory* notes perceptively that *The Red Badge of Courage* "is about the Civil War, but only one black person appears, and then only briefly."[3] After zooming in on his character, however, Ellison, like most other critics, seems at a loss concerning exactly what to make of the novel's unnamed black man. That they would have such difficulty is not at all surprising, given that the black man drops in (seemingly out of nowhere) for all of two sentences, and then he disappears, just as abruptly, never to be heard from again. The novel's opening scene shows Jim Conklin rushing back

from washing a shirt in order to broadcast excitedly, though erroneously, that the regiment will attack the following day. "To his attentive
audience," reports the narrator, Conklin

> drew a loud and elaborate plan of a very brilliant campaign. When he had
> finished, the blue-clothed men scattered into small arguing groups between
> the rows of squat brown huts. A negro [sic] teamster who had been dancing
> upon a cracker box with the hilarious encouragement of two-score soldiers
> was deserted. He sat mournfully down.[4]

I want to linger, for just a moment, on the variously dancing and
mournful character.

At its most basic level, the description is simply one of a black man
dancing, in typical minstrel fashion, so as to entertain a group of white
men.[5] This dancing black man and his amused audience, especially
with the rows of "squat brown huts" as backdrop, would appear to be
more at home in postbellum, romanticized defenses of slavery. Even
so, the three-sentence sideshow, when situated within the era's typical
portraits of African Americans, would not be particularly noteworthy
were it not for the fact, as Ralph Ellison reminds us, that Crane's is a
novel of the Civil War. Yet precisely because, the American Civil War
is the novel's subject,[6] this fleeting portrait of black-white interaction
actually drives to the very heart of *The Red Badge*. Why do Henry and
his colleagues enlist? Why are they fighting, risking and all too often
losing their lives? On this crucial point, even the characters themselves
remain unclear. By means of their "hilarious encouragement" of the
teamster and even more so their rudely abrupt departure, they do signal, however, that for them their black colleague is of little, if any, consequence. As a result, although we cannot determine exactly why they
are fighting, we can see rather clearly that abolition, Negro freedom,
and black uplift are far from the top of their agenda.

Amy Kaplan offers a more sympathetic reading. In a probing, subtly-
nuanced analysis, she maintains that in an effort to map new arenas for

warfare and for imaginative literature, Crane divorces both the Civil War from its historical context and his novel from generic narrative conventions.[7] Hence the opening scene, rather than an endorsement, is actually a rejection of minstrelsy. She explains that "[i]n the 1880s, tales of chivalric exploits . . . superseded the older narrative of emancipation." Crane, therefore, by divorcing his own narrative from these "former stories about freeing the slaves" actually "calls attention to the process whereby the history of emancipation has been reduced to a form of entertainment." The novel's sympathy, then, in Kaplan's view, rests not with the laughing two-score soldiers, but with the "deserted" teamster who "sits 'mournfully down' to lament his loss of an audience and his own passing as a figure for the subject of emancipation."[8]

Kaplan's reading, while not altogether convincing, is especially helpful to the extent that it locates the teamster center stage, rescuing him, at last, from the textual and critical margins. In so doing, she retards what Morrison has referred to as long-standing acts of "willful critical blindness."[9] Nonetheless, any number of critics continue to argue, as does Daniel Aaron, that Crane's soldiers ". . . have no antecedents to speak of, no politics, no prejudices. Negroes and Lincoln and hospitals and prisons," he maintains, "are not to be found in Crane's theater; these and other matters were irrelevant to his main concern— the nature of war and what happens to people who engage in it."[10] Here we are told that Crane focuses on people and that Negroes and other similar irrelevances are not to be found in his theater. Such readings so marginalize the novel's black man (and his interests) that he is all but pushed out of *The Red Badge* and rendered invisible. In contrast, the novel's young protagonist, Private Henry Fleming, finds it much more difficult to escape such matters as politics and prejudices, hospitals and Negroes.

Since my own analysis thus far has focused on how the laughing soldiers view the teamster, I also think it important, like Kaplan, to examine how he views them and even more importantly, how he views himself. As the twoscore soldiers depart, does the teamster actually sit mournfully down to lament his passing as a figure for the subject of emancipation, or does he merely lament his loss of an audience? If the latter is true, and I suspect that it is, then the teamster sees himself (or at least the novel would have us believe that he sees himself) as a subservient appendage to a group of other men. Rather than utter a healthy sigh of relief at their departure, he apparently prefers that they remain and continue their "hilarious encouragement." He thus measures his self-worth, as Du Bois would phrase it, through the eyes of those who "look on in amused contempt."[11] Notice, too, that the only visible role that the novel permits him is as entertainer for the dominant culture and according to the dominant culture's limited expectations. As a result, in this, the novel's opening scene, Crane has masterfully constructed a rigid, racialized hierarchy, one which dates back in American literature at least to Jefferson's *Notes on the State of Virginia* (1787). Simply put, Crane's dancing black man boosts the white soldiers' egos and their sense of self-worth, and in so doing he serves as a convenient device for cementing both his and their God-ordained place on the Great Racial Chain of Being.

As we flip to page two, the teamster is figuratively buried, never to be heard from again. In his place surfaces a more abstract, less concrete figuration of darkness, one which Morrison in a somewhat different context has labeled a "disrupting darkness."[12] What we might term "the great unseen presence in the text," therefore, persists. Chapter 16, for example, finds Henry reveling in his recently received red badge of courage. The narrator notes, somewhat derisively, that Henry "had performed his mistakes in the dark, so he was still a man. Indeed," he continues, "when he remembered his fortunes of yesterday, and looked at these from a distance he began to see something fine there. He had license to be pompous and veteran-like" (79). Here darkness is presented as a positive and perhaps even benevolent force. In keeping concealed the fact that Henry's wound, his bandage of courage, occurred as a consequence of his throwing down his rifle and running "like a rabbit" (35), the darkness enables, his manhood to remain intact. Of course the darkness does not blind Henry to the circumstances of his wound nor, by extension, to the substance of what he considers his "manhood." Hence in this scene we can begin to understand his ambivalence toward darkness, or what I prefer to call his love-hate relationship with blackness.

In the chapter's succeeding paragraphs, Henry undertakes a more sustained meditation on blackness. He is now a man of experience, an authentic hero, and he accordingly struts about and looks with scorn upon lesser men. To capture the passage's essence, I need quote at length:

> Some poets . . . had wandered in paths of pain and they had made pictures of the black landscape that others might enjoy it with them. He had, at that time, been sure that their wise, contemplating spirits had been in sympathy with him, had shed tears from the clouds. . . .
>
> But he was now, in a measure, a successful man and he could no longer tolerate in himself a spirit of fellowship with poets. He abandoned them. Their songs about black landscapes were of no importance to him since his new eyes said that his landscape was not black. People who called landscapes black were idiots. He achieved a mighty scorn for such a snivelling race. (80)

The antecedent of "snivelling race," I would argue, is intentionally vague. Does "snivelling race," for instance, refer to the poet race or, just as likely, to the black race? Here, as elsewhere throughout the novel, the passage is sufficiently complex to accommodate multiple readings. What seems indisputable, however, and what for me is the more salient point, is that within the passage, "blackness" takes on for Henry (as it does throughout Western civilization) a clear and unrelentingly negative connotation. What is equally clear is that the scene's biting irony renders Henry's judgment vain at worst and naive at best. Therefore, where the portrait of the teamster reinforces myopic conceptions of blackness and whiteness, Henry's ironized "scorn for such a snivelling race" challenges, perhaps unintentionally, all such constructions.

A later meeting between Henry and two members of the army's elite brings the novel's evolving depiction of "race" into even sharper focus. In chapter 19, Henry and another "foot-soldier" happen to overhear two officers insulting their regiment, the 304th. In this scene, we as readers are positioned with the foot soldiers, and we accordingly must similarly stand back and listen, unseen, and afterwards interpret the officers' conversation:

> The officer who rode like a cow-boy reflected for an instant. "Well," he said, "I had to order in th' 12th to help th' 76th an' I haven't really got any. But there's th' 304th. They fight like a lot 'a mule-drivers. I can spare them best of any." The youth and his friend exchanged glances of astonishment. The general spoke sharply. "Get 'em ready then. . . ." As the other officer tossed his fingers toward his cap and, wheeling his horse, started away, the general called out to him in a sober voice: "I don't believe many of your mule-drivers will get back." (92-93)

The uncomplimentary label "mule-drivers" bridges the color divide by figuratively linking Henry and his regimental brothers to the Negro teamster, who is literally a mule-driver. Once again, Morrison aids our interpretation. She writes in *Sula* of "old women who worried about such things as bad blood mixtures and knew that the origins of a mule and a mulatto were one and the same."[13] Indeed, an attentive examination of Henry's "glance of astonishment" reveals that he understands that which Morrison's old women understand, and like them he fears being collapsed into an arena of mules and other "mixed" beings, and thus placed on the bottom rung of humankind's evolutionary ladder. To be sure, Henry's gender and race set him above and apart from Morrison's old women. His race and phenotype do the same vis-à-vis the Negro teamster/mule-driver. Yet viewed through the general's eyes, they are all, at bottom, much the same. Crane's narrator reports that in listening to the officers "the most startling thing [for Henry] was to learn suddenly that he was very insignificant" (93). Henry certainly realizes, then, that the officers see him as mere cannon fodder, as one whose class renders him little better than Negroes and mules and such.

At first glance, Henry's romanticized encounter with a "dark girl," just prior to his leaving for the war, seems to further problematize stereotypic notions of blackness and whiteness. So, too, does the opening chapter's description of Henry's mother's "brown face" (6). Before turning to Henry and his brown-faced mother, whose extended conversation will shortly bring this paper to a close, I want to comment first on his encounter with the dark girl. We certainly need not look far into the canon of American literature to find synecdochical signifiers of race, more often than not ones mapped onto and played out by means of the female body. Let me offer three specific examples. In Cooper's *The Last of the Mohicans* (1826), Alice and Cora Munro brave a gauntlet of dangers to visit their father, a British officer fighting against the French in hostile Indian territory. During the course of their journey, dark-haired Cora, whose mother is West Indian,[14] is killed; her golden-haired, blue-eyed half-sister, Alice,[15] in contrast, lives and can thus marry and propagate the race in her own image. Hawthorne's *The Blithedale Romance* (1852) makes use of a similar pattern. Zenobia, a dark-haired woman drawn to recall and mock the pioneering feminist Margaret Fuller, drowns herself after being rejected by Hollingsworth.[16] Hollingsworth chooses, instead, "fair" Priscilla, who is painted as "perfectly modest, delicate, and virginlike."[17] Moreover, in the novel's famous last sentence, the narrator discloses that he, too, prefers Priscilla: "I—I myself—was in love—with—Priscilla!"[18] Even in Alcott's *Little Women* (1868), which like *The Red Badge* is set during the Civil War, it is a dark-haired sister, Beth, who catches scarlet fever and dies.[19] And it is her sister Amy, described as "A regular snow maiden with blue eyes, and yellow hair," who lives, eventually marrying the man whom Beth had fallen in love with and giving birth to a "golden-haired" baby girl.[20] Rather than cite additional instances of what eventually became a staple in nineteenth-century American literature, suffice it to say that Henry's longing for a dark girl stands this pattern on its head. Not only does he dismiss, rather decisively, a light-haired girl, and she him, but he finds (or at least he thinks that he does) in the dark girl his potential soul mate:

> From his home, he had gone to the seminary to bid adieu to many school-mates. They had thronged about him with wonder and admiration. . . . A certain lighthaired girl had made vivacious fun at his martial-spirit but there was another and darker girl whom he had gazed at steadfastly and he thought she grew demure and sad at the sight of his blue and brass. As he had walked down the path between the rows of oaks, he had turned his head and detected her at a window watching his departure. (6)

The above description of Henry desiring a dark girl rather than the un-attractive, stereotypical blonde-haired beauty challenges and arguably subverts common turn-of-the-century constructions of race and gender. Henry's relationship with his brown-faced mother, however, is less clear-cut. Henry's mother, similar to his light-haired female school-mate, "look[s] with some contempt upon the quality of his war-ardor and patriotism" (3). When he tells her that he has decided to enlist, she replies succinctly and bluntly, "Henry, don't you be a fool" (4). The en-suing verbal give-and-take between Henry and his mother, which is at bottom little more than a duel or a gendered battle,[21] draws to a close when Henry enlists. As he views it, "he had made firm rebellion against this yellow light thrown upon the color of his ambitions" (4).

Nonetheless, a short while later Henry finds himself wishing, with-out reserve, that he had heeded his mother's advice. In this rare mo-ment, for him, of clear thought, the yellow light personifies safety, courage, and insight, while brass buttons and red badges are merely the unfortunate by-products of a hyper and misguided masculine ethos. Feeling sorry for himself,

[h]e wish[es] without reserve that he was at home again, making the end-less rounds, from the house to the barn, from the barn to the fields, from the fields to the barn, from the barn to the house. He remembered he had often cursed the brindle-cow and her mates, and had sometimes flung milking-stools. But from his present point of view, there was a halo of happiness about each of their heads and he would have sacrificed all the brass buttons on the continent to have been enabled to return to them. (15)

This picture of a frustrated Henry milking cows, of him in fact as a milkmaid, captures compellingly the domestic realm which he had made firm rebellion against. But now, only a short while after having charged forth to become "a man," he would all too willingly retrace his steps. Indeed, he wishes with all his heart that he could step back over that dividing line which he had erroneously come to see as separating men from women, bulls from cows.

Unfortunately, this moment of lucidity does not last. A few chapters later he is again neck-deep in dreams of heroism and valor, of bloody battles and brass buttons. To cite one brief instance, toward the end of chapter sixteen he pictures himself back home

> in a room of warm tints telling tales to listeners. . . . He saw his gaping audi-ence picturing him as the central figure in blazing scenes. And he imagined the consternation and the ejaculations of his mother and the young lady at the seminary as they drank his recitals. Their vague feminine formula for beloved ones doing brave deeds on the field of battle without risk of life would be destroyed. (82)

Of course the irony here is too apparent to be missed. This vague femi-nine formula for beloved ones doing brave deeds on the field of battle which Henry details is neither his mother's nor his female classmate's. Instead, Henry is actually describing his own mistaken masculine for-mula, and it is the two women who have tried valiantly, though unsuc-cessful, to destroy it. Recall that when young Henry initially boasts of his forthcoming martial exploits, his mother cries out, in disgust, "Henry, don't . . . be a fool." Likewise, to the extent that the young woman at the seminary grows demure and sad at his departure, she, too, in all likelihood sees what he even by novel's end cannot see. The novel, therefore, in this and similar scenes, forcefully exposes and explodes what I earlier labeled Henry's misguided masculine ethos.

Hence for Henry to recognize and afterwards construct a more wholesome definition of manhood, he must first embrace his mother's teachings and thus collapse his flawed nations of the feminine and the masculine. No less important, constructing a healthier definition of personhood requires that he also move beyond hierarchical, dichotomous notions of race. Likely the novel's great message, then, for Henry and his critics alike, is that they look to the margins: to his dark-skinned potential lover, his African-American brother in arms, and his wise, though generally ignored, brown-faced mother.

From *CLA Journal* 40, no. 1 (September 1996): 60-71. Copyright © 1996 by the College Language Association. Reprinted with permission of the College Language Association.

Notes

Author's note: I wish to thank Professors Donald B. Gibson and John Clendenning for their help with this essay.

1. See Toni Morrison, "Unspeakable Things Unspoken: The Afro-American Presence in American Literature," *Michigan Quarterly Review* 28.1 (Winter 1989): 1-34.

2. Andrew Delbanco, "Melville in the '80's," *American Literary History* 4.4 (Winter 1992): 722.

3. Ralph Ellison, *Going to the Territory* (New York: Vintage, 1987) 237.

4. Stephen Crane, *The Red Badge of Courage* (1896; New York: Avon, 1982) 1. Hereafter cited parenthetically in the text by page reference only.

5. For an excellent analysis of minstrelsy, see Eric Lott, *Love and Theft: Blackface Minstrelsy and the American Working Class* (New York: Oxford UP, 1993).

6. The novel's full title is *The Red Badge of Courage: An Episode of the American Civil War.*

7. Amy Kaplan, "The Spectacle of War in Crane's Revision of History," in *New Essays on The Red Badge of Courage*, ed. Lee Clark Mitchell (New York: Cambridge UP, 1986) 78.

8. Kaplan 85.

9. Toni Morrison, *Playing in the Dark: Whiteness and the Literary Imagination* (New York: Vintage, 1993) 18.

10. Daniel Aaron, *The Unwritten War* (Madison, U of Wisconsin P, 1987) 214-15.

11. W. E. B. Du Bois, *The Souls of Black Folk* (1903; New York: Vintage, 1990) 8.

12. Morrison 91.

13. Toni Morrison, *Sula* (New York: Plume, 1973) 52.

14. James Fenimore Cooper, *The Last of the Mohicans* (1826; New York: Signet, 1980) 118, 187.

15. Cooper 20.

16. Nathaniel Hawthorne, *The Blithedale Romance* (1852; New York: Oxford UP, 1991) 15, 47.

17. Hawthorne 77.

18. Hawthorne 274; emphasis Hawthorne's.

19. Louisa May Alcott, *Little Women* (1868; New York: Penguin, 1989) 177, 183, 419.

20. Alcott 4, 489.

21. Chapter two contains another gendered battle. In this contest, the male is again found lacking and a young, pink-cheeked female proves his superior. "A rather fat soldier attempted to pilfer a horse from a dooryard. He planned to load his knapsack upon it. He was escaping with his prize when a young girl rushed from the house and grabbed the animal's mane. There followed a wrangle. The young girl, with pink cheeks and shining eyes, stood like a dauntless statue. . . . The regiment rejoiced at his downfall. Loud and vociferous congratulations were showered upon the maiden, who stood panting and regarding the troops with defiance" (14).

RESOURCES

Chronology of Stephen Crane's Life _____

1871	Stephen Crane is born on November 1 in Newark, New Jersey, to the Reverend John Townley Crane and Mary Peck Crane.
1874	The Crane family moves to Port Jervis, New York.
1880	Crane's father dies.
1883	Crane's mother moves the family to Asbury Park, New Jersey.
1885-1887	Crane attends Pennington Seminary.
1888-1890	Crane attends Claverack College and Hudson River Institute. He briefly attends Lafayette College, withdrawing shortly after the second semester begins.
1891	Crane briefly attends Syracuse University. He begins work on *Maggie: A Girl of the Streets* and meets Hamlin Garland in August. Crane moves to Lake View, New Jersey, and begins his journalism career with the *New York Tribune*. Crane's mother dies on December 7.
1892	Crane moves to New York City. "Sullivan County Sketches" are published.
1893	*Maggie* is privately printed. Crane meets William Dean Howells.
1894	An abbreviated version of *The Red Badge of Courage* is published as a newspaper serial.
1895	Appleton publishes the novel-length version of *The Red Badge of Courage*, and the poetry collection *The Black Riders, and Other Lines* is published. Crane travels to Mexico as a feature writer.
1896	*George's Mother* and *The Little Regiment, and Other Episodes of the American Civil War* are published, as well as a reissue of *Maggie*. Crane passes through Jacksonville, Florida, en route to Cuba and meets Cora Stewart, the owner of a brothel.

1897	Crane's ship runs aground as it leaves Florida for Cuba, and, with a few other passengers, Crane escapes from the wreck in a lifeboat. The incident inspires "The Open Boat." Crane and Stewart travel to Greece to report on the Greco-Turkish War and then to England, where Crane meets Joseph Conrad and writes *The Monster*, "Death and the Child," and "The Bride Comes to Yellow Sky." *The Third Violet* is published.
1898	*The Open Boat, and Other Tales of Adventure* is published. When the Spanish-American War breaks out, Crane returns to the United States to try to enlist in the armed forces. Rejected, he instead travels to Cuba as a correspondent for Joseph Pulitzer.
1899	*War Is Kind*, *Active Service*, and *The Monster, and Other Stories* are published. Crane returns to England with Stewart to live at Brede Place. On Christmas Day, he suffers a massive tubercular hemorrhage.
1900	Crane and Stewart travel to Badenweiler, Germany. Crane dies of tuberculosis on June 5. *Whilomville Stories* and *Wounds in the Rain* are published posthumously.
1901	*The Great Battles of the World* is published.
1902	*Last Words* is published.
1903	*The O'Ruddy* is published.

Works by Stephen Crane

Long Fiction
Maggie: A Girl of the Streets, 1893
The Red Badge of Courage: An Episode of the American Civil War, 1895
George's Mother, 1896
The Third Violet, 1897
The Monster, 1898 (serial), 1899 (novella; published in *The Monster, and Other Stories*)
Active Service, 1899
The O'Ruddy: A Romance, 1903 (with Robert Barr)

Short Fiction
The Little Regiment, and Other Episodes of the American Civil War, 1896
The Open Boat, and Other Tales of Adventure, 1898
The Monster, and Other Stories, 1899
Whilomville Stories, 1900
Wounds in the Rain: War Stories, 1900
Last Words, 1902

Poetry
The Black Riders, and Other Lines, 1895
A Souvenir and a Medley, 1896
War Is Kind, 1899

Drama
The Ghost, pr. 1899 (with Henry James; fragment)
The Blood of the Martyr, wr. 1898?, pb. 1940

Nonfiction
The Great Battles of the World, 1901
The War Dispatches of Stephen Crane, 1964

Miscellaneous
The University of Virginia Edition of the Works of Stephen Crane, 1969-1976 (10 vols.)

Bibliography

Anderson, Warren D. "Homer and Stephen Crane." *Nineteenth-Century Fiction* 19 (1964): 77-86.

Bassan, Maurice. *Stephen Crane: A Collection of Critical Essays*. Englewood Cliffs, NJ: Prentice-Hall, 1967.

Beaver, Harold. "Stephen Crane: The Hero as Victim." *Yearbook of English Studies* 12 (1982): 186-93.

Beidler, Philip D. "Stephen Crane's *The Red Badge of Courage*: Henry Fleming's Courage in Its Contexts." *CLIO* 20 (1991): 235-51.

Bender, Burt. "'The Chaos of His Brain': Evolutionary Psychology in *The Red Badge of Courage*." *Evolution and "the Sex Problem": American Narratives During the Eclipse of Darwinism*. Ed. Burt Bender. Kent, OH: Kent State University Press, 2004. 52-71.

_____. "Hanging Stephen Crane in the Impressionist Museum." *Journal of Aesthetics and Art Criticism* 35 (1976): 47-55.

Benfy, Christopher. "Badges of Courage and Cowardice: A Source for Crane's Title." *Stephen Crane Studies* 6.2 (Fall 1997): 2-5.

_____. *The Double Life of Stephen Crane*. New York: Alfred A. Knopf, 1992.

_____. "Two Cranes, Two Henrys." *Stephen Crane in War and Peace*. Ed. James H. Meredith. Spec. issue of *War, Literature & the Arts* (1999): 1-10.

Berryman, John. *Stephen Crane*. New York: William Sloane Associates, 1950.

Bickerstaff, Linda. *"The Red Badge of Courage" and the Civil War*. New York: Rosen, 2003.

Binder, Henry. "Donald Pizer, Ripley Hitchcock, and *The Red Badge of Courage*." *Studies in the Novel* 11 (1979): 216-23.

_____. "*The Red Badge of Courage* Nobody Knows." *Studies in the Novel* 10 (1978a): 9-47.

_____. "*The Red Badge of Courage* Nobody Knows." *The Red Badge of Courage*, by Stephen Crane. Ed. Henry Binder. New York: W. W. Norton, 1982. 111-58.

_____. "Unwinding the Riddle of Four Pages Missing from *The Red Badge of Courage* Manuscript." *Papers of the Bibliographical Society of America* 72 (1978b): 100-6.

Bowers, Fredson. "Regularization and Normalization in Modern Critical Texts." *Studies in Bibliography* 42 (1989): 79-102.

Bruccoli, Matthew J. *Stephen Crane, 1871-1971*. Columbia: Department of English, University of South Carolina, 1971.

Burhans, Clinton. "Judging Henry Judging: Point of View in *The Red Badge of Courage*." *Ball State University Forum* 15.2 (1974): 38-48.

Cady, Edwin H. *Stephen Crane*. Rev. ed. Boston: Twayne, 1980.

Clendenning, John. "Stephen Crane and His Biographers: Beer, Berryman, Schoberlin, and Stallman." *American Literary Realism* 28 (1995): 23-57.

_____. "Thomas Beer's *Stephen Crane*: The Eye of His Imagination." *Prose Studies* 14 (1991): 68-80.

Colvert, James B. "Crane, Hitchcock, and the Binder Edition of *The Red Badge of Courage*." *Critical Essays on Stephen Crane's "The Red Badge of Courage."* Ed. Donald Pizer. Boston: G. K. Hall, 1990. 238-63.

_____. "*The Red Badge of Courage* and a Review of Zola's *La Débâcle*." *Modern Language Notes* 71 (1956): 98-100.

_____. *Stephen Crane*. New York: Harcourt Brace Jovanovich, 1984.

_____. "Unreal War in *The Red Badge of Courage*." *Stephen Crane in War and Peace*. Ed. James H. Meredith. Spec. issue of *War, Literature & the Arts* (1999): 35-47.

Davis, Linda H. *Badge of Courage: The Life of Stephen Crane*. Boston: Houghton Mifflin, 1998.

Derrick, Scott. "Behind the Lines: Homoerotic Anxiety and the Heroic in Stephen Crane's *The Red Badge of Courage*." *Monumental Anxieties: Homoerotic Desire and Feminine Influence in Nineteenth Century U. S. Literature*. New Brunswick, NJ: Rutgers University Press, 1997. 170-90.

Detweiler, Robert. "Christ and the Christ Figure in American Fiction." *Christian Scholar* 47 (1964): 111-24.

Dooley, Patrick K. *An Annotated Bibliography of Secondary Scholarship on Stephen Crane*. New York: G. K. Hall, 1992.

_____. *The Pluralistic Philosophy of Stephen Crane*. Urbana: University of Illinois Press, 1993.

Dunn, N. E. "The Common Man's *Iliad*." *Comparative Literature Studies* 21 (1984): 270-81.

Dusenbery, Robert. "The Homeric Mood in *The Red Badge of Courage*." *Pacific Coast Philology* 3 (1968): 31-37.

Eby, Cecil D. "The Source of Crane's Metaphor, *Red Badge of Courage*." *American Literature* 32 (1960): 204-07.

_____. "Stephen Crane's 'Fierce Red Wafer.'" *English Language Notes* 1 (1963): 128-30.

French, Warren. "Stephen Crane: Moment of Myth." *Prairie Schooner* 55 (1981): 155-67.

Fryckstedt, Olaf W. "Henry Fleming's Tuppenny Fury: Cosmic Pessimism in Stephen Crane's *The Red Badge of Courage*." *Studia Neophilologia* 33 (1961): 265-81.

Gibson, Donald B. *"The Red Badge of Courage": Redefining the Hero*. Boston: Twayne, 1988.

Gullason, Thomas A., ed. *Stephen Crane's Career: Perspectives and Evaluations*. New York: New York University Press, 1972.

Hafer, Carol B. "The Red Badge of Absurdity: Irony in *The Red Badge of Courage*." *CLA Journal* 14 (1971): 440-43.

Halliburton, David. *The Color of the Sky: A Study of Stephen Crane*. New York: Cambridge University Press, 1989.

Hart, John E. "*The Red Badge of Courage* as Myth and Symbol." *University of Kansas City Review* 19 (1953): 240-56.

Hattenhauer, Darryl. "Crane's *The Red Badge of Courage*." *Explicator* 50 (1992): 160-61.

Hayes, Kevin J. "How Stephen Crane Shaped Henry Fleming." *Studies in the Novel* 22 (1990): 296-307.

Johnson, Claudia D. *Understanding "The Red Badge of Courage": A Student Casebook to Issues, Sources, and Historical Documents*. Westport, CT: Greenwood Press, 1998.

Knapp, Bettina L. *Stephen Crane*. New York: Frederick Ungar, 1987.

Krauth, Leland. "Heroes and Heroics: Stephen Crane's Moral Imperative." *South Dakota Review* 11 (1973): 86-93.

LaFrance, Marston. "Crane, Zola, and the Hot Ploughshares." *English Language Notes* 7 (1970): 285-87.

_____. *A Reading of Stephen Crane*. Oxford: Clarendon, 1971.

Lawson, Andrew. "The Red Badge of Class: Stephen Crane and the Industrial Army." *Literature and History* 14 (2005): 53-68.

Lentz, Perry. *Private Fleming at Chancellorsville: "The Red Badge of Courage" and the Civil War*. Columbia: University of Missouri Press, 2006.

Levenson, J. C. Introduction. *The Red Badge of Courage*. 1895. Vol. 2 of *The Works of Stephen Crane*. Ed. Fredson Bowers. Charlottesville: University Press of Virginia, 1975. xiii-xvii.

_____, ed. *Stephen Crane: Prose and Poetry*. New York: Library of America, 1984.

Lorch, Thomas M. "The Cyclical Structure of *The Red Badge of Courage*." *CLA Journal* 10 (1967): 220-38.

McDermott, John J. "Symbolism and Psychological Realism in *The Red Badge of Courage*." *Nineteenth-Century Fiction* 23 (1968): 324-31.

McIlvaine, Robert. "Henry Fleming Wrestles with an Angel." *Pennsylvania English* 12 (1985): 21-27.

Mailloux, Steven. "Literary History and Reception Study." *Interpretive Conversations: The Reader in the Study of American Fictions*. Ithaca, NY: Cornell University Press, 1982. 159-91.

_____. "*The Red Badge of Courage* and Interpretive Conventions: Critical Response to a Maimed Text." *Studies in the Novel* 10 (1978): 48-63.

Mangum, A. Bryant. "Crane's *Red Badge* and Zola." *American Literary Realism* 9 (1976): 279-80.

_____. "The Latter Days of Henry Fleming." *A N&Q* 13 (1975): 136-38.

Marcus, Mordecai, and Erin Marcus. "Animal Imagery in *The Red Badge of Courage*." *Modern Language Notes* 74 (1959): 108-11.

Maynard, Reid. "Red as a Leitmotiv in *The Red Badge of Courage*." *Arizona Quarterly* 30 (1974): 135-41.

Mitchell, Lee Clark. *New Essays on "The Red Badge of Courage."* New York: Cambridge University Press, 1986.

Monteiro, George. *Stephen Crane's Blue Badge of Courage*. Baton Rouge: Louisiana State University Press, 2000.

Morris, Roy. "On Whose Responsibility?: Historical Underpinnings of *The Red Badge of Courage*." *Memory and Myth: The Civil War in Fiction and Film*. Ed. David Sachsman. Lafayette, IN: Purdue University Press, 2007. 137-50.

Mulcaire, Terry. "Progressive Views of War in *The Red Badge of Courage* and *The Principles of Scientific Management*." *American Quarterly* 43 (1991): 46-72.

Myers, Robert M. "A Review of Popular Editions of *The Red Badge of Courage*." *Stephen Crane Studies* 6.1 (1997): 2-15.

_____. "'The Subtle Battle Brotherhood': The Construction of Military Discipline in *The Red Badge of Courage*." *Stephen Crane in War and Peace*. Ed. James H. Meredith. Spec. issue of *War, Literature & the Arts* (1999): 128-41.

Nagel, James. *Stephen Crane and Literary Impressionism*. University Park: Pennsylvania State University Press, 1980.

Parker, Hershel. "The Auteur-Author Paradox: How Critics of the Cinema and the Novel Talk About Flawed or Even 'Mutilated' Texts." *Studies in the Novel* 27.3 (1995): 413-26.

_____. "Getting Used to the 'Original' Form of *The Red Badge of Courage*." *New Essays on "The Red Badge of Courage."* Ed. Lee Clark Mitchell. New York: Cambridge University Press, 1986. 25-47.

_____. "*The Red Badge of Courage*: The Private History of a Campaign That—Succeeded?" *Flawed Texts and Verbal Icons: Literary Authority in American Fiction*. Evanston, IL: Northwestern University Press, 1984. 147-79.

_____. "Review of Recent Editions of *The Red Badge of Courage*." *Nineteenth-Century Fiction* 30 (1976): 558-62.

Pease, Donald. "Fear, Rage, and Mistrials of Representation in *The Red Badge of Courage*." *American Realism: New Essays*. Ed. Eric J. Sundquist. Baltimore: Johns Hopkins University Press, 1982. 155-75.

Pizer, Donald. "Henry Behind the Lines and the Concept of Manhood in *The Red Badge of Courage*." *Stephen Crane Studies* 10.1 (Spring 2001): 2-7.

_____. "Late Nineteenth-Century American Naturalism." *Realism and Naturalism in Nineteenth-Century American Literature*. Carbondale: Southern Illinois University Press, 1966. 11-32.

_____. "'*The Red Badge of Courage* Nobody Knows': A Brief Rejoinder." *Studies in American Fiction* 11 (1979): 77-81.

_____. "*The Red Badge of Courage*: Text, Theme, and Form." *South Atlantic Quarterly* 84 (1985): 302-13.

_____. "What Unit Did Henry Belong to at Chancellorsville, and Does It Matter?" *Stephen Crane Studies* 16.1 (Spring 2007): 2-13.

_____, ed. *Critical Essays on Stephen Crane's "The Red Badge of Courage."* Boston: G. K. Hall, 1990.

Rahv, Philip. "Fiction and the Criticism of Fiction." *Kenyon Review* 18 (1956): 276-99.

Renza, Louis. "Crane's *The Red Badge of Courage.*" *Explicator* 56.2 (1998): 82-83.

Reynolds, Kirk M. "*The Red Badge of Courage:* Private Henry's Mind as Sole Point of View." *South Atlantic Quarterly* 52 (1987): 59-69.

Richardson, Mark. "Stephen Crane's *The Red Badge of Courage.*" Vol. 1 of *American Writers Classics.* Ed. Jay Parini. New York: Scribner's, 2003. 237-55.

Robertson, Michael. *Stephen Crane: Journalism and the Making of Modern American Literature.* New York: Columbia University Press, 1997.

Schaefer, Michael. "'Heroes Had No Shame in Their Lives': Heroics and Compassion in *The Red Badge of Courage* and 'A Mystery of Heroism.'" *War, Literature & the Arts* 18.1-2 (2006): 104-13.

_____. "Sequential Art Fights the Civil War: The *Classics Illustrated* Version of *The Red Badge of Courage.*" *Stephen Crane Studies* 15.2 (Fall 2006): 2-17.

Schmitz, Neil. "Stephen Crane and the Colloquial Self." *Midwest Quarterly* 13 (1972): 437-51.

Shanahan, Daniel. "The Army Motif in *The Red Badge of Courage* as a Response to Industrial Capitalism." *Papers in Language and Literature* 32 (1996): 399-409.

Shaw, Mary Neff. "Henry Fleming's Heroics in *The Red Badge of Courage*: A Satiric Search for a 'Kinder, Gentler' Heroism." *Studies in the Novel* 22 (1990): 418-28.

Shulman, Robert. "*The Red Badge* and Social Violence: Crane's Myth of America." *Canadian Review of American Studies* 12 (1981): 1-19.

Solomon, Eric. "Another Analog for *The Red Badge of Courage.*" *Nineteenth-Century Fiction* 13 (1958): 64-67.

_____. "Stephen Crane, English Critics, and American Reviewers." *Notes and Queries* 12 (1965): 62-64.

_____. *Stephen Crane: From Parody to Realism.* Cambridge, MA: Harvard University Press, 1966.

_____. "The Structure of *The Red Badge of Courage.*" *Modern Fiction Studies* 5 (1959): 220-34.

_____. "Yet Another Source for *The Red Badge of Courage.*" *English Language Notes* 2 (1965): 215-17.

Sorrentino, Paul. "The Legacy of Thomas Beer in the Study of Stephen Crane and American Literary History." *American Literary Realism* 35 (2003): 187-211.

_____. *Student Companion to Stephen Crane*. Westport CT: Greenwood Press, 2006.

_____, ed. *Stephen Crane Remembered*. Tuscaloosa: University of Alabama Press, 2006.

Stallman, Robert W. "Fiction and Its Critics: A Reply to Mr. Rahv." *Kenyon Review* 19 (1957): 290-99.

_____. Introduction. *The Red Badge of Courage*. 1895. By Stephen Crane. New York: Modern Library, 1951. v-xxxiii.

_____. "The Scholar's Net: Literary Sources." *College English* 17 (1955): 20-27.

_____. *Stephen Crane: A Critical Bibliography*. Ames: Iowa State University Press, 1972.

Stevenson, James A. "Beyond Stephen Crane: *Full Metal Jacket*." *Literature/Film Quarterly* 16 (1988): 238-342.

Stone, Edward. *The Battle and the Books: Some Aspects of Henry James*. Athens: Ohio University Press, 1964. 150.

_____. "Crane and Zola." *English Language Notes* 1 (1963): 46-47.

_____. "Introducing Private Smithers" *Georgia Review* 16 (1962): 442-44.

_____. "The Many Suns of *The Red Badge of Courage*." *American Literature* 29 (1957): 322-26.

Stowell, Robert. "Stephen Crane's Use of Colour in *The Red Badge of Courage*." *Literary Criterion* 9 (1970): 36-39.

Weatherford, Richard M., ed. *Stephen Crane: The Critical Heritage*. Boston: Routledge & Kegan Paul, 1973.

Wertheim, Stanley. "*The Red Badge of Courage* and Personal Narratives of the Civil War." *American Literary Realism* 6 (1973): 61-65.

_____. *A Stephen Crane Encyclopedia*. Westport, CT: Greenwood Press, 1997.

_____. "Stephen Crane." *Hawthorne, Melville, Stephen Crane*. Ed. Theodore Gross and Stanley Wertheim. New York: Free Press, 1971. 201-301.

Wertheim, Stanley, and Paul Sorrentino. *The Crane Log: A Documentary Life of Stephen Crane, 1871-1900*. New York: G. K. Hall, 1994.

_____. "Thomas Beer: The Clay Feet of Stephen Crane Biography." *American Literary Realism* 22 (1990): 2-16.

_____, eds. *The Correspondence of Stephen Crane*. 2 vols. New York: Columbia University Press, 1988.

Woodress, James. "*The Red Badge of Courage*." *Reference Guide to American Literature*. Ed. D. L. Kirkpatrick. Chicago: St. James Press, 1978. 677-78.

CRITICAL INSIGHTS

About the Editor

Eric Carl Link is Professor of American Literature and Chair of the Department of English at the University of Memphis. He is the author of several books, including *The Vast and Terrible Drama: American Literary Naturalism in the Late Nineteenth Century* (2004), *Understanding Philip K. Dick* (2010), and *Neutral Ground: New Traditionalism and the American Romance Controversy* (coauthored with G. R. Thompson, 1999). He is also the founder and editor of *ALN: The American Literary Naturalism Newsletter* and coeditor, with Donald Pizer, of the Norton Critical Edition of *The Red Badge of Courage*, fourth edition (2008). Aside from these studies, he has published numerous essays on figures such as Stephen Crane, Frank Norris, Mark Twain, as well as articles on a variety of topics related to nineteenth-century aesthetic theory.

About *The Paris Review*

The Paris Review is America's preeminent literary quarterly, dedicated to discovering and publishing the best new voices in fiction, nonfiction, and poetry. The magazine was founded in Paris in 1953 by the young American writers Peter Matthiessen and Doc Humes, and edited there and in New York for its first fifty years by George Plimpton. Over the decades, the *Review* has introduced readers to the earliest writings of Jack Kerouac, Philip Roth, T. C. Boyle, V. S. Naipaul, Ha Jin, Ann Patchett, Jay McInerney, Mona Simpson, and Edward P. Jones, and published numerous now classic works, including Roth's *Goodbye, Columbus*, Donald Barthelme's *Alice*, Jim Carroll's *Basketball Diaries*, and selections from Samuel Beckett's *Molloy* (his first publication in English). The first chapter of Jeffrey Eugenides's *The Virgin Suicides* appeared in the *Review*'s pages, as well as stories by Rick Moody, David Foster Wallace, Denis Johnson, Jim Crace, Lorrie Moore, and Jeanette Winterson.

The Paris Review's renowned Writers at Work series of interviews, whose early installments include legendary conversations with E. M. Forster, William Faulkner, and Ernest Hemingway, is one of the landmarks of world literature. The interviews received a George Polk Award and were nominated for a Pulitzer Prize. Among the more than three hundred interviewees are Robert Frost, Marianne Moore, W. H. Auden, Elizabeth Bishop, Susan Sontag, and Toni Morrison. Recent issues feature conversations with Salman Rushdie, Joan Didion, Norman Mailer, Kazuo Ishiguro, Marilynne Robinson, Umberto Eco, Annie Proulx, and Gay Talese. In November 2009, Picador published the final volume of a four-volume series of anthologies of *Paris Review* interviews. *The New York Times* called the Writers at Work series "the most remarkable and extensive interviewing project we possess."

The Paris Review is edited by Philip Gourevitch, who was named to the post in 2005, following the death of George Plimpton two years earlier. A new editorial team has published fiction by André Aciman, Colum McCann, Damon Galgut, Mohsin Hamid, Uzodinma Iweala, Gish Jen, Stephen King, James Lasdun, Padgett Powell, Richard Price, and Sam Shepard. Poetry editors Charles Simic, Meghan O'Rourke, and Dan Chiasson have selected works by John Ashbery, Kay Ryan, Billy Collins, Tomaž Šalamun, Mary Jo Bang, Sharon Olds, Charles Wright, and Mary Karr. Writing published in the magazine has been anthologized in *Best American Short Stories* (2006, 2007, and 2008), *Best American Poetry, Best Creative Non-Fiction*, the Pushcart Prize anthology, and *O. Henry Prize Stories*.

The magazine presents two annual awards. The Hadada Award for lifelong contribution to literature has recently been given to Joan Didion, Norman Mailer, Peter Matthiessen, and, in 2009, John Ashbery. The Plimpton Prize for Fiction, awarded to a debut or emerging writer brought to national attention in the pages of *The Paris Review*, was presented in 2007 to Benjamin Percy, to Jesse Ball in 2008, and to Alistair Morgan in 2009.

The Paris Review was a finalist for the 2008 and 2009 National Magazine Awards in fiction, and it won the 2007 National Magazine Award in photojournalism. The *Los Angeles Times* recently called *The Paris Review* "an American treasure with true international reach."

Since 1999 *The Paris Review* has been published by The Paris Review Foundation, Inc., a not-for-profit 501(c)(3) organization.

The Paris Review is available in digital form to libraries worldwide in selected academic databases exclusively from EBSCO Publishing. Libraries can contact EBSCO at 1-800-653-2726 for details. For more information on *The Paris Review* or to subscribe, please visit: www.theparisreview.org.

Eric Carl Link is Professor of American Literature and Chair of the Department of English at the University of Memphis. He is the author of several books, including *The Vast and Terrible Drama: American Literary Naturalism in the Late Nineteenth Century* (2004), *Understanding Philip K. Dick* (2010), and *Neutral Ground: New Traditionalism and the American Romance Controversy* (coauthored with G. R. Thompson, 1999). He is also the founder and editor of *ALN: The American Literary Naturalism Newsletter.*

R. Baird Shuman, Professor Emeritus of English at the University of Illinois at Urbana-Champaign, has taught at the University of Pennsylvania, Drexel University, San José State University, and Duke University. He has published critical studies of Clifford Odets, William Inge, and Robert E. Sherwood. The editor of the thirteen-volume encyclopedia *Great American Writers, 20th Century*, he lives in Las Vegas, Nevada.

Barry Harbaugh lives in Brooklyn, New York, and has written for *Triple Canopy* and *Wired*, among other publications.

Matthew J. Bolton is Professor of English at Loyola School in New York City, where he also serves as Dean of Students. He received his doctor of philosophy degree in English from the Graduate Center of the City University of New York (CUNY) in 2005. His dissertation at the university was titled "Transcending the Self in Robert Browning and T. S. Eliot." Prior to attaining his Ph.D. at CUNY, he also earned a master of philosophy degree in English (2004) and a master of science degree in English education (2001). His undergraduate work was done at the State University of New York at Binghamton, where he studied English literature.

Patrick K. Dooley is Board of Trustees Professor of Philosophy at St. Bonaventure University. He is the author of *The Pluralistic Philosophy of Stephen Crane* (1994) and *Stephen Crane: An Annotated Bibliography of Secondary Scholarship* (1992), which he continues to update regularly with journal articles in *Stephen Crane Studies.*

Stanley B. Greenfield was Professor of English at the University of Oregon. Considered an expert in Old English literature, he taught courses spanning the topics of Old and Middle English and often focused strongly on the epic poem *Beowulf.* He is the author of *A New Critical History of Old English Literature* (1996) and *A Readable Beowulf* (1982).

James M. Cox is Professor Emeritus of English at Dartmouth College. His books include *Mark Twain: The Fate of Humor* (2002) and *Recovering Literature's Lost Ground: Essays in American Autobiography* (1989). His studies of Mark Twain, in particular, have contributed greatly to the understanding of the popular American writer. In 1997, he was the recipient of the Hubbell Medal for Lifetime Achievement.

Harold R. Hungerford is Professor Emeritus in the Department of Curriculum and

Instruction at Southern Illinois University at Carbondale. His contributions to environmental education are extensive, spanning more than thirty years and including such publications as *Essential Readings in Environmental Education* (2005) and *Ecology: An Introduction for Non-Science Majors* (1997).

Robert C. Albrecht is a Senior Fellow of EDUCAUSE Center for Applied Research. Upon his retirement in 2000, he was Chancellor Emeritus of Western Governors University. He has taught countless courses in American literature and has written much on the topics of distance learning and technology-supported learning.

Thomas L. Kent is Assistant Professor in the Department of English at Miami University in Ohio. His lectures center on American literature and composition. His essays on Stephen Crane have appeared in such literary journals as *Structuralist Review*, *American Literary Realism*, and *Modern Fiction Studies*.

Ben Satterfield taught English at the University of Texas at Austin in the early 1980s and has published articles in the *CLA Journal* and *Eureka Studies in Teaching Short Fiction*.

Donald Pizer is Pierce Butler Professor Emeritus of English at Tulane University, where he has taught since 1957. His books include *Dos Passos' "U.S.A.": A Critical Study* (1988) and *Twentieth-Century American Literary Naturalism: An Interpretation* (1982). He is the editor of several volumes of the works of Theodore Dreiser, Stephen Crane, Hamlin Garland, and Jack London.

Jacqueline Tavernier-Courbin is Emeritus Professor of English at the University of Ottawa. Considered an authority on Jack London, she has published several books and essays on the author and his works, including *The Call of the Wild: A Naturalistic Romance* (1994) and *Critical Essays on Jack London* (1983). She has also contributed to Cambridge Collections Online with essays on *"The Call of the Wild"* and Upton Sinclair's *The Jungle*.

James W. Tuttleton is Professor of English at New York University. He is a Fellow of the National Endowment for the Humanities and the author of *Thomas Wentworth Higginson* (1978), *Washington Irving: The Critical Reaction* (1993), and *The Novel of Manners in America* (1972). He is also the editor of *Voyages and Discoveries of the Companions of Columbus* (1986) and coeditor of *Edith Wharton: The Contemporary Reviews* (1992).

James Trammell Cox was a novelist, a poet, and an essayist who taught literature and creative writing at a variety of American universities, among them Florida State University and the University of Iowa. He won an O. Henry Award in 1963 for his story "That Golden Crane."

William B. Dillingham is Charles Howard Candler Professor Emeritus of American Literature at Emory University in Atlanta. He has published several works, including *Being Kipling* (2008), *Rudyard Kipling: Hell and Heroism* (2005), and *Humor of the Old Southwest* (1975). He is also coeditor, along with Floyd C. Watkins, of the *Practical English Handbook* (1996).

Robert M. Rechnitz was Professor of American Literature at Monmouth University, where he taught for more than thirty years. Currently serving as Executive Producer of Two River Theater Company, which he also founded, he continues to direct plays such as *Curse of the Starving Class*, *The Glass Menagerie*, and *True West*. His honors include the 2001 Monmouth University Maurice Pollak Award for Distinguished Community Service and the 2007 Monmouth County Arts Council's Celebration of Excellence Award.

Harold Kaplan is Professor Emeritus of English and American Literature at Northwestern University. He is the author of *Power and Order: Henry Adams and the Naturalist Tradition in American Fiction* (1981) and *The Passive Voice: An Approach to Modern Fiction* (1979).

Verner D. Mitchell is Associate Professor of English at the University of Memphis. His lectures span the popular works and authors of American literature, the Harlem Renaissance, and black feminist criticism. He is the author of *Western Echoes of the Harlem Renaissance: The Life and Writings of Anita Scott Coleman* (2008), *Where the Wild Grape Grows: Selected Writings by Dorothy West, 1930-1950* (2005), and *This Waiting for Love: Helene Johnson, Poet of the Harlem Renaissance* (2000). He is currently working on a biography of Dorothy West.

Acknowledgments _____

"Stephen Crane" by R. Baird Shuman. From *Dictionary of World Biography: The 19th Century*. Copyright © 1999 by Salem Press, Inc. Reprinted with permission of Salem Press.

"The *Paris Review* Perspective" by Barry Harbaugh. Copyright © 2011 by Barry Harbaugh. Special appreciation goes to Christopher Cox, Nathaniel Rich, and David Wallace-Wells, editors at *The Paris Review*.

"The Unmistakable Stephen Crane" by Stanley B. Greenfield. From *PMLA* 73, no. 5 (1958): 562-572. Copyright © 1958 by the Modern Language Association of America. Reprinted with permission of the Modern Language Association of America.

"*The Red Badge of Courage*: The Purity of War" by James M. Cox. From *Southern Humanities Review* 25, no. 4 (1991): 305-320. Copyright © 1991 by *Southern Humanities Review*. Reprinted with permission of *Southern Humanities Review*.

"'That Was at Chancellorsville': The Factual Framework of *The Red Badge of Courage*" by Harold R. Hungerford. From *American Literature* 34, no. 4 (1963): 520-531. Copyright © 1963 by Duke University Press. All rights reserved. Used by permission of the publisher.

"Content and Style in *The Red Badge of Courage*" by Robert C. Albrecht. From *College English* 27, no. 6 (1966): 487-492. Originally published by the National Council of Teachers of English.

"Epistemological Uncertainty in *The Red Badge of Courage*" by Thomas L. Kent. From *Modern Fiction Studies* 27, no. 4 (1981-1982): 621-628. Copyright © 1982 by Purdue Research Foundation. Reprinted with permission of the Johns Hopkins University Press.

"Subjectivism and *The Red Badge of Courage*" by Eric Carl Link. From *The Vast and Terrible Drama: American Literary Naturalism in the Late Nineteenth Century* (2004), pp. 129-140. Copyright © 2004 by The University of Alabama Press. Reprinted with permission of The University of Alabama Press.

"From Romance to Reality: The Accomplishment of Private Fleming" by Ben Satterfield. From *CLA Journal* 24, no. 4 (June 1981): 451-464. Copyright © 1981 by the College Language Association. Reprinted with permission of the College Language Association.

"*The Red Badge of Courage*: Text, Theme, and Form" by Donald Pizer. From *The South Atlantic Quarterly* 84, no. 3 (1985): 302-313. Copyright © 1985 by Duke University Press. All rights reserved. Used by permission of the publisher.

"Humor and Insight Through Fallacy in Stephen Crane's *The Red Badge of Courage*" by Jacqueline Tavernier-Courbin. From *Stephen Crane in War and Peace*, edited by James H. Meredith, special edition of *War, Literature & the Arts* (1999): 147-159. Originally published by the U.S. Air Force Academy Department of English.

"The Imagery of *The Red Badge of Courage*" by James W. Tuttleton. From *Modern Fiction Studies* 8, no. 4 (1962): 410-415. Copyright © 1962 by Purdue Research Foundation. Reprinted with permission of the Johns Hopkins University Press.

"The Imagery of *The Red Badge of Courage*" by James Trammell Cox. From *Modern Fiction Studies* 5, no. 3 (1959): 209-219. Copyright © 1959 by Purdue Research Foundation. Reprinted with permission of the Johns Hopkins University Press.

"Insensibility in *The Red Badge of Courage*" by William B. Dillingham. From *College English* 25, no. 3 (1963): 194-198. Originally published by the National Council of Teachers of English.

"Depersonalization and the Dream in *The Red Badge of Courage*" by Robert M. Rechnitz. From *Studies in the Novel* 6, no. 1 (Spring 1974): 76-87. Copyright © 1974 by the University of North Texas Press. Reprinted with permission of the University of North Texas.

"Violence as Ritual and Apocalypse" by Harold Kaplan. From *Power and Order: Henry Adams and the Naturalist Tradition in American Fiction* (1981), pp. 121-127. Copyright © 1981 by Harold Kaplan. Reprinted with permission of the author.

"Reading 'Race' and 'Gender' in Crane's *The Red Badge of Courage*" by Verner D. Mitchell. From *CLA Journal* 40, no. 1 (September 1996): 60-71. Copyright © 1996 by the College Language Association. Reprinted with permission of the College Language Association.

Index

Darwinism, 6, 29, 50-51, 216

Death and dying, 3, 19, 95, 104, 109, 116, 126-127, 129, 133, 141, 168, 186, 191, 201, 228, 231, 233, 238, 243, 245, 250, 269, 278, 284

"Death and the Child" (Crane), 12

Delbanco, Andrew, 47, 287

Derrick, Scott, 56

Detweiler, Robert, 49

Dietz, Rudolph F., 60

Dillingham, William B., 58

Domeraski, Regina, 43

Dooley, Patrick K., 173

Doubleness, 150, 152, 154-155, 157, 250

Dunn, N. E., 54, 56

Dusenbery, Robert, 56

Eby, Cecil D., 48, 50

Ellison, Ralph, 287

Existentialism, 74, 79, 85, 87, 161, 285

Feldman, Abraham, 56

Fisher, Benjamin F., 45

"Five White Mice, The" (Crane), 89, 112

Fleming, Henry (*The Red Badge of Courage*), 3, 17, 24, 46, 76, 89, 120, 136, 152, 161, 173, 190, 203, 219, 233, 240, 255, 263, 278, 289; and mother, 103, 124, 162, 222, 294

Follett, Wilson, 47

Food, 95, 99, 103, 186

Foote, Shelby, 47

Fraser, John, 52, 59, 200

French, Warren, 52

Fryckstedt, Olaf W., 51

Geismar, Maxwell, 201

George's Mother (Crane), 11, 134, 287

Gerstenberger, Donna, 160

Gettysburg, Battle of. *See* Battle of Gettysburg

Gibson, Donald B., 46, 56, 191

Great Battles of the World, The (Crane), 13, 146

Greenfield, Stanley B., 50, 150, 233, 240

Guinn, Dorothy Margaret, 51

Gullason, Thomas A., 40, 57

Gwynn, Frederic, 50

Habegger, Alfred, 35

Hafer, Carol B., 59

Haight, Gordon S., 57

Halliburton, David, 46

Hart, John E., 49, 52, 233, 253

Hattenhauer, Darryl, 51

Henry Fleming. *See* Fleming, Henry

Hergesheimer, Joseph, 46, 171

Heroism, 19, 76, 82, 96, 102, 106, 133, 162, 177, 181, 193, 221, 223, 231, 237, 252, 261, 278

Hitchcock, Ripley, 41, 44, 203

Hoffman, Daniel G., 52, 255, 261

Homeric references, 24, 31, 56, 80-81, 124, 237

Horsford, Harold C., 55

Howells, William Dean, 10, 122, 166

Hungerford, Harold R., 47

Hunter, Adrian, 28

Iliad (Homer), 56, 81, 121, 237

Imagery; animals, 51, 76, 103, 130, 151, 153, 158, 167, 178, 186, 188, 190, 193, 206, 224, 226, 236, 243, 247, 249; colors, 50, 76, 92, 124, 128-129, 243, 245, 250; corpses, 3, 125, 128-129, 150, 244-245, 248, 251, 267, 273; inferno, 167, 243, 250, 252; machinery, 5, 33, 59, 153, 182, 224,

DATE DUE

FOLLETT